BYRON'S POETRY

A CRITICAL INTRODUCTION

Riverside Studies in Literature

Riverside Studies in Literature

GENERAL EDITOR · GORDON N. RAY

Byron's Poetry

A Critical Introduction

LESLIE A. MARCHAND
Rutgers — The State University

Houghton Mifflin Company · Boston

Preface

My AIM IN THIS BOOK is simple and direct. I offer nothing surprisingly new in procedure, no startling revelations, no new critical system. My only purpose is to furnish to students and general readers some useful observations on Byron's poetry as a whole and on particular poems, not only those most read today but also those now little regarded which had an enormous vogue in the nineteenth century. A dispassionate rereading may at least discover whether *Childe Harold*, which was the Bible of the nineteenth century *Weltschmerz*, or *The Corsair*, which sold 10,000 copies on the first day of publication, have any merits other than their picturesque description or lurid autobiographical innuendoes.

In short, my purpose has been to write an introduction to Byron's poetry for twentieth century students and readers in the light of what is now known of the life, character, and pyschology of the poet, and of the intellectual and literary milieu in which he wrote. I have tried neither to overemphasize nor to neglect the biographical interpretation, always important for the understanding of the self-revelatory poetry of the Romantics. And at the same time I have tried to follow at least one precept of twentieth century criticism by looking closely at the poems themselves, both individually and in groups. If subjectivity has intruded while I have been trying to keep my eye on the object, my sin is at least no greater than that of other critics who have attempted a balanced appraisal of Romantic poetry.

My chief debt of gratitude is to the Rutgers Research Council for a Summer Fellowship in 1963 which gave me free time for the writing of the first draft of this book. My wife, Marion Marchand, has given me invaluable criticism and assistance in checking quotations and pruning ineptnesses and excess wordage. My debt to numerous laborers in Byronic fields has been acknowledged in the notes. I probably owe an unconscious debt also to numerous Byron scholars and students whose ideas have filtered into my mind. If I am accused of plagiarism I can say with Coleridge that the author "rejoices to find his opinions plumed and winged with the authority of venerable Forefathers."

L. A. M.

Contents

BYRON'S POETRY

A CRITICAL INTRODUCTION

1

Byron in the Twentieth Century

DOES BYRON'S POETRY have any significant value for us today? The answer depends largely on the depth and catholicity of our concepts of poetry. Poetry can be many things. If we see value in only one kind (as critics have tended to do in every age), we will naturally denigrate all that does not conform to our current taste. If we demand "high seriousness" in poetry, which in Matthew Arnold's use of the term meant a particular moral slant, we will speak disparagingly of Dryden and Pope as poets of "an age of prose and reason"; we will find Chaucer and Burns "poetically unsound" because they lack "the accent of high seriousness." If we demand, as many twentieth century critics do, that poetry embody irony and ambiguity and paradox in a complex and intricate structure of words weighted with symbolic meaning, we shall give short shrift to most other kinds of poetry, and particularly to the work of those poets who, like Byron, seem, in T. S. Eliot's phrase, to have an "imperceptiveness" to words, to be making "sonorous affirmations of the commonplace."[1]

But if we start with a broad definition of poetry as a something plus, a heightened realization of some idea, mood, or meaningful moment, and not something concentrated and distilled according to a single formula, then Byron's best poetry, at least, has merits

[1] Eliot's essay on "Byron" (*On Poetry and Poets*, 1961; the essay was first published in 1937) is an attempt to separate the good work from the bad, and he ends like most twentieth century critics by lauding *Don Juan*. He grants that in that poem Byron "has the cardinal virtue of being never dull." He praises Byron's "genius for digression," finds his banter and mockery "an admirable antacid to the high-falutin," and sees his ultimate virtue, as many others have, in his "reckless raffish honesty."

1

which can be appreciated by the most fastidious and sophisticated. Such an approach can clear the way for a better understanding and a fairer estimate of the work of a poet whose "sincerity and strength" have impressed critics from Goethe and Matthew Arnold to Eliot himself.

Among his merits are two which are peculiarly Byronic. By sheer genius he could make a statement of the commonplace ricochet past the platitude and lodge memorably in the mind, leaving reverberating harmonies of sound and sense. This is a virtue to be found in some stanzas of *Childe Harold* (Eliot notwithstanding) and in some of his tales and shorter lyrics, as well as in his satires. A second and greater merit is his facetious revelation of truths that are too threatening to the self-defensive ego to be presented without a comic mask. Byron was often most serious when he was most waggish. Mockery was the cover for intellectual and emotional honesty in a period solemnly tenacious of its own cant and complacent in its own certainties. When in his self-exile Byron achieved a kind of beyond-the-tomb freedom to speak his mind about all things, he found his true voice in *Don Juan*.

Byron had a sufficient contempt for "system," whether in criticism or poetry. After reading Leigh Hunt's manuscript of *Rimini*, he wrote Moore, "I told him that I deemed it good poetry at bottom, disfigured only by a strange style. His answer was, that his style was a system, or *upon system*, or some such cant; and, when a man talks of system, his case is hopeless."[2] Like most of the Romantics who indulged in the "spontaneous overflow of powerful feelings," Byron wrote many "unpremeditated" and uncorrected poems that cannot be defended. He apologized for them by saying: "I can never *recast* any thing. I am like the Tiger: if I miss the first spring, I go growling back to my jungle again; but if I *do hit*, it is crushing."[3]

For the most part one need not look for verbal subtleties in Byron. His irony is likely to be a brickbat, but hurled with such skill and force that when it does hit, it crushes. Writing to Murray after receiving a plea from his publisher to avoid "ap-

[2] *The Works of Lord Byron, Letters and Journals,* ed. R. E. Prothero, IV, 237. Letter of June 1, 1818. (This edition is hereafter cited as *Letters and Journals.*)

[3] *Letters and Journals,* V, 471. Letter of Nov. 3, 1821.

proximations to indelicacy" in *Don Juan*, Byron said: ". . . this reminds me of George Lamb's quarrel at Cambridge with Scrope Davies. 'Sir,' said George, 'he *hinted* at my *illegitimacy*.' 'Yes,' said Scrope, 'I called him a damned adulterous bastard'; the approximation and the hint are not unlike."[4]

One of the supposed weaknesses of Byron as a thinker which has lessened his stature among modern critics is his inability, or unwillingness, to adopt a fixed philosophy or permanent point of view. It is the same accusation that was made by Goethe and echoed by Arnold: "The moment he reflects, he is a child." But it may be that that very fact has given him a perennial freshness which makes him more congenial to the twentieth century than those of his contemporaries who adopted a "system" that can no longer answer the questions we perpetually ask about human life and destiny. If Coleridge may be thought a more profound philosopher, it is not because of the acceptance of absolutes and dogmas that made him an apologist for the contemporary orthodoxy in religion and politics. His reputation as a thinker rests rather on those "seminal" thoughts of his journals and conversations that penetrated to individual truths — truths which might have been disquieting to the systems he supported had his rationalizations been less persuasive.

It is probable that the mind that inquires and questions has always expanded philosophic as well as scientific knowledge more than the mind that affirms and accepts. In an era when blood transfusion is as universal a remedy as blood-letting was when Byron died at Missolonghi, it is easy to sympathize with the instinctive skepticism which made him resist the application of leeches. The symbolic significance should not escape us when we consider his skepticism of no less tenaciously held beliefs in other spheres.

In any reassessment of Byron's value to us as a thinker we can do no better than to repeat Professor Fairchild's statement: ". . . one may justly be irritated by the common assumption that a man who refrains from believing in lofty and inspiring ideas for which there is no evidence whatever necessarily has an inferior mind. Although no one would undertake to prove that Byron was a profound thinker, he possessed a quality which many supposedly profound thinkers lack — a sense of the toughness of facts and

[4] *Letters and Journals*, IV, 304–305. Letter of May 20, 1819.

an inability to dupe himself about them. . . . Beneath all his protective histrionism, his mind possessed a certain desperate integrity which should command respect."[5]

The quality which Lady Blessington and others among his contemporaries saw as a weakness was Byron's real strength: that sensitive response to the impression of the moment without regard to any "system" or principle of unity or consistency. Byron defined the term "mobility" as "an excessive susceptibility of immediate impressions — at the same time without *losing* the past."[6] As his "versified Aurora Borealis . . . flashes o'er a waste and icy clime," he throws the cold light of truth on human smugness. He has been accused, he says, of

> A tendency to under-rate and scoff
> At human power and virtue, and all that.

But, he replies,

> I say no more than hath been said in Dante's
> Verse, and by Solomon and by Cervantes;
>
> By Swift, by Machiavel, by Rochefoucault,
> By Fénélon, by Luther, and by Plato;
> By Tillotson, and Wesley, and Rousseau,
> Who knew this life was not worth a potato.
>   *   *   *   *   *   *   *   *   *
> Newton (that proverb of the mind), alas!
> Declared, with all his grand discoveries recent,
> That he himself felt only "like a youth
> Picking up shells by the great ocean — Truth."
>   (*Don Juan*, VII, 3–5)

In another digression he gives his answer to those who are "hot for certainties":

> 'T is true we speculate both far and wide,
> And deem, because we *see*, we are *all-seeing*: . . .
>
> "*Que scais-je?*" was the motto of Montaigne,
> As also of the first academicians:

---

[5] Hoxie Neale Fairchild, *The Romantic Quest*, 1931, p. 362.

[6] *The Works of Lord Byron, Poetry*, ed. E. H. Coleridge, VI, 600 (Hereafter cited as *Poetry*.)

That all is dubious which man may attain,
Was one of their most favourite positions.
There's no such thing as certainty, that's plain
As any of Mortality's conditions. . . .
(*Don Juan*, IX, 16–17)

In his disinclination to claim a truth he did not possess, and in his skepticism of absolutes, Byron finds a more sympathetic audience in the twentieth century than he found in the nineteenth. He gives voice to an era that is confused by the increase of knowledge and that no longer has confidence in intellectual leaders who seek easy answers. Byron had the strength to resist the demand for adherence to some creed, for acceptance of some simple and final interpretation of the only partly understood universe. He was aware that to keep an open mind on all subjects required courage.

The consequence is, being of no party,
I shall offend all parties. . . .   (*Don Juan*, IX, 26)

Keats complained of his friend Dilke — he was nearer to Byron here than either realized — that he was a man "who cannot feel he has a personal identity unless he has made up his mind about everything." That "Negative Capability" which Keats so admired in Shakespeare he might also have seen in Byron had he been able to look under the latter's flippant manner — "that is, when a man is capable of being in uncertainties, mysteries, doubts, without any irritable reaching after fact and reason."

It is easy to see why Byron has frequently been called a romantic paradox. The polarities of his life, opinions, and poetic productions are apparent enough. He was a Deist and free-thinker haunted by a Calvinistic sense of original sin. He espoused the cause of oppressed peoples in every land and yet was always conscious of his noble ancestry and sometimes displayed a child-ish aristocratic pride. He liked to think of himself as a Regency Dandy and yet he was sincere in admiration of Shelley's simplicity and unaffected manners. Occasionally with strangers, but seldom with his friends, he struck an attitude, though at bottom he had a "desperate integrity" and a disarming self-honesty. He was a leader of the Romantic revolution in poetry who clung to the literary ideals of Alexander Pope. He was a worshipper of the ideal whose leanings toward realism kept his feet on the ground.

But rightly seen, what appear to be contradictions are in the main only two sides of the same coin. The central problem for Byron, as for most of the Romantics, was to find a satisfying compromise between the demands of the real and the ideal. But with the strong strain of eighteenth century common sense in his nature, Byron's attitude toward the problem was different from that of most other Romantics.

There are several possible attitudes. One may deny that there is any disparity between the real and the ideal, either (a) by saying that the real is ideal (and then he is not a Romantic at all but has taken the so-called common sense view of Pope and the eighteenth century adherents of the "chain of being" philosophy, that seeming imperfections are only a part of the plan, that "all that is, is right"); or (b) by saying that the ideal is real, the only reality, and that the world of sense is only an appearance, an illusion through which the man of perception (let us say the poet) must penetrate in order to get a view of ultimate reality. This latter alternative is the one chosen by all the idealists from Plato to the present. With variations as to the means of perceiving ideal reality, this was the solution to which many of the nineteenth century poets (the so-called transcendental group) turned: Wordsworth, Coleridge, Shelley. Some of them were uneasy in that point of view, and like Wordsworth felt as they grew older that they could only fitfully command the power to see the ideal vision and so asked themselves:

> Whither is fled the visionary gleam?
> Where is it now, the glory and the dream?

This brought on a temporary melancholy, but their "will to believe" was too strong to permit them to rest there.

A second way of viewing the disparity between the real and the ideal is to see the gap as essentially unbridgeable: to come face to face with the necessity of dealing with the real world as real and the ideal world as ideal, as a creation of the mind. Within this possibility are two kinds and many degrees of attitudes: (a) One may be sensible (or insensitive, if you choose to call it so) enough to accept the separation of reality and ideality and feel no particular urge to bridge the gap between them. Such a person is not a Romantic but more nearly what we would call a realist. Or (b) one may be so constituted as to long for the ideal with an uncompromising zeal, and may be consequently disappointed and unhappy because the real fails to measure up to it, yet be too clear-sighted to confuse the two. He may then vary his mental occupations between a dwelling upon the ideal, which is his only true love, and a melancholy or a bitterly mocking reflection upon how disgustingly short of the ideal the real is and must always be. In this last description of an attitude we come as near as can any generalization to fixing the place of Byron among the Romantics. Of course Byron seemed at times to be admiring the classical (or neo-classical) acceptance of the world as it is. But because he was a child of his age, and could not detach himself sufficiently from the romantic longing for what the world does not give, he could seldom achieve the Augustan calm he admired in his idol Pope.

In one mood, that which permeates *Childe Harold,* he displays the melancholy and despair which accompany the recognition of the failure of the real to match the ideal. In another, he presents the comedy, sometimes bitter, sometimes roguishly facetious, of the disparity between real and ideal. With a keen delight he tears away the mask of sentimentalism, of hypocritical self-deception, of mock-ideality, of wishful thinking, and shows the plain or ugly face of reality. This is the mood that dominates much, but by no means all, of *Don Juan.*

We have the feeling now that the satiric Byron found himself, for it is this aspect of his work that most appeals to us. The melancholy Byron belongs more to his own time, though he too may voice a modern (and universal) *Weltschmerz.* But both moods pervade *Don Juan* and alternate in Byron's poetry throughout his career. Professor Fairchild has phrased it most aptly: "Aspiration, melancholy, mockery — the history of a mind too idealistic to refrain from blowing bubbles, and too realistic to refrain from pricking them."[7]

It is a common supposition that Byron began his career as a melancholy Childe Harold, a gloomy egoist, a Conrad (*The Corsair*) brooding over his "one virtue and a thousand crimes." Some biographers have pictured him standing on the sidelines at one of the London balls in his years of fame, wrapped in somber disillusionment and despair, "the wandering outlaw of his own dark mind." But it is just as likely that his curled lip of scorn indicated that he was about to voice a facetious witticism more appropriate to *Don Juan* than to *Childe Harold.* Judging not only from his letters and the record of his conversations at the time

[7] *The Romantic Quest,* p. 370.

but also from some of the poems he wrote early in his career, the satiric, realistic, mocking vein was strong in Byron from his Cambridge days, or before, until the end of his life. It only tended to be suppressed in his poetry after the success of the first two cantos of *Childe Harold* had fixed the pattern of his poetic production, and the flattering public demand for his tales of "pleasing woe" made it difficult for him to shatter the image of himself he had created.[8]

Though he had written some facetious and realistic (or cynical) verses before he ended his residence at Cambridge, only a very few were ventured upon the public, and those only in the privately printed volume *Fugitive Pieces*, intended to be circulated among friends. After that volume was suppressed and all but four copies destroyed because his parson friend John Becher objected that one of the poems ("To Mary") was "rather too warmly drawn," Byron retained only the more romantic, and less original, verses in his subsequent volumes. Many of the moods of *Childe Harold* appeared in *Hours of Idleness*, but no hint was given that the author possessed even at that time much of the mischievous good humor that later found expression in *Beppo*. Perhaps the *Edinburgh Review* critic would have been kinder to *Hours of Idleness* if its mawkishness had been leavened by the lively satire on sentimentalism from *Fugitive Pieces*: "To a Lady Who Presented to the Author a Lock of Hair Braided with His Own, and Appointed a Night in December to Meet Him in the Garden." Some of the lines suggest the mood if not the maturity of *Don Juan*.

> Why should you weep, like *Lydia Languish*,
> And fret with self-created anguish?
> Or doom the lover you have chosen,
> On winter nights to sigh half frozen. . . .

Byron's next attempt, stimulated rather than initiated by the attack in the *Edinburgh*, was a Popean satire begun at Cambridge under the influence of his friend Hobhouse and encouraged by

[8] I have discussed this point in the Introduction to my edition of *Don Juan* (Riverside Edition, Houghton Mifflin, 1958). Byron himself was aware of the stamp that *Childe Harold* and other poems in that vein had put upon him. In 1817 he asked Moore to assure Francis Jeffrey "that I was not, and, indeed, am not even *now*, the misanthropical and gloomy gentleman he takes me for, but a facetious companion, well to do with those with whom I am intimate, and as loquacious and laughing as if I were a much cleverer fellow." (*Letters and Journals*, IV, 72–74.)

Francis Hodgson, a translator of Juvenal. *English Bards, and Scotch Reviewers* owes something to the Roman satirist, but more to Pope and Gifford. Byron had read and admired Pope at Harrow, as most schoolboys who had any interest in poetry did at the time. But his immediate model was William Gifford, whose clever satires in the *Anti-Jacobin* and in *The Maeviad* and *The Baviad* roused Byron to emulation and to admiration scarcely this side idolatry. He would now try a *Dunciad* of his own: "The cry is up, and scribblers are my game."

Having made a success in this genre, imitative though it was, Byron henceforth felt that this was his forte. It was a style that was generally respected by those he most respected, and it did not bring ridicule on him but praise and admiration, even from some whom his barbs had stung. It was small wonder then that he tried to follow up his success by writing, while he was in Greece, *Hints from Horace* and that whenever he felt the urge to satiric expression he turned to the Popean couplet even when the subject and treatment were far from Pope.

Byron continued throughout his life to have a dual concept of poetry. On the one hand was the poetry of serious moral purpose (as he conceived Pope's to be). This was a poetry that would castigate the errors of the age with stringent wit, would point out deviations from good sense and good taste in brilliant balanced couplets, and would attack the corruptions and injustices in society with Juvenalian fierceness modified by Popean good temper.[9] It was the goal Byron had aimed at in *English Bards, and Scotch Reviewers*. It is significant that he set himself the task in that poem, beyond judging the little wits and poetasters of the day, of bringing "the force of wit" to bear on "Vice" and "Folly" as well as on literary lapses. It is significant too that he admired most the virtues of his models that he felt he could not achieve: the objectivity and the verbal skill that the very nature of his own character and genius made it most difficult for him to attain.

In the middle of his career, after he had finished the fourth canto of *Childe Harold* and thought it his best, he wrote to Murray: "With regard to poetry in general, I am convinced, the

[9] A close study of Byron's debt to the Roman satirists Horace and Juvenal has been made by Arthur Kahn (New York University doctoral dissertation). Aside from the obvious parallels in *Hints from Horace* and other poems in the Popean couplet, Kahn has found remarkable echoes of both the subject matter and the style of Horace, but many more and closer parallels with Juvenal in *Don Juan* particularly.

more I think of it, that . . . *all* of us — Scott, Southey, Wordsworth, Moore, Campbell, I, — are all in the wrong, one as much
as another; that we are upon a wrong revolutionary poetical
system, or systems, not worth a damn in itself, and from which
none but Rogers and Crabbe are free; and that the present and
next generations will finally be of this opinion. I am the more
confirmed in this by having lately gone over some of our classics,
particularly *Pope,* whom I tried in this way, — I took Moore's
poems and my own and some others, and went over them side by
side with Pope's, and I was really astonished (I ought not to have
been so) and mortified at the ineffable distance in point of sense,
harmony, effect, and even *Imagination,* passion, and *Invention,*
between the little Queen Anne's man, and us of the Lower
Empire. Depend upon it, it is all Horace then, and Claudian now,
among us; and if I had to begin again, I would model myself
accordingly."[10]

The other concept of poetry that guided Byron's literary
performance was the subjective Romantic one born of the impulse to "look in your heart and write." He adopted it perforce,
impelled by both his temperament and his environment, but he
continued to consider it second best and to speak disparagingly
of it, as he did in the letter just quoted. Having a conviction of
the lesser nature of the art he was practicing, he found a certain
satisfaction in deprecating poetry in general: "If one's years can't
be better employed than in sweating poesy, a man had better be
a ditcher."[11] It is characteristic of Byron that he could not compromise with his concept of the ideal in writing. He would live
in the world, but he would not bend his mind to call its imperfections ideal, even when it concerned his own performance.
"If I live ten years longer," he told Moore, "you will see, however, that it is not over with me — I don't mean in literature, for
that is nothing; and it may seem odd enough to say, I do not
think it my vocation."[12] As late as 1821, when he had found in
Don Juan a literary style that suited his genius far better than

10 *Letters and Journals,* IV, 169. Letter of Sept. 15, 1817. Byron would
have been flattered and pleased had he seen the note which Gifford, to
whom Murray showed the letter, wrote on the manuscript: "There is
more good sense, and feeling and judgment in this passage, than in any
other I ever read, or Lord Byron wrote."

11 *Letters and Journals,* IV, 284. Letter of April 6, 1819.

12 *Letters and Journals,* IV, 62. Letter of Feb. 28, 1817.

any imitation of Gifford or Pope, he wrote to Moore after the failure of the Neapolitan uprising had blighted his hopes for a similar revolt in the Romagna in which he could take an active part: "And now let us be literary; — a sad falling off, but it is always a consolation. If 'Othello's occupation be gone,' let us take to the next best; and, if we cannot contribute to make mankind more free and wise, we may amuse ourselves and those who like it. . . . I have been scribbling at intervals. . . ."[13]

Even before he had fully accepted his own limitations, Byron found an outlet for his energies and his feelings in poetry of the Romantic category. "All convulsions end with me in Rhyme,"[14] he wrote Moore in 1813. And again he spoke of poetry as "the lava of the imagination whose eruption prevents an earthquake."[15] His reluctance to publish *Childe Harold* was motivated as much by his anxiety that it would damage his claim as an Augustan wit, which he felt he had already staked out in *English Bards, and Scotch Reviewers*, as by his fear of revealing secrets of his private life and feelings. It would be an acknowledgment that he had enrolled himself in the camp of the Romantics who regarded poetry as nothing more than the safety valve of the emotions.

But the acclaim that greeted *Childe Harold*, together with the circumstances that led to the suppression of *English Bards* and the withdrawal of the manuscript of *Hints from Horace*, caused Byron to accept his role as a Romantic poet without ever giving up his conviction that the only ideal of poetry to which he could give full critical allegiance was that of the school of Pope. Swept along, however, by his phenomenal success in what he considered this lesser genre at a time when, frustrated in his ambition to be a political orator and statesman by the strait jacket of Whig politics, and pressed by the need for emotional relief for the impasses created by his fame and his passions, he succumbed to the poetry of self-expression as other men might to drugs or drink. But still he was from time to time stricken with remorse for having given up the ideal of poetic practice. Henceforth, except in these moments of critical contrition, he thought and spoke of poetry as a simple "lava of the imagination." While he was composing *The Bride of Abydos* he wrote Lady Melbourne: ". . . my mind has

13 *Letters and Journals*, V, 272. Letter of April 28, 1821.

14 *Letters and Journals*, II, 293. Letter of Nov. 30, 1813.

15 *Letters and Journals*, III, 405. Letter of Nov. 10, 1813, to Annabella Milbanke.

been from *late* and *later* events in such a state of fermentation, that as usual I have been obliged to empty it in rhyme, and am in the very heart of another Eastern tale."[16]

Most of what Byron wrote henceforth grew directly or indirectly out of his personal need for emotional release, and through practice of this "inferior" art he became adept in voicing the pangs not only of himself but of his generation. Like "wild Rousseau" he "threw / Enchantment over passion, and from woe / Wrung overwhelming eloquence." In *Childe Harold*, in the Oriental and other tales, and also in shorter lyrics and in pieces with supposedly more objective themes like "The Prisoner of Chillon," personal catharsis of turbulent moods was the dominant motive for composition.[17] Likewise in his speculative dramas, *Manfred, Cain, Heaven and Earth*, and *The Deformed Transformed*, the driving force is always the poet's desire to work out a solution to his own deepest quandaries. And it might be said that whatever merit these poetic dramas have lies in the depth and sincerity of the personal revelation rather than in any resolution of a philosophical problem.

Fidelity to the mood of the moment was Byron's forte, and failure to acknowledge this has befuddled Byron criticism from the time the poems were published until the present day. There has been a persistent refusal to accept Byron's own frankest statements, and to recognize that honesty and self-honesty were almost an obsession with him. Somerset Maugham once wrote a story of a man who got a tremendous reputation for being a humorist merely by telling the simple truth about himself and others. So Byron acquired the reputation of being a great poseur because no one would believe that anyone would be as honest in literature as people may frequently be in private conversation.

Among his contemporaries, those who felt the strong spell of his passionate revelation of the romantic ego, but disapproved of the unconventional conduct or opinions of the hero, were constrained to apologize for Byron by saying that he was not drawing from his own experience but was only assuming a Satanic pose. A

16 *Lord Byron's Correspondence*, ed. John Murray, I, 214. Letter of Nov. 4, 1813.

17 There is no doubt that Byron's deep hatred of personal restraint as well as of governmental tyranny made the story of Bonivard's imprisonment a subject congenial to him. The passionate interest it aroused in him is best seen in the "Sonnet on Chillon": "Eternal Spirit of the chainless Mind!"

typical statement is that of one of the Cambridge "Apostle" editors of the *Athenaeum*, who wrote not long after Byron's death: "Among the states of feeling which he describes with so much intensity, we doubt whether any great proportion were really painted from his own feelings."[18] But recent biographical evidence shows convincingly that no writer was ever more patently autobiographical in the creations of his imagination. In fact, this became so much a habit of his mind and of his composition that even when he deliberately set out to write objectively, as in his historical dramas, in which he prided himself on fidelity to the written records of characters and events, he could not but make the major figures over into personalities like himself with problems that were his own.

Byron's supreme literary achievement, however, was developed almost by accident, though its ingredients had been long heated in the crucible of his own experience and literary practice. When he discovered in the Italian ottava rima the possibilities for both colloquial ease and rhetorical brilliance, for kaleidoscopic but natural shifts from serious to comic, he had found his métier and his medium. When he tried it out in *Beppo* he saw that it offered the freest outlet for all the thoughts and feelings of his mobile personality. The darker moods had already found adequate expression in the third and fourth cantos of *Childe Harold* and in *Manfred.* He had achieved something like calm again in Venice, which, he wrote Moore, "has always been (next to the East) the greenest island of my imagination."[19] At last, he felt freed by his self-exile from the necessity of fitting his life or his verse into an English pattern. By November, 1816, he was already willing to become a citizen of the world. If he could only arrange his financial affairs in England, he told Kinnaird, "you might consider me as *posthumous,* for I would never willingly dwell in the 'tight little Island.' "[20] He could now indulge in literature that facetious and satiric bent which had been largely confined to his letters since *Childe Harold* had diverted his talents into the single track of the "Romantic Agony."

When the success of *Beppo* encouraged him to continue the same style and manner in *Don Juan,* Byron was not fully conscious of the significance of the change that was being wrought

[18] *Athenaeum,* Jan. 23, 1828, p. 55.

[19] *Letters and Journals,* IV, 7. Letter of Nov. 17, 1816.

[20] *Lord Byron's Correspondence,* II, 24. Letter of Nov. 27, 1816.

not only in his poetic subject matter and style but also in his concept of the poetic function. While he was increasingly aware of the value of *Don Juan* as a production that possessed candor and life and truth more than any other literary work of the day, and while he defended it facetiously against the attacks of his squeamish friends in England, he never fully understood why it engrossed his loyalty more than anything else he had written. The fact was that he had found a genre which satisfied his deepest feelings about the moral function of poetry and at the same time allowed the completest cathartic escape for his feelings, whether serious or comic.

It is true that by the very nature of the medium and the style he had adapted from the ottava rima mock-heroic poems of the Italians, Byron's work has less of the neat compactness of Pope's best couplets. But on the other hand, by following his own genius with a freedom of artistry that forgets art, Byron cuts deeper with his broadsword through the armor of conventional pretenses to the living flesh of the human condition than Pope ever does with his more pointed rapier. Byron swung wildly at times, but in more than half of *Don Juan* he did hit and the blow was crushing.

2

Early Poems

IN STUDYING the early work of any poet, the significant things to observe are evidences and inklings of an authentic voice. It is to be expected that the bulk of such juvenile verse will be imitative. Tennyson's early poems are full of echoes, first of Byron and then of Keats, the poetic voices that resounded most melodiously to his boyish ears. But there was also a true Tennysonian quality in some of the pieces in his earliest published volumes. Nothing in Byron's early work stands out on its own merits so shiningly as Tennyson's "Lady of Shalott," "Œnone," or "The Lotus-Eaters," for Byron was slow to develop his best talents, but it is easy to find the unmistakable Byronic accent in a number of poems written before 1809.

Many of the poems in *Fugitive Pieces*[1] are close imitations of the early poems of Thomas Moore which had appeared pseudonymously in 1801 as *The Poetical Works of the Late Thomas Little* and had gone into nine editions by 1808. Moore's verses are full of voluptuous images cloaked in sentimental phrases: "her ripe lips," "rapture's rite," "Warmly I felt her bosom thrill," "my Julia's burning kiss." Byron wrote Moore in 1820: "I have just been turning over *Little*, which I knew by heart in 1803, being then in my fifteenth summer. Heigho! I believe all the mischief I have ever done, or sung, has been owing to that confounded book of yours."[2] Certainly *Fugitive Pieces* includes some of the

---

[1] There were four separate printings of Byron's early poems, each successive volume containing some of the poems in the preceding ones, suppressing some, and adding more new ones. For details see the contents in the first volume of E. H. Coleridge's edition of the *Poetry*.

[2] *Letters and Journals*, V, 42. Letter of June 9, 1820.

most mawkish poems Byron ever wrote. The theme of the fleetingness of love and the inconstancy of lovers was one which appealed to the adolescent then in the throes of his unrequited love for Mary Chaworth. Byron did, however, imitate well some of the lilting anapestic lyrics of Moore, and sometimes improved on them. His facility in some of the lyric measures he learned from Moore was one of the chief merits of his occasional verse and was to bear fruit in *Hebrew Melodies* and in some of his early verses that sprang from genuine emotions, like "Hills of Annesley! bleak and barren."

Though he took his cue from Moore in these poems celebrating passion subdued to sentiment, in several respects he went beyond his model. In the first place, it is evident that Byron was not merely imitating a style or a poetic jargon but was writing in "red-hot earnest"; the fever of the feeling sometimes burns away the "fictions of flimsy romance" as in "The First Kiss of Love," and a two-bladed Byronic theme appears: the superiority of truth to fiction and the nostalgia for an idealized youthful innocence. The smirk and the condescension of Moore toward his "nymphs" somehow disappear and even some of Byron's conventional phrases carry a ring of sincerity.

> I hate you, ye cold compositions of art,
>   Though prudes may condemn me, and bigots reprove;
> I court the effusions that spring from the heart,
>   Which throbs, with delight, to the first kiss of love.

Byron's inclination toward truth in poetry is already indicated in a kind of sad farewell "To Romance" in *Hours of Idleness*.

> Parent of golden dreams, Romance!
>   Auspicious Queen of childish joys . . .
> No more I tread thy mystic round,
>   But leave thy realms for those of Truth. . . .
>
> Romance! disgusted with deceit,
>   Far from thy motley court I fly,
> Where Affectation holds her seat,
>   And sickly Sensibility. . . .

It is characteristic of Byron also that he should outdo Moore in voluptuousness and that his realism should at times balance on the brink of irony. When he attempted to show the romance of passion in the poem "To Mary," which caused the suppression of

Fugitive Pieces, he was on the verge of a mood later expressed in
Don Juan:

> And the sad truth which hovers o'er my desk
> Turns what was once romantic to burlesque.
>
> (IV, 3)

And finally, even in the poems that owe most to "the late
Thomas Little" there is a directness of phrasing and a correspondence between feeling and phrase, even when it is trite, that somehow save them from the mere pampered prettiness of Moore's
lyrics.

Byron's imitations of conventional eighteenth century poetry
in heroic couplets were on the whole little better than most college exercises in that genre at the time, except perhaps in occasional bursts of Byronic gusto in "Thoughts Suggested by a College Examination." But in serious attempts at declamation and
high-flown sentiments, as in the prologue which he wrote for the
private theatricals at Southwell and in "Childish Recollections,"
there is little suggestion of the Popean wit or Byronic sparkle
that shortly after enlivened the best parts of *English Bards, and
Scotch Reviewers.* In these the trite ink-horn phrases ("deathless
fame," "cricket's manly toil," "the river's spoil") were scarcely
relieved by any originality, even when he was extolling friendships
that meant much to him.

In other imitations Byron was at least as successful as most
young poets. "The Death of Calmar and Orla" shows his skill in
capturing the melancholy aura of *Ossian* as well as the easily
parodied style. He would probably later have agreed with Dr.
Johnson's dictum that "a man might write such stuff for ever, if
he would *abandon* his mind to it."

Byron's imitations and translations from the classics are interesting both for what they reveal of his tastes in classical literature
and for the character of the rendering. Some of these were school
exercises but all indicate unmistakable Byronic biases. He made
several translations and imitations from Catullus, the Roman poet
of woeful passion, three from Anacreon's Odes (the graceful
amatory lyrics which Moore had translated in his own fashion),
one from Horace, one from the *Medea* of Euripides, and the
episode of Nisus and Euryalus, paraphrased from the ninth book
of the Aeneid. As a schoolboy Byron also made a number of
translations and imitations of the Epigrams of Martial, a satirical

genre for which he showed a fondness to the end of his days (see, for example, his epigrams on Castlereagh). The fragment which he translated at Harrow from the *Prometheus Vinctus* of Aeschylus has special interest as evidence of his early absorption in the Promethean character which came out in the poem "Prometheus" written at Diodati in 1816, the semi-Promethean Childe Harold, and the clearer identification in the defiant and indomitable Manfred.[3]

The two voices that emerge in the early poems as clearly Byron's own, however, have the peculiar accents of melancholy and mockery which were to gain resonance in the poet's later and maturer work. The most persistent note of melancholy in these early poems, and the one which apparently inspired his best and most sincere expression, was to be heard again in *Childe Harold* and to echo hauntingly in many of his later lyrics. It is a sentimental (and frequently sweetly lyrical) dwelling upon beauty of person or feeling or experience in the past, tempered with the sad reflection that it is irrevocably gone though it had been evanescently beautiful. The romantic haze of distance in time or place lends enchantment to it. It is the nostalgia for innocence which gives greatest poignancy to the Byronic longing for an ideal. It may be seen in such poems as "On a Distant View of the Village and School of Harrow on the Hill, 1806," "To a Beautiful Quaker," "The First Kiss of Love," "On the Death of a Young Lady, Cousin to the Author, and Very Dear to Him," and "Epitaph on a Beloved Friend." It is an undertone of other poems too, such as "On Leaving Newstead Abbey" and "To an Oak at Newstead." It rings clearest in some of his nostalgic poems of Scotland: "I Would I Were a Careless Child," "Lachin y Gair," and "When I Roved a Young Highlander." For all the undistinguished triteness of the phrasing, the feeling comes through, as for example in "Lachin y Gair":

> Though cataracts foam 'stead of smooth-flowing fountains,
>   I sigh for the valley of dark Loch na Garr.

The theme of idealized innocence and the beauty of boyhood loves finds more poignant if not more individual expression in

---

[3] It is with a Promethean defiance that Byron challenges the world and the gods of its idolatry in *Don Juan*. There is an element of Prometheus in all the Byronic heroes, from Bonivard through the protagonists of the Oriental tales to Sardanapalus.

"Stanzas to Jessy" (addressed to the Cambridge chorister Edleston):

> There is a Voice whose tones inspire
>   Such softened feelings in my breast
> I would not hear a Seraph Choir,
>   Unless that voice could join the rest.

The same might be said of "The Adieu," which becomes almost a nostalgic history of his youth and the loves that are past but not forgotten.

But the realistic-satiric vein in Byron found expression in a number of pieces, published and unpublished, that have the authentic Byronic wit and liveliness, even when they are not completely original in form or phrasing. The saucy tone of "To Lesbia" rises from present flirtation rather than the idealized past loves of his boyhood.

> Sixteen was then our utmost age,
>   Two years have lingering pass'd away, love!
> And now new thoughts our minds engage,
>   At least, I feel disposed to stray, love!

This and "To Woman" are only a refinement, with perhaps a little more mockery and cynicism than sentiment, of some of Thomas Little's themes. The realistic tone appears again in "Reply to Some Verses of J. M. B. Pigot, Esq., on the Cruelty of His Mistress":

> Why, Pigot, complain
> Of this damsel's disdain,
> Why thus in despair do you fret?
>   For months you may try,
>   Yet, believe me, a *sigh*
> Will never obtain a *coquette.*
>
> Would you teach her to love?
> For a time seem to rove;
> At first she may *frown* in a *pet;*
>   But leave her awhile,
>   She shortly will smile,
> And then you may *kiss* your *coquette.*

The sequel, "To the Sighing Strephon," carries the unrepentant realism a step further:

> I will not advance,
> By the rules of romance,
> To humour a whimsical fair. . . .
>
> While my blood is thus warm,
> I ne'er shall reform,
> To mix in the Platonists' school;
> Of this I am sure,
> Was my Passion so pure,
> Thy *Mistress* would think me a fool.

The light jeering tone appears in a few other poems published posthumously. For the most part they were occasional pieces and *jeux d'esprit* of the sort that Byron later wrote frequently and enclosed in letters from Italy. Their only importance is their indication of a style and a mood thus early displayed.

Two poems that voiced Byron's irritation at the hypocritical Puritan reaction in Southwell to his first volume give some foretaste of his later Popean satires. "To a Knot of Ungenerous Critics," written in tetrameter couplets, portrays Truth triumphing over the "baffled friends of Fiction," tearing the mask from all their pretensions. We see his model when he says, "Why should I point my pen of steel / To break 'such flies upon the wheel?' " In his "Soliloquy of a Bard in the Country" Byron uses the heroic couplet with something like the dexterity he was to display in *English Bards, and Scotch Reviewers.*

But when Byron approached the public with his first published volume, *Hours of Idleness,* he timorously suppressed all the lighter pieces, the ones that might have suggested the realism and the wit which were inherent in his personality and which certainly supplied the greater part of the originality in his early poems. It took the shock of the *Edinburgh Review* critique to reopen the satiric vein in print. It was never closed again in his letters or in his life.

3

Popean Satires

OF ALL THE SATIRES that Byron wrote in the heroic couplet in emulation of his great master Alexander Pope, the first one, *English Bards, and Scotch Reviewers*, was the most successful both in the sharpness of its satiric barbs and in the vigor of its audacious wit. E. H. Coleridge has said that it "appeals with fresh delight to readers who know the names of many of the 'bards' only because Byron mentions them, and count others whom he ridicules among the greatest poets of the century."[1]

The key to that success is the unaccountable manner in which by sheer force of a personality Byron endows with freshness the hackneyed themes, and phrases even, of times past or present. In fact, that is the formula by which we must measure Byron's success in all his poetry. We are constantly being surprised into listening without distaste to commonplaces that in another voice would be intolerable. He makes us feel that he is seeing the world for the first time and with his own eyes, and even well-worn tropes take a twist that makes them seem his own. But Byron generally suffers from quotation of individual lines, for it is the overall or cumulative effect rather than the concentrated essence in word or figure that adds up to an impression of strength and sincerity.

It is not my purpose here to repeat the often-told history of the composition of *English Bards, and Scotch Reviewers*. But it is important to observe that the poem suffered from Byron's method of composition. Like *The Giaour* it was a "snake of a poem" that added lengths to its tail as the white heat of indignation or inspiration directed. When he began *British Bards* at Cambridge in the

[1] *Poetry*, I, 295.

autumn of 1807 his purpose was simply to castigate and ridicule
"the scribbling crew" of his own day by measuring them against
a time when "sense and wit" were "with poesy allied." While the
Dunciad was his far-off shining model, he had no notion of
imitating its elaborate machinery of myth, nor did his talents lie in
that direction. His inspiration came rather from the whole of
"Pope's pure strain" by which he judged the extravagance, folly,
and dullness of his contemporaries. Following a brief introduction
extolling the days when Pope "Sought the rapt soul to charm,
nor sought in vain" and "great Dryden pour'd the tide of song,"
he sets out to catalogue the dullards of his own day "From soaring Southey down to grovelling Stott." After the *Edinburgh
Review* had roused his anger he added not only the satire on
Jeffrey and Lord Holland but also a number of other sections
which he fitted into the manuscript of the original poem. The
520 lines of *British Bards* had grown to 696 lines by the time he
published the first edition of *English Bards, and Scotch Reviewers.*
When he prepared the second edition before going abroad, he
added 102 lines at the beginning, including some gibes at "hoarse
Fitzgerald" (thus immortalizing a nonentity in the opening line),[2]
the mock-heroic invocation to his grey goose-quill (borrowed
from Pope's "Epistle to Dr. Arbuthnot"), a justification of his
taking up the cry against "knaves and fools," an apology for his
early verses, a return to Jeffrey and an attack on critics, and the
conclusion that it is "Better to err with Pope than shine with
Pye." This with other additions, such as the lampoon on Hewson
Clarke, who had ridiculed him in *The Satirist*, increased the length
to 1050 lines.

While the poem in its final state sometimes gives the impression of being fragments pieced together with little logic and some
repetition, there is an overall singleness of purpose and a concept
of the poetic ideal that is superimposed on the hodgepodge of
unrelated flayings of dunces. The theme as stated in the preface
— to make others write better — is an afterthought, but there is
the general aim consistent with Byron's constant belief in the
superiority of Dryden, Pope, and Gifford and the school of poetry
they represent to all the innovators of his own day.

It is not surprising that the poem is unequal. But the paradox
is that the most telling parts are not always the most original.
The "grey goose-quill," borrowed from Pope, becomes for Byron

---

[2] Byron wrote in 1816 in an annotated copy of the fourth edition after
this first line: "Right enough; but why notice such a mountebank?"

"That mighty instrument of little men" and is dipped in ink that is indelibly Byron's own. And so with the judgments of individual writers: most of them are not wildly original but reflect the views expressed by Gifford and other critics oriented to the standards and tastes of the Augustans. Part of his attack on "the ballad-monger Southey" owes something to Gifford's poem to Southey in the *Anti-Jacobin*, but it is Byron's lines rather than Gifford's that are remembered: "While Southey's epics cram the creaking shelves," and " 'God help thee,' Southey, and thy readers too."

There was nothing in the aspersions on Wordsworth that had not been repeated many times in the critical journals, but here truly in a few lines is "What oft was thought, but ne'er so well expressed."

> That mild apostate from poetic rule,
> The simple Wordsworth, framer of a lay
> As soft as evening in his favourite May,
> Who warns his friend "to shake off toil and trouble,
> And quit his books, for fear of growing double";
> Who, both by precept and example, shows
> That prose is verse, and verse is merely prose;
> Convincing all, by demonstration plain,
> Poetic souls delight in prose insane;
> And Christmas stories tortured into rhyme
> Contain the essence of the true sublime.
> Thus, when he tells the tale of Betty Foy,
> The idiot mother of "an idiot Boy";
> A moon-struck, silly lad, who lost his way,
> And, like his bard, confounded night with day;
> So close on each pathetic part he dwells,
> And each adventure so sublimely tells,
> That all who view the "idiot in his glory"
> Conceive the Bard the hero of the story.
>
> (E. B., 236–254)

In 1816 Byron wrote opposite this passage in a copy of the fourth edition: "Unjust." Unjust it was certainly to Words-worth's work as a whole and particularly to his best work, but no one has ever summed up Wordsworth's weaknesses and sillinesses more amusingly or more tellingly. "And Christmas stories tor-tured into rhyme": that line itself is a devastating critique of "Old Wordy's" self-conscious attempts to wring pathos out of events and characters of common life, as in "Simon Lee" or "Alice Fell." And the account of "The Idiot Boy" puts the cap

on all the ridicule that has been heaped on that most unfortunate
of Wordsworth's poems.

Byron was also reflecting the critical bias of the day when he
ridiculed, more unjustly, Coleridge, whose best work he gen-
uinely admired. But the barbs had enough of sharpness to stick,
and they still delight even Coleridge's greatest admirers.

> Yet none in lofty numbers can surpass
> The bard who soars to elegize an ass:
> So well the subject suits his noble mind,
> He brays, the Laureate of the long-eared kind.
>
> (*E. B.*, 261–264)

His lines on "Monk" Lewis, "Who fain would make Parnassus
a church-yard," neatly dispose of the Gothic tales, but his next
most crushing characterization is that of the Rev. William Lisle
Bowles, "The maudlin prince of mournful sonneteers." Byron
entered the fray with particular relish because his gorge had risen
when he saw the attack on Pope, on moral grounds, in the introduction to an edition of Pope's works which Bowles published
in 1806. The task of flaying Bowles for his abuse of Pope he had
delegated to Hobhouse, whose lines appear in the first edition.
But when he published the second with his name on the title
page he substituted his own caustic, retaining only Hobhouse's
first and best line: "Stick to thy Sonnets, Man! — at least they
sell." Byron had sufficiently sported with the sentimental son-
neteer in the first edition. Now he turned to Bowles the critic.
But the satire was less effective than he had intended, as he himself recognized. He wrote in 1821: "I am grieved to say, that in
reading over those lines, I repent of their having so far fallen
short of what I meant to express upon the subject of B's edition
of *Pope's Works*."[3] Perhaps the reason these lines failed to come
off the ground was that they bore too heavy a weight of Pope's
style for Byron to be quite himself in them.

His ire at Jeffrey, supposed author of the mocking critique of
his early poems, inspired a burst of wit and ferocity that is more
typically Byronic. His comparison of the editor of the *Edinburgh*

---

[3] Byron wrote this in his first letter in the Bowles-Pope controversy.
See *Letters and Journals*, V, 539. He began the paragraph: "Although I
regret having published *English Bards, and Scotch Reviewers*, the part
which I regret the least is that which regards Mr. B. with reference to
Pope."

Review with the hanging Judge Jeffreys is a tour de force that succeeds by its sheer audacity. The climax comes when the Judge's shade presents Jeffrey with a rope and hails him:

> Heir to my virtues! man of equal mind!
> Skilled to condemn as to traduce mankind,
> This cord receive! for thee reserved with care,
> To wield in judgment, and at length to wear.
>
> (*E. B.*, 456–459)

But Byron could not leave it there; he carried the attack into personalities in his ridicule of the farcical duel between Moore and Jeffrey, "When Little's leadless pistol met his eye," and in the accusation that "banquets spread at Holland House" corrupted the critics, while Lady Holland censored the critiques (in the *Edinburgh Review*) by breathing "o'er the page her purity of soul."

Byron's seemingly gratuitous assault on Moore probably had its source in ambivalent feelings about the poetry which had influenced so deeply his early life and verses. His relish for the amorous lyrics of Thomas Little was tinged with guilt, partly because he had adopted the Popean concept of the poet as one who "not in fancy's maze . . . wandered long, / But stoop'd to truth, and moralized his song," and partly because he was already a little ashamed of having been under the spell of such sickly sentimental poetry. Yet a regretful fondness hovers over his condemnation, which seems as much addressed to himself as to Moore.

The attack on Scott is more inexplicable, though one may make certain surmises based on a general knowledge of Byron's literary biases. His satiric summaries of *The Lay of the Last Minstrel* and *Marmion* give an inkling of the reasons for his dislike of this kind of "stale romance." Lovers of Scott in Byron's day as well as later must have felt that he was needlessly and cruelly breaking the fine border tales on the wheel of his own caprice. But Byron had already developed a native distaste for fanciful tales divorced from life. He could as truthfully have said then what he later wrote to John Murray: "But I hate things *all fiction.* . . . There should always be some foundation of fact for the most airy fabric, and pure invention is but the talent of a liar."[4]

[4] *Letters and Journals*, IV, 93. Letter of April 2, 1817.

It is significant that even after he became a warm admirer of
Scott as man and writer Byron never retracted what he had said
about the absurdity of the poetic border tales.[5] In the final
analysis his judgment of Scott's poetry, like his pert appraisal of
many other writers, does not vary greatly from our own. That
is why we can read his irreverent description with so much relish.
While schoolboys may still thrill to the rhythm of the song of
young Lochinvar, Scott's poetry scarcely holds us beyond the
sixth grade. Byron voiced our feelings in one of his lines on
Bowles: "All love thy strain, but children like it best."

When Byron turned to the drama he had an open field and he
unleashed his whole pack of expletives on the absurdities that
filled the stage at the time. If notes are required for an understanding of the topical allusions, that is a measure of the barren-
ness of theatrical writing in Byron's England. Only Sheridan, on
whom he calls to resuscitate Comedy, stands out, and Sheridan
had left the theater for politics and parties.

Byron was understandably self-conscious in attacking the vices
of the town, but he felt that in order to be a Popean moralist he
must include such a diatribe. To those who knew he had served
his apprenticeship to those vices he made apology:

> E'en I — least thinking of a thoughtless throng,
> Just skilled to know the right and choose the wrong,
> Freed at that age when Reason's shield is lost,
> To fight my course through Passion's countless host,
> Whom every path of Pleasure's flow'ry way
> Has lured in turn, and all have led astray —
> E'en I must raise my voice, e'en I must feel
> Such scenes, such men, destroy the public weal:
> Altho' some kind, censorious friend will say,
> "What art thou better, meddling fool, than they?"
> And every Brother Rake will smile to see
> That miracle, a Moralist in me.   (E. B., 689–700)

It was here that Byron again called on Gifford to raise his
voice "To drive this pestilence from out the land." And then he
turned to the "smaller fry" among the poets and took occasion to
make a bitter assault on "The paralytic puling of Carlisle," the

[5] It must be noted that in a later passage in *English Bards, and Scotch
Reviewers* (lines 911–948) Byron singled Scott out from among the lesser
crew of scribblers as deserving the highest praise if he would only undertake something worthy of his talents: "Thou, with powers that mock the
aid of praise, / Should'st leave to humbler bards ignoble lays."

guardian to whom he had dedicated his *Hours of Idleness* but who had inflicted a wound to his pride by failing to introduce him in the House of Lords. After praising a few lesser men like Rogers, Campbell, and Crabbe, who had clung to the heroic couplet and a semblance of Augustan dignity, though their themes were romantic, he admonished the best of the poets he had damned to mend their ways and "Restore the Muse's violated laws." Following a few more digressions and recapitulations, he ended with a defiant apology:

> But now, so callous grown, so changed since youth,
> I've learned to think, and sternly speak the truth;
> Learned to deride the critic's starch decree,
> And break him on the wheel he meant for me. . . .
>   if my incondite lay
> Hath wronged these righteous times, let others say:
> This, let the world, which knows not how to spare,
> Yet rarely blames unjustly, now declare.
>   (*E. B.*, 1057–1060, 1067–1070)

What has the world declared? In his own day it chuckled and thought him a very clever young Lord, both because he defended the traditional literary standards against romantic innovators and because the world delights to see high reputations humbled by ridicule whether it considers the satire justified or not. After Byron's anger had cooled and after he had made friends of a number of people he had attacked such as Moore and Scott, he could say that he wished "this miserable record of misplaced anger and indiscriminate acrimony" consigned to the flames. And in 1816 he wrote: "The greater part of this satire I most sincerely wish had never been written — not only on account of the injustice of much of the critical, and some of the personal part of it — but the tone and temper are such as I cannot approve."[6]

But Byron's repentance should not blind us to the genuine merits of much of *English Bards, and Scotch Reviewers.* As for the judgments themselves of individual writers, how often was Byron wrong if we measure them against the critical judgments of time, or at least of our own time? We could not take much exception to what Byron actually said about a few writers whose total work we now value more highly — as Byron himself did later. But what he said about the weaknesses of Wordsworth, Coleridge, and Scott still rings a bell in the twentieth century.

---

[6] *Poetry*, I, 381.

Our only real quarrel now would be with his overrating of such writers as Rogers, Campbell, and Gifford; but that blindness was a natural consequence of his bias toward the school of Pope.

With respect to the literary qualities of the poem, it is fair to say that, imitative as it is, the true Byronic spark often ignites lines that seem to be following a model. It goes without saying that if he had pruned the poem it would have been better. It seems to trail off on pedestrian wanderings after the first slashing blow at Jeffrey. But in the best parts it is not sacrilege — though Byron himself might have thought it so — to say that he surpasses Pope. There is a ringing candor springing from a freshness of vision that is his own, matched by a neat and appropriate phrase that is the product of his own wit, as in some of the lines on Wordsworth quoted above. But what makes him more congenial to the twentieth century than Pope is his skeptical realism that despite his deference to tradition will not allow him to feign any belief or emotion he does not feel. Byron's brash *lèse-majesté* contrasts sharply with the bland (and essentially timid) respect for the conventional and the traditional among the Augustans.

If Byron had been more successful in *English Bards* — successful not only in terms of popular approval and applause but also in terms of genuine satisfaction with *his* accomplishment as compared with that of Pope and Gifford — would he have become a true Augustan of the nineteenth century? Given his temperament and the literary and intellectual climate of his time, it seems unlikely. The pressures and the conflicts, both internal and external, were too strong. Even if *Childe Harold* had not swept him into the camp of the Romantics, could he have withstood the wave of Romanticism? He tried, and he scarcely gave up even after the wave had swept over him. But he knew he would never reach the haven of Popean assurance.

Hints from Horace was a deliberate attempt on Byron's part to follow up the success of *English Bards, and Scotch Reviewers*. In his subtitle he called it a sequel, but it became something more than that. Seemingly he was merely following his intention, expressed in the preface of the earlier satire, to make others write better. Here are the rules laid down by Horace in the *Ars Poetica*, the Bible of the neo-classicists. He is merely bringing them up to date and furnishing modern examples. But the rules, though sometimes stated in Horace's own tropes, seem to be derived from Byron's personal observation. As a schoolboy he had hated Horace as a symbol of "The drilled dull lesson, forced down word by word / In my repugnant youth." But rereading the *Ars Poetica* in Athens in 1811 he saw an opportunity to improve on Horace's didactic dullness while teaching his own lesson to the present — a lesson essentially based on the common sense of the classic writers.

It is interesting to see how Horace's platitudes take on the Byronic tone and color. Horace's famous "Mountains will labor, and there will be born a ridiculous mouse" takes at once a personal cast: "He sinks to Southey's level in a trice, / Whose Epic Mountains never fail in mice!" He follows Horace's passage on the ages of man but lightens it with personal asides and additions of a typical Byronic flavor.

> Behold him Freshman! forced no more to groan
> O'er Virgil's devilish verses and his own;
> Prayers are too tedious, Lectures too abstruse,
> He flies from Tavell's frown to "Fordham's Mews";
> (Unlucky Tavell! doomed to daily cares
> By pugilistic pupils, and by bears,)[7]
> Fines, Tutors, tasks, Conventions threat in vain,
> Before hounds, hunters, and Newmarket Plain.
> Rough with his elders, with his equals rash,
> Civil to sharpers, prodigal of cash;
> Constant to nought — save hazard and a whore,
> Yet cursing both — for both have made him sore:
> Unread (unless since books beguile disease,
> The P–x becomes his passage to Degrees);
> Fooled, pillaged, dunned, he wastes his terms away,
> And unexpelled, perhaps, retires M.A....
>   (*H. H.*, 225–240)

Having drawn this much from his own experience and observation, he projected the future of the English gentleman with Swiftian candor and spleen: he marries for money, is sunk in avarice, and finally,

> Peevish and spiteful, doting, hard to please,
> Commending every time, save times like these;
> Crazed, querulous, forsaken, half forgot,
> Expires unwept — is buried — Let him rot!
>   (*H. H.*, 259–262)

[7] The Rev. G. F. Tavell was Byron's tutor at Trinity College, Cambridge, during his last term in 1807. Byron had some tussles with his tutor regarding the keeping of a tame bear in his rooms, which he had brought there, he said, "to teach the Fellows manners," and "to *sit for a fellowship*."

Though never slavish in his restatement of Horace's sensible advice on literary propriety, Byron followed rather closely the themes and points of view and sometimes gave almost a literal rendering of the generalizations in the *Ars Poetica* for the first 300 lines. His illustrations, of course, are his own and usually contemporary, or at least reflect his own taste in authors of the past. The facetious or ferocious tone contrasts with Horace's more sober and even-tempered protests against absurdity. But when Byron turned to the drama, which was Horace's major concern, he went off on his own abusive harangue against the Opera.

From this point on Byron wandered at will with many digressions, though he touched nearly all the themes of the Latin poet and in the duller parts merely paraphrased them. His recollection of the theater brought forth a personal address to Hobhouse (he later substituted the classical name):

> Moschus! with whom once more I hope to sit,
> And smile at folly, if we can't at wit;
> Yes, Friend! for thee I'll quit my cynic cell,
> And bear Swift's motto, "Vive la bagatelle!"
> Which charmed our days in each Ægean clime,
> As oft at home, with revelry and rhyme.
>
> (H. H., 341–346)

At several points Byron voiced views that have no parallel in Horace, as when he attacked the Licensing Act that constituted a censorship of frankness and broad humor on the stage, such as prevailed in the Restoration plays. He laid the blame for part of the current squeamishness on the Methodists.

> Faith cants, perplexed apologist of Sin!
> While the Lord's servant chastens whom he loves,
> And Simeon kicks, where Baxter only "shoves."[8]
>
> (H. H., 380–382)

Byron explained in a note: "Mr. Simeon is the very bully of beliefs, and castigator of 'good works.' He is ably supported by

[8] Byron's note: *"Baxter's Shove to heavy-a---d Christians,* the veritable title of a book once in good repute, and likely enough to be so again." Byron was mistaken in the author and title; it was a tract or sermon entitled *An Effectual Shove to the heavy-arse Christian,* by William Bunyan (1768).

John Stickles, a labourer in the same vineyard: — but I say no more, for, according to Johnny in full congregation, 'No hopes for them as laughs.' "

There follow tributes to Swift and "matchless Hudibras," facetious references to Wordsworth and Southey, amplified in the notes, and a long apostrophe to Jeffrey, taunting him for not replying to *English Bards, and Scotch Reviewers*. One has the feeling that while Byron wished to show his general approval of the Augustan standards of propriety, taste, and wit by citing the authority of Horace, the chief pleasure he found in the task came from the freedom it gave him (or that he seized in the process) to comment on the world about him as the spirit moved him. It gave an outlet to the critical, realistic, humorous, or caustic side of his nature whose expression had been confined mainly to his letters since the suppression of his early verses. *English Bards*, by comparison, is more soberly addressed to the castigation of Vice and Folly in the approved manner of Pope. With all its looseness of construction it has fewer deviations from the spirit of the model. In parts of *Hints from Horace* Byron is more relaxed and more himself. In some ways, in scope and range, if not in style, the *Hints* anticipated the free form of *Don Juan*, and that may have accounted for his tenacious fondness for it. He read it over in 1820 and wanted to publish it. He wrote Murray: "As far as versification goes, it is good; and, on looking back to what I wrote about that period, I am astonished to see how *little* I have trained on. I wrote better then than now; but that comes from my having fallen into the atrocious bad state of the times — partly."[9]

It is customary to say, as E. H. Coleridge does, that Byron's preference for the *Hints* above most of his other works is an instance of his blindness in judging his own poetry, and that is true in that much of it is imitative, not only in subject but also in style, of the traditional poetry of the eighteenth century. But in the passages, which are not few, where he gives free rein to his own genius for sense and wit enshrined in the apt phrase, he equals the best in *English Bards*.

The Curse of Minerva, written in Athens about the same time as *Hints from Horace*, is in many ways the dullest of Byron's satires. In spite of the *saeva indignatio* against Lord Elgin for his rape of the Grecian marbles, a theme better handled in *Childe Harold*, it is scarcely more than a humdrum humorless diatribe in

[9] *Letters and Journals*, V, 77. Letter of Sept. 23, 1820.

conventional couplets. It is significant that the glowing sunset
picture at the beginning,

> Slow sinks, more lovely ere his race be run,
> Along Morea's hills the setting Sun;
> Not, as in northern climes, obscurely bright,
> But one unclouded blaze of living light. . . .
>
> (C. of M., 1–4)

was transferred without violence to its spirit, and with some
appropriateness, to the beginning of the third canto of *The
Corsair*.

Byron chose to make the maimed and mourning Pallas Athena
hurl her execrations on Elgin the spoiler, worse than Turk and
Goth, and the country whence he came. The poet, sinking his
own nostalgia for the land beyond the Tweed, replies that
"England owns him not . . . thy plunderer was a Scot."

> And well I know within that bastard land
> Hath Wisdom's goddess never held command. . . .
>
> (C. of M., 131–132)

Nothing better can be expected from a land whose thistle sym-
bolizes its "stern sterility," "A land of meanness, sophistry, and
mist." But Pallas will not accept this apology. Her vengeance
will be "To turn my counsels far from lands like thine," and to
fix her curse on Elgin and his seed: "Be all the sons as senseless as
the sire." She then goes on to picture, in a less heroic and a more
Byronic mood, Elgin's "stone shop" in London, viewed by the
gawking populace. "While many a languid maid, with longing
sigh, / On giant statues casts the curious eye," and observing
"the mighty back and length of limb," concludes, "These Greeks
indeed were proper men!" and "Alas! Sir Harry is no Hercules!"

Then by a curious transition Athena turns her accusations
against British policies abroad and at home:

> Hers were the deeds that taught her lawless son
> To do what oft Britannia's self had done.
>
> (C. of M., 211–212)

First she points to England's brazen seizure of the Danish fleet
at Copenhagen in 1807, the uprisings in India, "where Ganges'
swarthy race / Shall shake your tyrant empire to its base," and
finally the British bungling and failures in the Peninsular cam-

paigns, citing the Battle of Barossa as evidence that the Spanish did not like or trust their British allies. At home the picture is no brighter: "loud though Revel howls, / Here Famine faints, and yonder Rapine prowls." Athena proclaims, "Your strength a name, your bloated wealth a dream," while "The starved mechanic breaks his rusting loom."

There is evidence here that Byron had become a citizen of the world during his travels and that he was taking an increasing interest in foreign and domestic affairs such as led him to make his maiden speech in Parliament a defense of the "starved mechanic." But his poetry had sunk to a jog-trot of pedestrian propaganda unrelieved by more than a hint of his usual sparkling wit.

The Waltz, written in the autumn of 1812 after his first season of fame had introduced him to Whig society and the balls and waltzing parties of Caroline Lamb, has a bouncing bitterness and an occasional waggish pungency. Here as in *The Curse of Minerva* he has left the subject matter of Pope and Gifford. The manner and mood are nearer to Swift, and the whole tone suggests something of the Swiftian inverted romantic Puritanism: revulsion against physical display and physical contacts. In Byron it becomes something like the prudery of the libertine. There is no doubt that the savagery of the satire owes much to the psychic repressions of his lameness, which prevented him from dancing.

> Imperial Waltz! imported from the Rhine
> (Famed for the growth of pedigrees and wine) ...
> Through the full veins thy gentler poison swims,
> And wakes to Wantonness the willing limbs.
> 				(*Waltz*, 29–30, 37–38)

Sometimes the sheer burlesque erupts into some memorable quips, as when in his mock praise of George the Third he lauds him "For graciously begetting George the Fourth." But the prurient Puritanism overwhelms the wit in all but a few lines.

> Waltz — Waltz alone — both legs and arms demands,
> Liberal of feet, and lavish of her hands;
> Hands which may freely range in public sight
> Where ne'er before — but — pray "put out the light."
> 				(*Waltz*, 113–116)

But Byron's reluctance to acknowledge the poem was not due mainly to moral trepidation. His flippant references to royalty (obviously the Prince Regent) might well have caused political repercussions:

> Round all the confines of the yielded waist,
> The strangest hand may wander undisplaced:
> The lady's in return may grasp as much
> As princely paunches offer to her touch.
> Pleased round the chalky floor how well they trip
> One hand reposing on the royal hip!
>
> (*Waltz*, 192–197)

The Humphry Clinkerish letter "To the Publisher," by Horace Hornem, the supposed author of the poem, has more of the normal Byronic humor than most of the too-earnest couplets which suggest the rash impetuosity of Swift's attacks on the bodily functions and passions of men and women.

After composing *The Waltz*, Byron did not attempt any extensive satire in the heroic couplet again until 1821.[10] This was due largely, no doubt, to the diversion of his talents into the melancholy romantic vein by the success of *Childe Harold*. He continued to show a fondness for the couplet, however, and used it, with variations (sometimes in tetrameters, as in *The Giaour, The Bride of Abydos*, and *Mazeppa;* sometimes relieved by alternate rhyme and even anapests, as in the *Bride*), in all his romantic narratives from the Oriental tales to *The Island*. When he took up satire again in 1817 he had found the more congenial measure of the ottava rima. But though he had ceased to have hopes of rivaling Pope, he returned to the couplet satire twice more.

On August 7, 1821, he wrote to Murray: "I send you a thing which I scratched off lately, a mere buffoonery, to quiz *The Blues*, in two literary eclogues. If published, it must be *anonymously:* . . . You may send me a proof, if you think it worth the trouble. . . ."[11] It was the concoction of an idle moment, and Byron knew it would not add to his fame. Six weeks later he countermanded the order for proofs, saying it was not meant for publication; but he could seldom resist publishing anything he

---

[10] Exception must be made for a few occasional pieces like "A Sketch," and for *jeux d'esprit* enclosed in letters, such as the satire on Sam Rogers and the "delicate declension" of Dr. Polidori's tragedy written for Murray. His malicious wit usually overflowed in that form, but most of these pieces were published posthumously.

[11] *Letters and Journals*, V, 338.

had written, and he allowed it to appear anonymously in the third number of *The Liberal* in 1823.

The subject was a favorite one with Byron. His letters and journals are full of persiflage on boring literary ladies (and gentlemen), to whom the word "Blues," or "Blue-stockings," had been applied since the late eighteenth century.[12] And he had already made some of his most witty remarks on the breed in *Beppo* and *Don Juan*, the best perhaps being the ironic description of the learned lady Donna Inez in the first canto of his mock-epic. *The Blues* is a disappointment from the beginning, particularly in comparison with his better satire on the same subject elsewhere. The dialogue interrupts, perhaps purposely, the rhythm of the lines. The humor is too well worn and obvious, as in references to poetry ending up at the pastry-cook's. The heroic couplet has descended to a very unheroic jog-trot, with irregular metre and atrocious rhymes: "lead in — reading," "patience — publications," "hours — pours," "ether — together." Occasional anapests give a swing to one line which is not matched in the next. A few rhymes, however, suggest the intentional facetiousness for comic or ironic effect that is so common a feature of *Don Juan:* "shock it — pocket," "speaking of Scamp ill — set an example." The satiric thrusts at Scamp the lecturer (Hazlitt), Botherby the Bore (Sotheby), Mouthy (Southey), Wordswords (Wordsworth), Miss Lilac (Annabella Milbanke), and Lady Bluebottle (Lady Holland) rarely run into cleverness.

Byron made one more ambitious attempt to wield the Popean couplet in serious satire. *The Age of Bronze* was intended for anonymous publication in *The Liberal*. (It was finally published separately by John Hunt.) Although he wrote deprecatingly of it to Leigh Hunt, he felt that he had given the best of his mind and talents to the composition, for it dealt with matters that deeply concerned him. He told Hunt: "It is calculated for the reading part of the million, being all on politics, etc., etc., etc.,

[12] Boswell in his *Life of Johnson* (Oxford Standard Authors Edition, II, 412) gives this account of the origin of the Blue-stocking Clubs: "One of the most eminent members of those societies, when they first commenced, was Mr. Stillingfleet, whose dress was remarkably grave, and in particular it was observed, that he wore blue stockings. Such was the excellence of his conversation, that his absence was felt as so great a loss, that it used to be said, 'We can do nothing without the *blue stockings*'; and thus by degrees the title was established."

and a review of the day in general, — in my early *English Bards* style, but a little more stilted, and somewhat too full of 'epithets of war' and classical and historical allusions."[13] But the tone is quite different from that of his early satire. The aim now is not so much the clever witticism attained by means of zeugma and other Popean devices; it is rather the propounding of bold and bitter truth with sharpened irony in balanced and telling phrases. At its best the poem suggests the swing and power of "great Dryden" rather than the neat packaging of Pope.

The theme centers on the exile and death of Napoleon, with recollections of his career, and the Congress of Verona, where the Allied monarchs gathered to make Europe less free. From this Byron turns to the landed and other interests who profited from the war. Their one concern is that the peace has brought a reduction in the price of corn.

> Safe in their barns, these Sabine tillers sent
> Their brethren out to battle — why? for rent! ...
> Blood, sweat, and tear-wrung millions — why? — for rent!
>   (*A. of B.*, 618–619, 621)

Byron had already expressed his mixed feelings about Napoleon in his Ode and in the third canto of *Childe Harold*. Now he could "Sigh to behold the Eagle's lofty rage / Reduced to nibble at his narrow cage." Although he could feel the pathos of Napoleon's exile and lonely death, the final sorrow is the thought of what this Promethean figure might have been:

> A single step into the right had made
> This man the Washington of worlds betrayed:
> A single step into the wrong has given
> His name a doubt to all the winds of heaven. ...
>   (*A. of B.*, 233–236)

But hope for the future lies in the awakening spark of liberty in Spain, in Greece, and in the New World. His mind and his verse glow with the theme:

> 'T is the *old* aspiration breathed afresh,
> To kindle souls within degraded flesh,
> Such as repulsed the Persian from the shore
> Where Greece *was* — No! she still is Greece once more.
>   (*A. of B.*, 268–271)

---

[13] *Letters and Journals*, VI, 161. Letter of Jan. 10, 1823.

Byron's ardor lends a heroic quality to the couplets, but the spirit and mood are those of *Childe Harold*. He returns to sardonic satire in describing the Congress at Verona where the royal guests "Crowd to the theatre with loyal rage, / The comedy is not upon the stage." There is a good deal of caustic in his pictures of "the coxcomb Czar, / The Autocrat of waltzes and of war!" and gourmand Louis, "A scholar always, now and then a wit, / And gentle when Digestion may permit." One need not go all the way with E. H. Coleridge, who says that there is evidence in the poem that Byron had "learned to think and to feel," that in *The Age of Bronze* he had "wedded 'a striking passage of history' to striking and imperishable verse." But the poem certainly gives evidence of Byron's "sincerity and strength" and of his ability to impress his personality on conventional forms.

4

Childe Harold, Cantos I-II

Childe Harold's Pilgrimage is not only the greatest confessional poem of the Romantic Period in English literature. It is
also the most authentic record of the *Weltschmerz* of the era that
followed the disillusionments of the French Revolution and the
Napoleonic wars. These are the qualities which account in largest
measure for its popularity in its own day and its continued influence throughout Europe and America during the nineteenth century. That it also served as a picturesque travelogue for people
who could not travel no doubt added to its appeal but could not
in itself have caused its tremendous impact and its hold on the
popular imagination. Byron wrote what may be called the first
Childe Harold (Cantos I and II) "amidst the scenes which it
attempts to describe," beginning it in Jannina in October, 1809,
and finishing the second canto at Smyrna in March, 1810. He had
been reading some extracts from Spenser and so began his
"fictitious" poem of the wandering pilgrim in the Spenserian
stanza.

Perhaps the whole cycle of Byronic melancholy can be traced
in *Childe Harold*. But these multiple and changing moods all
center on the inexorable dilemma of the romantic ego: the com-
pulsive search for an ideal and a perfection that do not exist in
the world of reality. *Childe Harold* is the record of that search
and of the states of mind that follow recognition of its inevitable
failure: bitterness, remorse, sweet sadness, cynicism, forced
stoicism, or exhausted resignation (and a dozen others that merge
into each other). But the foredoomed pilgrimage goes on, for the
longing that drives the Pilgrim is insatiable and it feeds on bright
glimpses of the strange and unexplored, the far away and long

38

ago, though they inevitably fade into the light of common day on nearer approach.

One manifestation of Byron's longing for the ideal and his perception of the failure of the real to satisfy it we have already seen in some of his early poems: an idealization of innocent and evanescent beauty. A perfect example is the tribute to Ianthe (Lady Charlotte Harley, the eleven-year-old daughter of Lady Oxford) prefixed to the first canto in the seventh edition, 1814:

> Ah! may'st thou ever be what now thou art,
> Nor unbeseem the promise of thy Spring —
> As fair in form, as warm yet pure in heart,
> Love's image upon earth without his wing,
> And guileless beyond Hope's imagining!

He congratulated himself that, twice her age, he could safely view the "ripening beauties" of this "Young Peri of the West," but disillusionment, which he kept out of the verses, had already intruded, for he wrote Lady Melbourne on April 5, 1813, that Lady Charlotte was one "whom I should love for ever if she could always be only eleven years old, and whom I shall probably marry when she is old enough, and bad enough to be made into a modern wife."[1]

A severer melancholy arises from contemplation of the fact that reality viewed closely is a sham or does not satisfy the mind's craving for the ideal, the perfect. The mind seeks an escape, or at least a psychologically satisfying way of viewing the dilemma. One can relish one's misery and find relief in parading the extent of the suffering of one's supersensitive soul attuned to the ideal but forced to face hard reality and the cruelty of disillusionment. Or one can meet the monster by pretending to oneself or others that one has achieved a sort of philosophic calm, by rising above the lot of mankind, and with stoical restraint or cynical detachment one can then assume an attitude of godlike superiority to both the insatiable desire for perfection in the experiences of life and love, and the common disappointment in the imperfection of the world as it is. Byron dramatized these moods spectacularly in *Childe Harold,* even in the later more mature cantos. The mawkish and sentimental tone of parts of the first two cantos is largely responsible, especially in later criticism of his poetry, for the belief that he was a poseur, that he magnified his sins and the

[1] *Lord Byron's Correspondence,* I, 145.

acuteness of his mental sufferings. Perhaps the attempt at archaic language, where it is used, helps to give the impression of affectation, but without defending the poetry in these passages one may still say that Byron faced frankly and honestly the basic emotional problems of himself and his time.

Let us look more closely at some of these Byronic "poses" and see how they relate to the general romantic dilemma as Byron presented it in *Childe Harold*. The so-called "Satanic pose," the confession of satiety and a sense of sin with which the first canto opens, was only a too literal statement of what was not false but only seems so because of the sentimental clichés into which his feelings naturally fell. Byron was a victim of his taste for the elegant and gilded generalizations of eighteenth century poetry, and the habit dogged his best efforts in the romantic vein. But he was telling the truth in verse when he said he had "felt the fulness of Satiety" and "through Sin's long labyrinth had run." He had come face to face with the hardest reality for the Romantic to bear: the imperfection of human nature.

The "lonely soul" mood follows. "Apart he stalked in joyless reverie" because he is supersensitive and stands above, in aspirations if not in deeds, that part of mankind which is content to live in the world of dull reality. In that mood the wild aspects of nature, not the tame Wordsworthian lakes and pastures, soothe his mind. He sees a reflection of his own uncompromising spirit in the torrent, the craggy mountain, the ocean, and the deep woods, "Where things that own not man's dominion dwell."

The worldly wisdom, akin to that in his early verses to John Pigot, except that the tone is melancholy rather than facetious, grows from observation of the frailty of human nature:

> Maidens, like moths, are ever caught by glare,
> And Mammon wins his way where Seraphs might despair.
>
> (I, 9)

And again:

> Not much he kens, I ween, of Woman's breast,
> Who thinks that wanton thing is won by sighs. . . .
> Disguise ev'n tenderness, if thou art wise;
> Brisk Confidence still best with woman copes:
> Pique her and soothe in turn — soon Passion crowns thy
>   hopes.   (II, 34)

The sadness of things past, the regretted farewell to people, experiences, or things, once beautiful but now only a memory, the beauty and melancholy of things far away in time or place, or unfamiliar, are all a part of the ineffable romantic longing for perfection which is constantly disappointed. "Bound to the earth, he lifts his eye to heaven."

And so with the love of the picturesque and dramatic, the temporary idealizing of the past and the unfamiliar. The pilgrim finds Lisbon from the Tagus a beautiful vision of white houses on the hills, but disillusionment follows immediately when he lands and sees "A nation swoln with ignorance and pride," and the "dingy denizens . . . reared in dirt." And the pageantry of the battles in Spain ends with the reflection, à la Falstaff, of the sophistry of honor. The heroes are the "broken tools, that tyrants cast away." Only the Spanish maidens, seen briefly in Seville, are spared in the general unmasking. Not even the Houris can match "Spain's dark-glancing daughters." They have "Beauties that even a cynic must avow." The description of the bull fight at Cadiz follows the familiar pattern. The colorful spectacle is built up in chivalric terms until the horse is mangled and the scene ends in blood and cruelty, "sweet sight for vulgar eyes."

The moralizing on the ruins and on history, the *sic transit gloria mundi* theme, which has come to be considered the dominant one in *Childe Harold*, does not appear often in the first canto, and in the second, though "the glory that was Greece" seems to be the central theme, it takes some peculiar forms. In viewing the ruins of Greece Byron does not so much stress the vanity of ambition (as he does in the stanzas on the Roman ruins in Canto IV) as the evidence of a living and deathless spirit in the ancient monuments — a lesson to the slavish modern Greeks and to the world at large which has profited from Greek culture, and now, in the person of Lord Elgin, is basely plundering those relics. There is the complaint that the modern Greeks are not like their ancestors:

> Where are thy men of might? thy grand in soul?
> Gone — glimmering through the dream of things that
> were. . . .   (II, 2)

There is recognition of the inevitable passing of cultures and religions:

Look on this spot — a Nation's sepulchre!
Abode of Gods, whose shrines no longer burn.
Even Gods must yield — religions take their turn:
'T was Jove's — 't is Mahomet's — and other Creeds
Will rise with other years, till Man shall learn
Vainly his incense soars, his victim bleeds;
Poor child of Doubt and Death, whose hope is built on reeds.

(II, 3)

But it is the Greece of "lost gods and godlike men" that holds
him in the end:

Where'er we tread 't is haunted, holy ground;
No earth of thine is lost in vulgar mould,
But one vast realm of wonder spreads around,
And all the Muse's tales seem truly told,
Till the sense aches with gazing to behold
The scenes our earliest dreams have dwelt upon. . . .

(II, 88)

Other moods in *Childe Harold* are all different facets of the
same thwarted search which is the heart of romantic aspiration
and despair. Cries against restraint and tyrants are born of the
desire for freedom from all limitations of the spirit and mind of
man. Expressions of the beauty and bitterness of love always are
coupled with the implied theme that the unpossessed is sweetest
("Love has no gift so grateful as his wings"). Momentary exultation in scenery or situations (the convoy on the dark Ionian Sea,
"Monastic Zitza" overlooking the high mountains of Albania, the
"glittering minarets of Tepalen," the kilted Albanian soldiers
dancing around the night-fires) lift the spirit to half-believed
transcendence over drab reality. Disillusionment is held at a
distance while these picturesque moments last, but over them
hovers the sadness of transience, and there follow moods of disappointment, cynicism, world-weariness, or resignation.

However, the rereading of the whole of *Childe Harold* shows
a balance of the pleasantly picturesque with the melancholy in
the first two cantos, as compared with the gloomy egoism of the
last two. One has the feeling that in spite of himself Byron was
so carried away by his own native zest for experience and the
novelty that his travels presented as to hold his gloom in abeyance or make the "pleasing woe" complement the descriptions.
In these early cantos once Harold is on his way, "More restless

than the swallow in the skies," he tends to forget his "early youth misspent" and to concern himself more objectively with the scenes of his travels than in the third and fourth cantos. He has not yet grown so "agèd in this world of woe" or so blasé "that no wonder waits him," as Byron pictured Harold (or himself) in Canto III. More than two-thirds of the second canto deals objectively with the Albanian journey and the plight of Greece. The most dismal stanzas, those which end the canto, were added later after he learned of the death of Edleston, the Cambridge chorister, and they are not an integral part of the "Romaunt."

In the rambling scheme of the poem, with its many asides and digressive comments, as well as in the alternate blowing and pricking of bubbles, the Byronic method later developed with more assurance and skill in *Don Juan* is already apparent. The disparity between desire and fulfillment, the unquenchable thirst for ideality and the dissatisfaction with reality, is the common theme. In *Childe Harold* the unmasking reveals the melancholy face of the real world; in *Don Juan* the face is more often seen as grotesque and deserving only irony and mockery. That the ironic mood was present in Byron when he wrote *Childe Harold* and that he barely suppressed it is evident in the fact that the song he wrote to follow stanza 84 of the first canto, "The Girl of Cadiz," both in its spirit and in its rollicking rhythm and even its rhymes, is suggestive of *Don Juan:*

> Oh never talk again to me
>   Of northern climes and British ladies;
> It has not been your lot to see,
>   Like me, the lovely Girl of Cadiz. . . .
>
> Our English maids are long to woo,
>   And frigid even in possession;
> And if their charms be fair to view,
>   Their lips are slow at Love's confession.

It was only after he saw that it was quite out of tone with *Childe Harold* that he substituted the more insipid "To Inez."

Byron was warned by Hobhouse and other friends that the thin veil of fiction would not hide the autobiography in the poem. He had some trepidations and so tried to throw dust in the eyes of the public: "It has been suggested to me by friends," he wrote in the preface, ". . . that in this fictitious character,

'Childe Harold,' I may incur the suspicion of having intended some real personage: this I beg leave, once for all, to disclaim — Harold is the child of imagination, for the purpose I have stated. In some very trivial particulars, and those merely local, there might be grounds for such a notion; but in the main points, I should hope, none whatever." But knowing how much of his life and feelings had gone into the poem, his friends cautioned him before publication that Harold's "Monastic Dome," where "laughing dames . . . long had fed his youthful appetite," might too easily be identified with Newstead Abbey, where he had amused himself with the pretty chambermaids before he went abroad. Byron wrote to his worried literary agent Dallas: "If in parts I may be thought to have drawn from myself, believe me it is but in parts, and I shall not own even to that. . . . I would not be such a fellow as I have made my hero for all the world."[2]

But when the whole world refused to accept his denial and even assumed that he had only hinted at deeds that were darker than any he portrayed, Byron protested again in the preface to the fourth edition that Harold was only a fictitious character. "Had I proceeded with the Poem, this character would have deepened as he drew to the close; for the outline which I once meant to fill up for him was, with some exceptions, the sketch of a modern Timon, perhaps a poetical Zeluco."

Byron liked to picture himself as a poetical Zeluco, a character in a novel of that name by John Moore which he had read as a boy and which deeply impressed him. Zeluco, a guilt-ridden figure, is fated to do evil because environmental circumstances of his youth have misshaped his character: his father's early death, his mother's indulgence and neglect, and his false education made him a cruel sensualist and a misanthrope. But there were vast differences between Zeluco and Harold, mainly because Harold resembled Byron more than he did the hero (or villain) of Moore's novel. Harold was not cruel and was easily roused by cruelty to others, and his "lonely soul" mood was a passing one that did not prevent him from espousing the cause of humanity against tyranny. In refusing to identify himself with his hero, however, Byron did not wholly falsify, for in one sense Harold is not Byron; he *is* the child of Byron's imagination. When he wrote, Byron escaped into an alter ego which was only a part of himself and gave expression to aspects of his nature of which his common sense could not quite approve.

[2] *Letters and Journals*, II, 66. Letter of Oct. 31, 1811.

Actually the affectations of the "poetical Zeluco" scarcely go beyond the introductory stanzas, where the half-hearted attempt at Spenserian archaisms increases the silliness of the sentimentalized Satanism. As soon as he leaves this mawkish self-portrait and moves on to the more objective scenes of travel, the affectation diminishes; and while the poetry may still be commonplace or trite in phrasing, it is characterized by a directness of observation and an honesty of reflection. Though it seldom reaches the passionate eloquence or the depth of feeling of the third and fourth cantos, some lines and stanzas lift it above the mere sentimental *Weltschmerz* it is credited with being. Such is stanza 27, one of the few admired by the hard-headed Hobhouse, the one containing the line "More restless than the swallow in the skies," and ending "But as he gazed on truth his aching eyes grew dim." And some of the picturesque descriptions, of Cintra, of Spain, of "Andalusia's maids," of the bull fight, and especially of the Greek landscape and monuments, are superb. They glow with a fervor that lifts them above their own commonplace phrasing and makes them resound ringingly in the memory. Nor are the reflections childish. When Byron admonished the Greeks,

> Hereditary Bondsmen! know ye not
> *Who* would be free *themselves* must strike the blow?
> (II, 76)

he voiced a political realism that was prophetic and displayed a wisdom far in advance of his day.

5

Childe Harold, Cantos III-IV

No SOONER had Byron left England, shaking its dust from his feet after the scandal of the separation, than he began the third canto of *Childe Harold*. The first stanzas were composed in Brussels following his visit to the field of Waterloo on May 4, 1816. The canto was completed by the 4th of July at the Villa Diodati above the Lake of Geneva after a boat trip with Shelley to Montreux and Lausanne. The experiences of his four years of fame and the conviction of his own "delinquencies" gave him the right to say without affectation that he had "grown agèd in this world of woe, / In deeds, not years, piercing the depths of life, / So that no wonder waits him." Yet his mind was "rife / With airy images, and shapes which dwell / Still unimpaired, though old, in the Soul's haunted cell."

A weight fell from him as he left England and all the compulsions of his fame. As he took up the theme again of Childe Harold, "The wandering outlaw of his own dark mind," he felt free to speak in his own voice without subterfuge or pretense of fiction. Henceforth Harold is Byron's own self, or his acknowledged alter ego. The poetic tone has improved with the genuineness of the expression. But like other romantic poets in moods of dejection — like Wordsworth in his famous Ode and Coleridge bewailing the loss of his "shaping spirit of imagination" in a poem that demonstrates it at its height — Byron too had misgivings about his ability to sing his woe with the clear voice of his youth:

> Since my young days of passion — joy, or pain —
> Perchance my heart and harp have lost a string —
> And both may jar: it may be, that in vain
> I would essay as I have sung to sing. . . .   (III, 4)

But if anything his heart and harp had gained a string, one whose notes added to the richness and the poignancy of the melody. Here is "Byronism" in its most poetic statement and finest sweep. At his best he comes close to the transcendental dream of achieving reality in ideal forms, the creations of his mind that somehow through the alchemy of art take a life of their own.

> 'T is to create, and in creating live
> A being more intense that we endow
> With form our fancy, gaining as we give
> The life we image, even as I do now —
> What am I? Nothing: but not so art thou,
> Soul of my thought! with whom I traverse earth,
> Invisible but gazing, as I glow
> Mixed with thy spirit, blended with thy birth,
> And feeling still with thee in my crushed feelings' dearth.
>   (III, 6)

Although his brain was at the beginning "A whirling gulf of phantasy and flame," he had found at times a certain tranquility beyond tragedy and was able to make a calmer appraisal of the human situation and his own than had been possible in the hectic autobiographic outpourings of the first cantos.

> Self-exiled Harold wanders forth again,
> With nought of hope left, but with less of gloom;
> The very knowledge that he lived in vain,
> That all was over on this side the tomb,
> Had made Despair a smilingness assume. . . .[1]
>   (III, 16)

Though Hobhouse did not like the third canto — it was filled with "mystery and metaphysics" — as well as the first two, which recounted in part a shared experience in the East, the admiration of Gifford and Moore gave Byron confidence. He wrote to Moore on January 28, 1817: "I am glad you like it; it is a fine indistinct piece of poetical desolation, and my favourite. I was half mad during the time of its composition, between metaphysics, mountains, lakes, love unextinguishable, thoughts unutterable, and the nightmare of my own delinquencies." Then the facetiousness

---

[1] It is indicative of how easily Byron could flip the coin and look at the other side that the remainder of this stanza — "as on the plundered wreck / When mariners would madly meet their doom / With draughts intemperate on the sinking deck" — almost exactly parallels, except in mood, the mocking, cynical account of the shipwreck in *Don Juan.*

which was inappropriate to the poem broke out in the letter: "I should, many a good day, have blown my brains out, but for the recollection that it would have given pleasure to my mother-in-law; and, even *then*, if I could have been certain to haunt her. . . ."[2]

With burning recollections of the chagrin and frustration of the separation, of his love for his half-sister Augusta, of the human weaknesses that had seemed to bring his world crashing down at the height of his fame, Byron was never at a lower depth of dis-illusionment with the realities of the world and of his own nature, and out of that depth he rose to magnificent poetic achievement. Lady Caroline Lamb, who knew Byron as well as anyone, shrewdly observed after the publication of the third canto of *Childe Harold*: ". . . misfortune and rage have occasioned this, and whenever he may speak of *himself* Lord Byron will succeed. Self is the sole inspirer of his genius — he cannot, like Homer, Dante, Virgil, Milton, Dryden, Spenser, Gray, Goldsmith, Tasso, write on other subjects well; but what he feels he can describe extravagantly well. . . ."[3] But perhaps Lady Caroline did Byron some injustice, for when his mind was fired with a subject he sometimes wrote with equal fervor and eloquence on matters as objective as those which stirred Dante, or Virgil, or Milton. At least the subjects which touched him deeply and inspired his egocentric genius had as close a bearing on the general human condition as those of most of the writers she mentioned.

If Byron dragged across Europe "the pageant of his bleeding heart" he gave voice and solace at the same time to many other romantic idealists disillusioned with their world after the end of the Napoleonic wars had brought the final collapse to hopes born in the French Revolution. "Gaul may champ the bit / And foam in fetters; — but is Earth more free?" Standing on the field of Waterloo Byron had ample cause for reflection on the *sic transit gloria mundi* theme. The passage which begins with the memor-able dramatization of the Duchess of Richmond's ball in Brussels — "There was a sound of revelry by night" — and ends with contemplation of the futility of the bravery and blood spilled upon the plain leads to the analysis of the character and career of Napoleon, in "Whose spirit, antithetically mixt," Byron saw much of his own. "Extreme in all things," he had conquered the

---

[2] *Letters and Journals*, IV, 49.

[3] George Paston and Peter Quennell, "*To Lord Byron*," pp. 78–79. Letter of Oct. 13, 1816.

earth, but now was nothing "save the jest of Fame." He could crush an empire, but could not govern his own "pettiest passion." And finally,

> When Fortune fled her spoiled and favourite child,
> He stood unbowed beneath the ills upon him piled.
>
> (III, 39)

It was obvious that Byron was writing of himself when he analyzed the drive that carried Napoleon to his fame and fall, but he was at the same time eloquently summing up the quandary of all romantic souls compelled by inner fires to "aspire / Beyond the fitting medium of desire."

The mirror is even clearer in the stanzas on "the self-torturing sophist, wild Rousseau." Though Byron took pains later to explain to his diary how much he differed from Rousseau, he etched here in brilliant tones those traits in which the resemblance is unmistakable.

> The apostle of Affliction, he who threw
> Enchantment over Passion, and from Woe
> Wrung overwhelming eloquence . . .
> yet he knew
> How to make Madness beautiful, and cast
> O'er erring deeds and thoughts, a heavenly hue
> Of words, like sunbeams, dazzling as they past
> The eyes, which o'er them shed tears feelingly and fast.
>
> His love was Passion's essence — as a tree
> On fire by lightning; with ethereal flame
> Kindled he was, and blasted; for to be
> Thus, and enamoured, were in him the same.
> But his was not the love of living dame,
> Nor of the dead who rise upon our dreams,
> But of ideal Beauty, which became
> In him existence, and o'erflowing teems
> Along his burning page, distempered though it seems.
>
> (III, 77–78)

But Byron did not stop with the Rousseau of the *Confessions* and the *Nouvelle Héloïse*, much as those works stirred him. Rousseau was also one who uttered "oracles which set the world in flame, / Nor ceased to burn till kingdoms were no more: / Did he not this for France? which lay before / Bowed to the

inborn tyranny of years?" From this Byron proceeded to express
a view that he knew to be very unpopular in Tory England at the
time, that the Terror and the excesses of the French Revolution
were only the natural result of long oppression:

> They were not eagles, nourished with the day;
> What marvel then, at times, if they mistook their prey?[4]
>
> (III, 83)

And with reference to the reaction that had restored dungeons
and thrones, he expressed a prophetic optimism that many disillusioned idealists of his time did not share. It was a concept of
the value of the Revolution that was not to gain currency until
well into the Victorian period:

> But this will not endure, nor be endured!
> Mankind have felt their strength, and made it felt.
>
> (III, 83)

Byron's tour around the lake inspired tributes to two other
fiery iconoclasts who had lived near its borders, Voltaire and
Gibbon:

> They were gigantic minds, and their steep aim
> Was, Titan-like, on daring doubts to pile
> Thoughts which should call down thunder, and the flame
> Of Heaven, again assailed, if Heaven, the while,
> On man and man's research could deign do more than smile.
>
> (III, 105)

The shift in point of view at the end of this stanza is an
example of the ironic turn that was later sharpened and became a
distinctive device of Byron's satire in *Don Juan*. Byron the
enemy of conventional beliefs, "Titan-like" defying the gods, suddenly perceives that the gods may be indifferent to puny man's
gesticulations, whether of worship or of wrath. While this device
was eminently successful for the ironic or humorous purposes of
the satire, it may at first glance seem to weaken the forceful
defense of the iconoclastic rebels in the more serious poem. But
it may also be seen as Byron's greatest strength, the mobility of

[4] Unknown to Byron, Wordsworth had made a similar apology for the
Terror in his revolutionary youth, and recorded it faithfully in an autobiographical poem (*The Prelude*) which was not published until after his
death. The difference was that Wordsworth later repudiated the Revolution and what it stood for, and Byron did not.

mind that made him aware of the equal validity of many points
of view, and his inability to delude himself into the belief that
there was only one right one. In any event Byron believed that
these were rebels against the foolishness, the superstitions, and
the cruelties of men, and that it was only their enemies who invoked the gods and saw their rebellion as an attack on heaven.

The "lonely soul" theme appears again in all its notable forms
in the third canto and is generally allied with the most picturesque
descriptions of and most eloquent apostrophes to nature, to "All
that expands the spirit, yet appals." His spirit expanded as soon
as he left Dover and the waves bounded beneath him "as a steed /
That knows his rider." In fact, the third canto radiates the freedom of spirit Byron felt on leaving the "tight little island" and
the artificialities of social life into which he had tried to fit himself. He had felt the strain of holding a mask before his real
self. "Secure in guarded coldness, he had mixed / Again in
fancied safety with his kind." He had sought "fit speculation"
in the crowd, "But soon he knew himself the most unfit / Of
men to herd with Man."

> He would not yield dominion of his mind
> To Spirits against whom his own rebelled.   (III, 12)

His romantic self now sought companionship in all the wild and
lonely aspects of nature, the high mountains, "desert, forest, cav-
ern, breaker's foam."

The Rhine journey offered ample subjects for meditation to
the lonely soul. Here the robber barons' ruined castles started
reflections on the *sic transit* theme and heightened the melancholy beauty of the ancient river's crags and vine-clad shores.
The Drachenfels inspired a song to his sister, tender and sentimental rather than bitter.

Lake Leman and the Alps, and daily association with Shelley,
drew Byron closer to a transcendental concept of nature than he
had ever come before or was ever to reach again. The lonely soul
is nourished by "Nature's pages glassed by sunbeams on the
lake." Here loneliness could "renew / Thoughts hid, but not less
cherished than of old, / Ere mingling with the herd had penned
me in their fold." In this mood he sought to escape not only "the
hum / Of human cities" but the very "clay-cold bonds which
round our being cling." And here for a moment he felt the
thrill of the transcendental belief he had caught from Shelley:

> I live not in myself, but I become
> Portion of that around me; and to me
> High mountains are a feeling. . . .
>   I can see
> Nothing to loathe in Nature, save to be
> A link reluctant in a fleshly chain,
> Classed among creatures, when the soul can flee,
> And with the sky — the peak — the heaving plain
> Of Ocean, or the stars, mingle — and not in vain.
>   (III, 72)

It was an exhilarating thought, which was captivating to one who had seen with such devastating clarity the imperfections of the human lot and the limitations and weaknesses of the flesh. It was tempting to think, as Shelley did, that by sheer will and thought one might remount with a fresh pinion "on delighted wing" and escape the fleshly bonds that curb the spirit.

> And when, at length, the mind shall be all free
> From what it hates in this degraded form . . .
> When Elements to Elements conform,
> And dust is as it should be, shall I not
> Feel all I see less dazzling but more warm?
> The bodiless thought? the Spirit of each spot?
> Of which, even now, I share at times the immortal lot?
>   (III, 74)

Then he passed on to a pantheistic stanza which sprang from his reading of Wordsworth at Shelley's behest:

> Are not the mountains, waves, and skies, a part
> Of me and of my Soul, as I of them?
> Is not the love of these deep in my heart
> With a pure passion?[5]
>   (III, 75)

---

[5] Wordsworth in his letters and later in talking to Moore complained of Byron's plagiarisms from him. As Moore recorded the conversation, Wordsworth said: ". . . the whole third canto of 'Childe Harold' founded on his style and sentiments. The feeling of natural objects which is there expressed, not caught by B. from nature herself, but from him (Wordsworth), and spoiled in the transmission. 'Tintern Abbey' the source of it all. . . ." (Moore, *Memoirs*, III, 161.) But this is nonsense. While some of the phrasing of this passage may suggest "Tintern Abbey," the whole impact and tone of the third canto is extremely un-Wordsworthian. Nature has no power "to chasten and subdue" Byron but is only a symbol and a solace to his own untamed nature. And the moods which nature inspired in him were direct and not from books.

He would not exchange such feelings for "the hard and worldly phlegm / Of those whose eyes are only turned below, / Gazing upon the ground, with thoughts which dare not glow." But Byron was too hard-headed and his genius had too much affinity with reality, imperfect as it might be, to soar too far from the earth, however strong his wish to escape the "clay-cold bonds" of fleshly existence. It was only "at times" that he could raise himself to a half-belief in the possibility of the transcendental leap, and even then he knew it was a feeling fathered by the wish. When confronted with it later he was a little sheepish and told Medwin: "Shelley, when I was in Switzerland, used to dose me with Wordsworth physic even to nausea."[6]

Although Byron's nature descriptions are drawn from direct observation, he is inclined to rhapsodize rather than to describe accurately, but "Clear, placid Leman" wooed him from the wild world he dwelt in to a closer look at nature's features. There follow some stanzas with a restrained power unusual in *Childe Harold:*

> There breathes a living fragrance from the shore,
> Of flowers yet fresh with childhood; on the ear
> Drops the light drip of the suspended oar,
> Or chirps the grasshopper one good-night carol more.
>
> (III, 86)

It is a sweet rather than a bitter melancholy that pervades the description of the storm on the lake and of Clarens, associated with Rousseau's *Nouvelle Héloïse.* But in the end he returns to the proud defiance of the Promethean rebel, which is the dominant motif of the canto:

> I have not loved the World, nor the World me;
> I have not flattered its rank breath, nor bowed
> To its idolatries a patient knee. . . .   (III, 113)

As he began with an apostrophe to his daughter, so he ended:

> The child of Love! though born in bitterness,
> And nurtured in Convulsion! Of thy sire
> These were the elements. . . .   (III, 118)

---

[6] Thomas Medwin, *Conversations of Lord Byron,* II, 40. Byron owed more to Shelley than to Wordsworth in these "transcendental" stanzas. The passion to break the bonds of the cold clay and to become a "bodiless thought" is pure Shelley. Here is a much closer parallel to passages in Shelley's "Julian and Maddalo" than to anything in Wordsworth.

The fourth canto of *Childe Harold* interweaves the pageant of
Byron's bleeding heart with the pageant of Italy from Venice to
Rome and achieves the finest statement of the *sic transit* theme,
retracing Roman history in the "marble wilderness" of that "city
of the soul." The autobiographical part has less of the hectic
urgency to relieve the pain of "love unextinguishable" and
"thoughts unutterable" (though the sense of desolation is still
there) than in the third canto. To a certain extent Byron had
learned to live with "the nightmare of . . . [his] own delinquencies." Although the dull pain of unfulfilled romantic longing persisted, the sense of loss was deeper but less acute. The
sickness was there but the fever had subsided. After a few months
in Venice he confessed that he was "in very good contentment."[7]
In this strange environment, with an opera setting for common
life, he had relaxed and had accepted common pleasures. He
wrote to Douglas Kinnaird on November 27, 1816: "I have books
— a decent establishment — a fine country — a language which
I prefer — most of the amusements and conveniences of life —
as much of society as I choose to take — and a handsome woman,
who is not a bore. . . ."[8]

It was a novelty for Byron to be in love and not, like Rousseau,
kindled "with ethereal flame . . . and blasted." His new love,
Marianna Segati, he wrote his sister, "does not plague me (which
is a wonder) and I verily believe we are one of the happiest —
unlawful couples on this side of the Alps. . . . This adventure
came very opportunely to console me . . . I have been very tran-
quil, very loving, & have not so much embarrassed myself with
the tortures of the last two years. . . ."[9] It is significant that in
this relaxing environment Byron did not write much poetry, except for an occasional *jeu d'esprit* like "So we'll go no more
a-roving," enclosed in letters which are witty, crisp, and wholly
delightful. The carnival came and went and Byron lingered in
Venice though Hobhouse urged him to come to Rome. It was
the middle of April before he could tear himself away from
Marianna and start on his pilgrimage. And it was not until he
had taken a villa on the Brenta at La Mira in the summer that he
turned again to serious composition. The fourth canto, unlike
the first and third, does not begin with an agonized statement of

7 *Letters and Journals*, IV, 14. Letter of Nov. 25, 1816, to Murray.

8 *Lord Byron's Correspondence*, II, 24.

9 *Astarte*, 1921, p. 279. Letter of Dec. 18, 1816.

his own quandary. It is still intensely subjective, but it is a
personal view of Venice and her beauty and decay. In the prefatory letter to Hobhouse Byron referred to the canto as "the most
thoughtful and comprehensive of my compositions . . . as a mark
of respect for what is venerable, and of feeling for what is
glorious, it has been to me a source of pleasure in the production.
. . ." And he disclaimed finally any pretense to fiction in the
character: ". . . there will be found less of the pilgrim than in
any of the preceding [cantos], and that little slightly, if at all,
separated from the author speaking in his own person. The fact
is, that I had become weary of drawing a line which every one
seemed determined not to perceive."

Venice, still the "greenest isle" of his imagination, inspired in
him a kind of rapt veneration for her past glory when she "sate
in state, throned on her hundred isles," and her present glamour
in decay:

> She looks a sea Cybele, fresh from Ocean,
> Rising with her tiara of proud towers.   (IV, 2)

The brass steeds over the portal of St. Mark's were now bridled,
for Venice was under the Austrian yoke and "Her thirteen hundred years of freedom done, [she] / Sinks, like a sea-weed, unto
whence she rose!" But as he stood on the Bridge of Sighs and
"saw from out the wave her structures rise / As from the stroke
of the Enchanter's wand," he recreated the spell that the "mighty
shadows" of the past evoked. And he spoke directly of the
special enchantment which Venice had for him:

> I loved her from my boyhood — she to me
> Was as a fairy city of the heart,
> Rising like water-columns from the sea —
> Of Joy the sojourn, and of Wealth the mart;
> And Otway, Radcliffe, Schiller, Shakespeare's art,
> Had stamped her image in me. . . .   (IV, 18)

The personal interpolations, and there are frequent ones, do
not, as in earlier cantos, divert the light for long from the objective
theme. The first one develops a thought touched upon in the
third canto, the transcendental quality of the mind's creations:

> The Beings of the Mind are not of clay:
> Essentially immortal, they create
> And multiply in us a brighter ray

And more beloved existence. That which Fate
Prohibits to dull life in this our state
Of mortal bondage, by these Spirits supplied,
First exiles, then replaces what we hate. . . .   (IV, 5)

Then he speaks of his own exile, a thought that was filling his
letters at the time: "I've taught me other tongues — and in
strange eyes / Have made me not a stranger." But if he had
permanently left his native land, he would still twine his hopes
of being remembered "with my land's language." He had
reached a stage where "no changes bring surprise," and the mood
of the canto begins in stoic resignation:

Existence may be borne, and the deep root
Of life and sufferance make its firm abode
In bare and desolated bosoms. . . .   (IV, 21)

But ever and anon there comes a token of "griefs subdued" like
a "scorpion's sting." The best solace is to "meditate amongst
decay." After a tribute to Italy, "the Garden of the World, the
Home / Of all Art yields," he began the pilgrimage. The first
stop was at Arqua, the quiet hamlet in the hills where "repose /
The bones of Laura's lover." Although Byron was not in complete sympathy with Petrarch (he could say with Sismondi, "I am
tired of this veil always lowered"), it was the setting in the
beautiful Euganean Hills that gave rise to his meditations.

At Ferrara, Tasso's cell was the symbol for him of the oppression suffered by the poet at the hands of the despot Alfonso. But
Tasso was still the "Victor unsurpassed in modern song!" Florence
roused images of the "bards of Hell and Chivalry," Dante and
Ariosto, the southern Scott. Although he was not a great admirer of sculpture or painting, the Venus de Medici carried him
back to the Greek legends out of which the goddess was born.

With the Roman section, which begins in stanza 78, the
perfunctory record of impressions of travel gives way to something that surpasses even the glowing tribute to Venice in the
opening stanzas. The living evidence of that dead world in the
ruins of Rome kindled his melancholy imagination into in-
candescence:

Oh, Rome! my Country! City of the Soul!
The orphans of the heart must turn to thee,
Lone Mother of dead Empires! and control
In their shut breasts their petty misery.
What are our woes and sufferance? Come and see

> The cypress — hear the owl — and plod your way
> O'er steps of broken thrones and temples — Ye!
> Whose agonies are evils of a day —
> A world is at our feet as fragile as our clay.
>
> The Niobe of nations! there she stands,
> Childless and crownless, in her voiceless woe;
> An empty urn within her withered hands,
> Whose holy dust was scattered long ago. . . .
>
> (IV, 78–79)

In this shifting world, so dramatized in Rome's ruins, the only thing, he felt again, that had a kind of immortality was the word, the "soul of thought":

> Alas, for Tully's voice, and Virgil's lay,
> And Livy's pictured page! — but these shall be
> Her resurrection; all beside — decay.   (IV, 82)

It was not with exultation but with sadness that Byron followed the historical pageant of the grandeur that was Rome to the inevitable *sic transit* ending.

> Alas, for Earth, for never shall we see
> That brightness in her eye she bore when Rome was free!
>
> (IV, 82)

Tracing Rome's history from the legendary "she-wolf," nurse of its founder, down to all the Caesars gave him ample opportunity to extract the obvious lessons concerning the vanity of ambition and the passing of tyrants, a theme whose clear applications in the present he was careful to point up.

Then came a lull and he was carried from the historical panorama into contemplation once more of the ideal visions which neither perpetual frustrations nor common pleasures and achievements could assuage in the romantic bosom. The sight of the supposed fountain of Egeria, a legendary spirit who loved a mortal, set up a train of thought that grew into the most eloquent and poignant statement of romantic longing and desolation.

> Oh, Love! no habitant of earth thou art —
> An unseen Seraph, we believe in thee, —
> A faith whose martyrs are the broken heart,
> But never yet hath seen, nor e'er shall see
> The naked eye, thy form, as it should be;
> The mind hath made thee, as it peopled Heaven,
> Even with its own desiring phantasy. . . .

> Where are the forms the sculptor's soul hath seized?
> In him alone. Can Nature show so fair?
> Where are the charms and virtues which we dare
> Conceive in boyhood and pursue as men,
> The unreached Paradise of our despair . . . ?
>   (IV, 121–122)

Then comes again the ultimate complaint of the "immedicable soul" of the romantic that "Our life is a false nature — 't is not in / The harmony of things." This is a Satanism that is not deliberate or posed; it is based on a solid conviction that "This uneradicable taint of Sin," the imperfection of human nature, is an "all-blasting tree, / Whose root is Earth — whose leaves and branches be / The skies which rain their plagues on men like dew."

In this desolate world there is still one inviolable retreat: the indomitable and uncompromising mind of man. There is less hope now that it can make the Shelleyan leap to the transcendental world, but in its own redoubt it is unconquerable.

> Yet let us ponder boldly — 't is a base
> Abandonment of reason to resign
> Our right of thought — our last and only place
> Of refuge; this, at least, shall still be mine:
> Though from our birth the Faculty divine
> Is chained and tortured — cabined, cribbed, confined,
> And bred in darkness, lest the Truth should shine
> Too brightly on the unprepared mind.   (IV, 127)

This thought colors his reflections in the Coliseum, which he sees as a symbol of Time's revenges, and out of it comes, by a somewhat devious digression on the wrongs he has suffered, the often-quoted lines:

> But there is that within me which shall tire
> Torture and Time, and breathe when I expire;
> Something unearthly, which they deem not of,
> Like the remembered tone of a mute lyre. . . .
>   (IV, 137)

After this digression which revived the moods of earlier cantos, he returned to the Coliseum and painted a series of subjective-objective pictures: the dying gladiator, "Butchered to make a Roman holiday," the Pantheon, Hadrian's "mole" or mausoleum (the Castle of St. Angelo), St. Peter's church, and finally the

Laocoön and the Apollo Belvedere. The pilgrimage ends at Albano, where the view of the ocean revives old memories, recalling some of the happier "lonely soul" moods of earlier cantos. And so "to mingle with the universe" in nature became a substitute for the transcendental leap. In that environment the mind could become all free from what degraded it in the earthly form.

> Oh! that the Desert were my dwelling-place,
> With one fair Spirit for my minister. . . .
>
> There is a pleasure in the pathless woods,
> There is a rapture on the lonely shore. . . .
> (IV, 177–178)

On this note of exuberance the canto ends, though the concluding stanzas take on a tinge of melancholy — the melancholy of parting:

> My task is done — my song hath ceased — my theme
> Has died into an echo.   (IV, 185)

Byron already had the feeling that the *Childe Harold* theme had "died into an echo." Before he had finished the fourth canto he was deeply engrossed in the boisterous mockery of *Beppo*.

But the echo of *Childe Harold*'s melancholy music lingers in the reader's memory, for its cumulative effect somehow transcends the commonplaces of its individual statements. The conviction remains that Byron has voiced the common thoughts of all men to a degree. Seen in the light of its own time it surpasses anything else in romantic autobiography in unclouded clarity of statement and revelation of an active and troubled mind. In the third and fourth cantos the Spenserian stanza is no longer imitative. Byron has made it over into an instrument of his own, subtly sounding every note of the romantic agony.

6

Oriental and Other Tales

BYRON'S VERSE TALES — all of them, but particularly the Oriental tales — served as escape valves for "the lava" of his imagination. But the enormous energy of his creative drives carried into them much that was not merely a part of the emotional purgation. In addition to their self-revelation they are notable among Byron's poems for their colorful settings and their lyrical mood pictures. Whether the scene is the craggy coast of Greece and the blue waters of the Aegean which he knew at first hand, or the Friendly Islands of the South Pacific which he had read about in an account of the mutiny on the *Bounty*, he lends it an energetic immediacy which does much to create a willing suspension of disbelief in the reality of the tale. The lyric descriptions of Greece in the Oriental tales are among the "Beauties of Byron" so admired in his own day, and they still hold a reader who comes upon them for the first time without prejudice. The opening lines of *The Giaour* and *The Bride of Abydos* may seem stagy and overblown to the modern reader, but they still contain phrases that persist in the memory.

The same tendency to digression that may be observed in most of Byron's longer poems, from *Childe Harold* to *Don Juan*, has slowed and sometimes confused the narrative in some but not all of the tales. *The Giaour* seems to have no chronology, proceeds by fits and starts, and is developed by innuendo. The narrative is as indirect as in a novel of Conrad. *The Bride of Abydos*, *The Prisoner of Chillon*, and *The Island*, on the other hand, all have straightforward and for the most part uninterrupted narratives.

It has been said that in the Oriental tales Byron deliberately set out to follow up the success of *Childe Harold,* but this is not quite true. The initial impulse was as usual the need for an outlet for an emotional impasse. Whenever he reached a crisis in his personal affairs during the years of fame following the publication of *Childe Harold,* he yearned to return to the East where, in retrospect, he felt he had known a carefree happiness he could find nowhere else. He did not need more fame, and he did not conceive of the Oriental tales as likely to add to his literary reputation; later he apologized for them as having been written in four nights or a week without revision. As for money, he was still giving away his copyrights.

The Giaour was written in the spring and added to in the summer and autumn of 1813, when his amatory entanglements were becoming impossible to unravel and when escape to the East was a recurrent note in his letters. In it are mingled themes of love — beautiful, lawless, and unextinguishable — revenge, remorse, and unrepentant defiance. The story of a Turkish girl cast into the sea for infidelity, and the revenge of the "Christian" lover on the cruel husband, Byron adapted partly from stories he had heard in the East (Ali Pacha had sacked and drowned a goodly number of unfaithful women in the lake at Jannina) and partly from an episode in which he was personally involved at Athens in a way that he darkly hinted at but never told, even to his journal.[1]

As new moods and quandaries demanded catharsis he added lines to "this snake of a poem" in successive editions. Those he

[1] For details of what little is known of the factual background of the story of *The Giaour* (pronounced *Jä-oor,* and meaning "infidel," from the Mohammedan point of view, i.e., "Christian") see the introduction to the poem in E. H. Coleridge's edition of the *Poetry,* III, 75–76, and the sources cited by Coleridge; see also Marchand, *Byron,* I, 257–258. The letter of Lord Sligo reporting what he had heard in Athens concerning Byron's rescue of a Turkish girl who had been sewn in a sack and was about to be thrown into the sea did not apparently tell the whole story. This letter, which Byron circulated to counter some rumors that were "a little too close to the text," is now in the Murray collection. If the fourteen lines that are blotted out could be read they might or might not clarify Byron's connection with the event. That he was emotionally involved is hinted at in his letters and journals. In his diary for Dec. 5, 1813, he wrote: "But to describe the feelings of *that situation* were impossible — it is *icy* even to recollect them."

wrote during the summer reflected directly the mingled feelings
of guilt and exultancy in his love for his half-sister Augusta:

> I loved her — Love will find its way
> Through paths where wolves would fear to
> prey; ...
> I did not vainly seek, nor sigh:
> Yet sometimes, with remorse, in vain
> I wish she had not loved again....
> Yes, Love indeed is light from heaven;
> A spark of that immortal fire
> With angels shared, by Alla given,
> To lift from earth our low desire.
> (*Giaour*, 1048–1049, 1053–1055, 1131–1134)

Granted that the emotional foundations of the tale were based
firmly in Byron's own troubled feelings, yet when he began to
write certain objective interests surged up. Chief among these
was his nostalgic love of Greece, which made him recall every
detail of landscape, character, and costume. These in addition to
the white heat of emotion gave a seeming authenticity to Byron's
Eastern tales that set them in the popular mind far above other
more fantastic Oriental stories like Moore's *Lalla Rookh*. The
theme that kindled Byron's finest feelings and poetry was the life
in death still to be seen in Greece. The passage beginning "He
who hath bent him o'er the dead" is perhaps too theatrical for
modern taste, though it was much admired by Byron's contemporaries and has some lines that may still strike a spark:

> 'T is Greece, but living Greece no more!
> So coldly sweet, so deadly fair,
> We start, for Soul is wanting there.
> (*Giaour*, 91–93)

Byron has attempted to give dramatic force to the tale by
making the narrator a Turkish fisherman who has just landed his
boat at Port Leone (Piraeus) and who sees the Giaour come
"thundering . . . on blackest steed" and witnesses most of the
events. Then the narration (or rather description) is taken over
by a monk in a monastery where the Giaour has retired to meditate but not to repent. And finally the Giaour tells his own story
with its emotional overtones to the tolerant Abbot.

In spite of the gnarled narrative technique, it is easy to understand the popularity of the tale. Byron has pulled all the stops, picturesque and emotional. He has drawn on his knowledge of Eastern customs for exotic coloring and has thrown in facile references to caïques, capotes, ataghans, the "solemn sound of 'Alla Hu,' " the Koran, and the Houris. For people who had no movies it was an excellent emotional release, with the musical accompaniment of the tetrameter couplets:

> Sullen it plunged, and slowly sank,
> The calm wave rippled to the bank....
> (*Giaour*, 374–375)

Certainly the poetry lifts it above the Grade C movie which Hollywood supplies for twentieth century catharsis. In fact, it is surprising that Hollywood has not discovered the possibilities of the theme; but perhaps the cast is too small.

The Bride of Abydos was the product of an even more agonizing personal quandary. The frustration of his love for Lady Frances Webster, an affair which Lady Melbourne had hoped would distract him from a more dangerous liaison with his half-sister Augusta, only complicated his feelings without solving his emotional problem. "It was written in four nights to distract my dreams from * *," Byron wrote in his journal. To the same journal he confided: "I began a comedy, and burnt it because the scene ran into *reality*; — a novel, for the same reason. In rhyme, I can keep more away from facts. . . ." He did keep more away from facts in the poem (though he at first had made the lovers brother and sister, he later changed the relationship to cousins), and one result is that it is a more coherent dramatic presentation than *The Giaour*, with a more swiftly moving narrative. Though the love speeches of Selim reflect some of Byron's own passion, the story seems to be a more objective Oriental tale with authentic background of Moslem customs.

The poet as his own narrator keeps better control. The swinging anapests of the opening are effective in giving the romantic aura through which the passions of the tale are to be seen:

> Know ye the land where the cypress and myrtle
>   Are emblems of deeds that are done in their clime? ...
> Where the citron and olive are fairest of fruit,
> And the voice of the nightingale never is mute;
> Where the tints of the earth, and the hues of the sky,

> In colour though varied, in beauty may vie,
> And the purple of ocean is deepest in dye;
> Where the virgins are soft as the roses they twine,
> And all, save the spirit of man, is divine —
> 'T is the clime of the East — 't is the land of the Sun —
> Can he smile on such deeds as his children have done?
> Oh! wild as the accents of lovers' farewell
> Are the hearts which they bear, and the tales which they tell.
>
> (*Bride*, I, 1–2, 9–19)

Then the swift-moving tetrameter couplets take up the narrative. The story is wholly melodramatic, and the characters, except in so far as they voice Byronic moods and feelings, are quite unrealistic. Byron has tried to make them stoical Orientals, but an overbalance of romantic sensibility in their actions and speeches reveals the conventional romantic hero, heroine, and villain, rather than stolid Turks. Giaffir, thought to be modeled on the suave but cruel Ali Pacha, becomes sentimental over his daughter and her mother. Selim puts Zuleika on a pedestal in a manner that Byron would have ridiculed in his later satires, for he knew that in the East "wedlock and padlock mean the same." But, of course, however much he may have tried to objectify the events of the story and to give it authentic background, the emotions of the poem were entirely subjective and Byronic. Relief for these emotions was his admitted purpose in writing, as he frankly told Lady Melbourne and his journal.

The Corsair and its sequel *Lara* tell a tale of piracy and passion with an Eastern setting, but the protagonist is a patent self-portrait, at least a profile or half-face of the melancholy Byron. Conrad is Childe Harold projected into melodrama. Though he has qualities of Ali Pacha and of Lambro, the pirate father of Haidée, these traits are subordinated to the brooding melancholy of his own dark mind. We see him first in *The Corsair* as "That man of loneliness and mystery." His pirate crew respect him as a leader but do not dare to disturb his private thoughts. More than Childe Harold he becomes a kind of "poetical Zeluco":

> Warped by the world in Disappointment's school,
> In words too wise — in conduct *there* a fool;
> Too firm to yield, and far too proud to stoop,
> Doomed by his very virtues for a dupe. . . .
> He knew himself a villain — but he deemed
> The rest no better than the thing he seemed. . . .
>
> (*Corsair*, I, 253–256, 265–266)

But Conrad, the cold corsair, has one "softer feeling," that for Medora, whether wife, mistress, or slave, we are never told. She is, like all the heroines of the Oriental tales, an idealized version of the Eastern woman, dark, lush, softly yielding, with no pretensions to learning but a flattering utter devotion to her lord. Aside from this Medora has no character of her own; her merit is in seeing Conrad's, and that makes her a perfect prototype of all the romantic Byronic heroines.

Conrad is a little appalled, however (as Byron would have been), when another woman carries that devotion to its logical extreme and murders her lord to save the corsair and then follows him with doglike fidelity. But Conrad reflects the romantic Byronic ideal again in being a one-woman man. He has thoughts only for Medora, and when she dies his love life is ended, though he allows Gulnare to follow him as a devoted servant, whose reward for saving his life is one chaste kiss, "The first, the last that Frailty stole from Faith." It is significant that even in this conventional picture of fidelity demanded by romantic melodrama Byron recognized the limits of Conrad's virtue:

> Perchance, but for the bodings of his breast,
> His latest virtue then had joined the rest.
> (*Corsair*, III, 1715–1716)

But Byron was not very successful in picturing Conrad as a Zeluco. The Corsair is too softly sentimental, too weakly humanitarian under the suffering, cold, proud exterior to be the villain he admits.

> His heart was formed for softness — warped to wrong,
> Betrayed too early, and beguiled too long. . . .
> (*Corsair*, III, 1830–1831)

The stolid pirate wept, though not when anyone could see, at the loss of Medora and then disappeared mysteriously.

> He left a Corsair's name to other times,
> Linked with one virtue, and a thousand crimes.
> (*Corsair*, III, 1863–1864)

But we cannot believe in his crimes, for we have never seen them, and his character belies them; in fact, he is wholly Byronic.

Byron knew that he would be identified with Conrad as he had been with Childe Harold and he made a gesture of denial in the prefatory letter addressed to Thomas Moore, though feebler than before: ". . . if I have deviated into the gloomy vanity of 'drawing from self,' the pictures are probably like, since they are unfavourable: and if not, those who know me are undeceived. . . ." But of course the Conrad in him was hidden from his facetious friends. And at most the Corsair was only half of him, and that other Janus face was unmasked after the dinners or soirees when the lava of the imagination overflowed into rhyme. And the curious paradox was that he idealized the portrait of that face, whether of a Harold or a Conrad, and the only realistic features were the brooding pride and the sense of guilt.

In his preface Byron defended his use of the heroic couplet in a poem that was far from Popean in either manner or matter: ". . . I have attempted not the most difficult, but, perhaps, the best adapted measure to our language, the good old and now neglected heroic couplet. The stanza of Spenser [used throughout *Childe Harold*] is perhaps too slow and dignified for narrative; though, I confess, it is the measure most after my own heart: Scott alone, of the present generation, has hitherto completely triumphed over the fatal facility of the octosyllabic verse . . . in blank verse, Milton, Thomson, and our dramatists, are the beacons that shine along the deep, but warn us from the rough and barren rock on which they are kindled." It was the first time Byron had used the pentameter couplet for extended romantic narrative, and he made it a supple instrument for his need, just as he had fashioned the Spenserian stanza into something of his own. Certainly in the famous description of the Greek sunset at the opening of the third canto the ringing couplets add to rather than detract from the magic, and even anesthetize the reader to its worst faults as poetry: its trite tropes and conventional sentiments.

Lara carries the history of the man of "loneliness and mystery" to the inevitable tragic end. Lara has abandoned the life and name of the Corsair and has returned from the colorful Aegean to the feudal castle which was his ancestral home. Of course he is followed by a page boy Kaled (Gulnare in disguise). The poem has fewer of the glowing descriptions inspired by the Eastern setting, and more of gloomy Byronic self-analysis:

> Left by his Sire, too young such loss to know,
> Lord of himself, — that heritage of woe,
> That fearful empire which the human breast
> But holds to rob the heart within of rest!
>
> (*Lara*, I, 13–16)

But now there was a change. His brow spoke of "passion past":

> The pride, but not the fire, of early days,
> Coldness of mien, and carelessness of praise;
> A high demeanor, and a glance that took
> Their thoughts from others by a single look;
> And that sarcastic levity of tongue,
> The stinging of a heart the world hath stung. . . .
> *(Lara,* I, 69–74)

The tortured confessional and apologia goes on for pages. No-where, not even in *Childe Harold,* had Byron more explicitly diagnosed his own case, and in doing so he exposed to view the chief symptoms of the universal romantic malady:

> His early dreams of good outstripped the truth,
> And troubled Manhood followed baffled Youth;
> With thought of years in phantom chase misspent,
> And wasted powers for better purpose lent;
> And fiery passions that had poured their wrath
> In hurried desolation o'er his path. . . .
> *(Lara,* I, 323–328)

This diagnosis, perhaps even more than the gory and melancholy ending, made the poem immensely popular even when it was published anonymously with Rogers' *Jacqueline.* Murray sold six thousand copies as soon as it was published. But Byron was a little shamefaced about it, particularly before those friends from whom he had concealed the most melancholy side of his nature. He spoke lightly of it to Moore as having been written "amidst balls and fooleries, and after coming home from masquerades and routs, in the summer of the sovereigns."[2]

Here the so-called Oriental tales ended. On the subjective side they projected the Childe Harold image into picturesque settings and melodramatic situations where Byron perhaps naïvely felt that it would be less recognizable as his own. But the more he tried to distort the image into that of Zeluco, the more he saw his reflection in the melancholy mirror. The tales had served their purpose as emotional eruptions that prevented an earthquake in his personal affairs. But the strain to camouflage these self-revelations in exotic environments give the tales an artificiality that is rare in Byron's poetry. With all their "beauties" of in-

---

[2] *Letters and Journals,* VI, 81. Letter of June 8, 1822.

dividual lines and descriptions, they do not have that vital contact
with reality which is the distinguishing mark of his best work.

The Siege of Corinth, written during the year of his marriage,
which was barren of any literary work of note except the
Hebrew Melodies, was an attempt to poetize an episode in the
siege and capture of the citadel from the Venetians by the Turks
in 1715. Byron had only slight knowledge of the historical background, though he may have picked up local color and details
from oral tradition ("We have heard the hearers say"). The
protagonist, Alp, a renegade Venetian who had joined the Turks
to seek revenge because his countrymen had wronged him, is only
slightly Byronic: he is proud and broods on his wrongs, he ideal-
izes a woman torn from him, he is lonely and fate-directed.
Renegade though he is, Byron gives him some of the feelings of
Childe Harold as he wanders over remnants of ancient glory the
night before the battle. For the rest, the perverted heroism of Alp
and the details of the carnage are tinged with Byronic feelings of
pride and remorse.

Byron's writing had never been more careless. He had reverted
to the octosyllabic couplet but used it with great irregularity,
with bad rhymes and halting rhythms. When Gifford, Murray's
reader, went over the manuscript he was shocked by grammatical
errors and bad taste in many of the lines. One has the suspicion
that it is not a poem spun out of immediacy of feeling such as one
senses in even the most unreal of the Oriental tales. It may be
significant that it was the first poem (along with *Parisina*) for
which Byron accepted money from his publisher.

Parisina, a tale of incest and horror taken from an account by
Gibbon of the Marquis of Este's bastard son who cuckolded his
father and was beheaded, is a strangely moving story, superior in
poetic nuances of character and situation to anything in Byron's
previous narrative poems. Undoubtedly the theme of forbidden
love fascinated him, but the curious thing is that, contrary to his
general practice, he chose a setting quite unfamiliar (he had not
yet been in Ferrara, or even in Italy), and that the story moves
forward without either digressive descriptions or self-analysis.
His empathy with the characters, not only Hugo, the guilty son,
but also Parisina, and even the father, is without undue intrusion
of the Byronic ego. And though the story is as melodramatic as
that in *The Siege of Corinth* or any of the Eastern tales, one is less
aware of the melodrama than of the poetic realization of the pas-

sions involved. The verse flows smoothly, as it usually did when his pen was dipped in genuine feelings. Like Rousseau he "threw / Enchantment over passion." Murray, who had opened the manuscript with trepidation because of the theme, wrote that he had found it "a Pearl." The figure is not wholly inappropriate: it may be an artificial pearl, but it seems simple and natural and smoothly pure.

While the horror of the beheading is described with too much bloody detail, for the rest the scene is invested with a sad beauty and naturalness like that surrounding the story of Francesca of Rimini. Again one is at a loss to find apt quotations; it is the cumulative effect that counts. From the idyllic love tryst in the beginning to the blasted tree image of the father in the end there is a sustained harmony of tone. Hugo's self-justification (Azo had wronged his mother and stolen the bride meant for him) has a different ring from that of the Giaour. Yet Hugo accepts the judgment upon him without complaint, like a fated hero of tragedy. But lest we lose critical perspective by viewing *Parisina* in comparison with Byron's earlier verse tales, let it be said at once that it is not his best work for the very reason that he was not distilling the essence of his own experience. There is feeling but little profundity in the portrayal of character, and despite the smoothness of the verse the melodrama shows through.

The directness, simplicity, and restraint which are the most apparent virtues of *Parisina* were carried to their highest perfection in a dramatic tale in *The Prisoner of Chillon*, written after a visit to the dungeon where François Bonivard had been kept a political prisoner. Even though Byron got the story of Bonivard in garbled form, the contemplation of injustice, cruelty, and the chaining of body and spirit roused his feelings and enlivened his pen. With the first person narrative he stepped into the being of Bonivard with perfect sympathy. He became the "Eternal Spirit of the chainless Mind." Byron packed tremendous dramatic force into the simple narrative of a man who "suffered chains and courted death" for an idea.

There is no polemic as such, but the simple narrative of the prisoner's sufferings carries a heavier indictment of injustice and man's inhumanity to man than reams of rhetorical protest. Byron has not spared emotion in Bonivard's account of the death of his brothers chained beside him, of his blankness of mind from the shock:

> I had no thought, no feeling — none —
> Among the stones I stood a stone,
> And was, scarce conscious what I wist,
> As shrubless crags within the mist. . . .
> <div align="right">(<i>Prisoner</i>, 235–238)</div>

And the narrative hovers on the brink of the sentimental when he tells of his revival by a bird's song, his pacing the dungeon floor, his friendly feeling for the spiders and the mice, his climbing up the wall to see through the barred window the mountains with their "thousand years of snow," the lake, and the "small green isle" with young flowers growing on it. But it somehow stays within the bounds of realizable feeling. There is a quiet persuasiveness in the description of both setting and feelings that is enhanced by the rhythm of the octosyllabic verse, which does not suggest doggerel but rather the accompaniment of a distant drum-beat.

The Prisoner of Chillon is the closest knit of all Byron's narrative poems. Once he has imagined the character, he allows him a unity of tone and sentiment uninterrupted by Byronic mobility or digression. The conclusion, in view of Bonivard's story, is a decisive coup:

> My very chains and I grew friends,
> So much a long communion tends
> To make us what we are: — even I
> Regained my freedom with a sigh.
> <div align="right">(<i>Prisoner</i>, 389–392)</div>

Mazeppa, a framework tale based on an incident mentioned by Voltaire in his *History of Charles XII*, demonstrates Byron's delight in a startling dramatic story, particularly one involving love adventures. Told as an episode of his youth by a Polish gentleman who had become a Prince of the Ukraine and then defected to Charles, it carries the reader along by its vigor of style and its sharp realization of the feelings of suffering and endurance. Only in the beginning does Mazeppa slip into levity a little out of tone with the romantic texture of the tale:

> Not that he had no cares to vex;
> He loved the Muses and the Sex;
> And sometimes these so froward are,

> They made him wish himself at war;
> But soon his wrath being o'er, he took
> Another mistress — or new book. . . .
> (*Mazeppa*, 137–142)

And in the picture of the young wife of the old count whose decoration with horns led to Mazeppa's involuntary ride on a wild horse, Byron ran full tilt into the accents and attitudes of *Don Juan*. The Countess, he says, grew tired of her husband, thirty years her senior,

> And, after wishes, hopes, and fears,
> To Virtue a few farewell tears,
> A restless dream or two — some glances
> At Warsaw's youth — some songs, and dances,
> Awaited but the usual chances,
> Those happy accidents which render
> The coldest dames so very tender,
> To deck her Count with titles given,
> 'T is said, as passports into Heaven. . . .
> (*Mazeppa*, 170–178)

But once the ride begins and Mazeppa is borne naked on the wild horse's back through burning day and cold night, the narrative becomes rapid and the sensations of the rider are depicted with sharp realism tinged with romantic coloring.

> And my cold sweat-drops fell like rain
> Upon the courser's bristling mane. . . .
> (*Mazeppa*, 444–445)

Only in the end, as if exhausted by the overstrained emotion, does Byron revert to irony: when Mazeppa finished his dramatic tale, told to distract Charles from the loss of the Battle of Poltáva, "The King had been an hour asleep!"

The Island; or, Christian and His Comrades is a strange Byronic performance. The last long poem and the last dramatic tale which he composed, it reveals both his excellences and his weaknesses in that genre. Written at a time when his imagination was fired by dreams of escape from the routine domestic existence into which he had fallen in Italy, and completed just before the opportunity of the Greek adventure opened up avenues of activity to him, he found it a most congenial subject. He had toyed with the idea of leaving Europe for the "free" environment of South America, where he imagined an idealized democratic society that would give tribute to worth and genius, and at the same time would pay respect (and presumably rents) to a benevolent landholder. The Noble Savage dream that was so popular a part of eighteenth and early nineteenth century romanticism had a strong appeal to one side of Byron's nature, but after playing with it for a time, whether in *Childe Harold* or in *Don Juan*, his knowledge of human nature, his cynical realism, caused him to prick that bubble sooner or later. Even Haidée, his most idealized child of nature, seems in the end to love the luxury of her father's ill-gotten gains too much.

But the South Sea islands were far enough away from Byron's experience to quiet the cynic in his blood. Mariner's *Account of the Natives of the Tonga Islands* furnished him the setting for a last romantic escape from the gray commonplace into which life tended to subside. William Bligh's narrative of the mutiny on the *Bounty* gave him the dramatic machinery for the introduction of the tale. The first canto, which follows Bligh's account of the mutiny, is the least interesting. It is curious that Byron, not having read the evidence brought into the trials respecting the savage cruelty and brutality of the commander of the *Bounty*, allied his sympathies with Bligh and played down, though he did not eliminate entirely, an attempt to understand the feelings of the mutineers. If he had known all the facts he would undoubtedly, with his natural hatred of tyranny and his tendency to espouse the cause of the rebellious underdog, have taken the side of Christian and his comrades. As it was, there was an undercurrent of sympathy for their desire to remain at Otaheite:

> The gentle island, and the genial soil,
> The friendly hearts, the feasts without a toil,
> The courteous manners but from nature caught,
> The wealth unhoarded, and the love unbought. . . .
> (*Island*, I, 107–110)

For the rest, the conventional couplets extolling Duty and Conscience, at war with the natural desire of the mariners to escape the toils of the sea, seem rather perfunctory. Even without knowledge of the brutality that caused the mutiny, he could not conceal sympathy for the "Young hearts, which languished for some sunny isle," despite his "correct" disapproval of their unlawful act. Greater warmth enters into the account of the motives of the mutineers.

Men without country, who too long estranged,
Had found no native home, or found it changed,
And, half uncivilised, preferred the cave
Of some soft savage to the uncertain wave. . . .
The wish — which ages have not yet subdued
In man — to have no master save his mood. . . .
(*Island*, I, 29–32, 37–38)

Byron was aware that this ambivalence had put a damper on his free handling of the theme. He wrote to Leigh Hunt that he wanted to avoid running "counter to the reigning stupidity altogether, otherwise they will say that I am eulogizing *Mutiny*. This must produce tameness in some degree."[3]

But when the mutineers had returned to Toobonai, Byron abandoned all constraint in picturing the Noble Savage life of the islands, and particularly the glowing idyll of Neuha, "the gentle savage of the wild," and the "fair-haired Torquil," who, nurtured in the Scottish Highlands, was in his innocence and purity as true a child of nature. Byron has lavished more detail on the description of Neuha than on any other of his fictional heroines. Even Haidée in *Don Juan* is less minutely described. Neuha was "lovely, warm, and premature; / Dusky like night, but night with all her stars." She had "eyes that were a language and a spell, / A form like Aphrodite's in her shell." She was voluptuous yet full of life. She was "highborn," for she came from a long line of "naked knights of savage chivalry."

Glowing also is the account of how the island life

Did more than Europe's discipline had done,
And civilised Civilisation's son! (*Island*, II, 270–271)

A reference to the Highland scenery that nourished Torquil's youth ends with a digressive reminiscence of Byron's own nostalgia for Scotland:

The infant rapture still survived the boy,
And Loch-na-gar with Ida looked o'er Troy.
(*Island*, II, 290–291)

Some of the digressions — a habit carried over from *Don Juan* — change the tone of the piece and seem incongruous. Such is the apostrophe to "Sublime Tobacco!" ending with the couplet:

"Yet thy true lovers more admire by far / Thy naked beauties —
Give me a cigar!" Such also is the lengthy comical description
of Ben Bunting, an unromantic sailor who brought the news of a
strange sail in the offing in a somewhat forced colloquial dialogue.

Byron finally resolved the ambivalence of sympathies apparent
in the beginning of the tale by centering the guilt and the remorse
of the erring mariners in their leader Christian. He, "of a higher
order, stood / Like an extinct volcano in his mood." When they
are about to be captured or killed, he absolves the innocent Torquil of guilt, blames himself, and concludes:

> For me, my lot is what I sought; to be,
> In life or death, the fearless and the free.
>
> (*Island*, III, 163–164)

At this point the faithful, loving, and competent Neuha
rescues her Torquil and carries him to a natural cave reached by
diving under the sea. The happy ending of the idyll of Torquil
and his Noble Savage bride makes the tale unique among Byron's
verse narratives. It is unique too in its picture of an ideal world
unspoiled by the cynical intrusions of the critical intelligence.
This is one bubble Byron blew that he refrained from pricking.

7

Speculative Dramas

BYRON WROTE four poetic dramas which, for want of a better term, I call "speculative": *Manfred, Cain, Heaven and Earth,* and *The Deformed Transformed* (the last two unfinished). Each is in some way connected with his contemplation of the mysteries beyond the known and the knowable, with the inability of man's mind to reach out beyond the "clay-cold bonds" of its fleshly habitation, and with the capacity of the mind to compensate for that limitation. Each demonstrates, with varying success, the dual thesis, already suggested in *Childe Harold,* of the spirit's inevitable slavery to the limited human condition, and the defiant Promethean invincibility of the mind and will. Although all of these grew directly out of personal emotional quandaries, their speculative interest lifts them above the mere sensational Gothic drama of the supernatural, for they touch the human situation at vital points.

Manfred is the most clear-cut and the most successful in giving poetic realization to those themes. There is not space here, nor is it necessary except incidentally, to go into the biographical background of events, emotions, and ideas that induced the composition of this dramatic poem. It embodied so much that was close to Byron's thought and feelings that he was defensively apologetic about it. He mentioned it first to his publisher as "a kind of Poem in dialogue (in blank verse) or drama . . . but of a very wild, metaphysical, and inexplicable kind."[1] More even than the third canto of *Childe Harold* it might be said to have been the distillation of "metaphysics" (his discussions with Shelley on the·lake and in the evenings at the Villa Diodati), "mountains" (the

[1] *Letters and Journals,* IV, 54–55. Letter of Feb. 15, 1817.

initial idea and the setting came to him during his tour of the
Bernese Alps with Hobhouse in September, 1816), "love unextinguishable, thoughts unutterable, and the nightmare of . . .
[his] own delinquencies" (the whole complex of guilt, remorse,
and frustration growing out of the separation, his relations with
Augusta, his exile, and the blasted hopes of an ideal career in
politics or poetry).

The Faustian form led to accusations that he had plagiarized
Marlowe or Goethe. But Byron was truthful when he told
Murray that "it was the *Staubach* [sic] and the *Jungfrau*, and
something else, much more than Faustus, that made me write
Manfred. The first Scene, however, and that of Faustus are very
similar."[2] Byron maintained that he had never read the *Faustus*
of Marlowe, but admitted that "Monk" Lewis had translated
orally parts of Goethe's *Faust* for him at Diodati, and that no
doubt gave him the opening and the general idea of calling up the
spirits. But the ways in which Byron departed from the Faust
story are more striking than the resemblances. Manfred does
not sell his soul to the devil nor to any spirit. He will not bow
down to them nor admit that they have any power over him; he
commands them and defies them to the end. Moreover, Manfred's
world-weariness and death wish prevent him from desiring, like
Faust, power, wealth, love, fame, or worldly pleasures. When
the spirits he has called up offer him "Kingdom, and sway, and
strength, and length of days," Manfred replies: "Accursed! what
have I to do with days? / They are too long already."

The ostensible theme is remorse for some sin or sins hinted at
and only partly revealed. But it is balanced by a Promethean
aspiration which in the end dominates the poem. Jeffrey in the
Edinburgh Review remarked that the "tone and pitch" as well as
the diction reminded him of Aeschylus. Byron happily acknowledged the influence: "Of the *Prometheus* of Aeschylus I was
passionately fond as a boy (it was one of the Greek plays we read
thrice a year at Harrow). . . . The *Prometheus*, if not exactly in
my plan, has always been so much in my head, that I can easily
conceive its influence over all or any thing that I have
written. . . ."[3] The pervading theme is stated clearly in Manfred's
haughty reply to the spirits in the first scene:

[2] *Letters and Journals*, V, 37. Letter of June 7, 1820.

[3] *Letters and Journals*, IV, 174–175. Letter of Oct. 12, 1817, to John
Murray.

> The Mind, the Spirit, the Promethean spark,
> The lightning of my being, is as bright,
> Pervading, and far darting as your own,
> And shall not yield to yours, though cooped in clay!
> (*Manfred*, I, i, 154–157)

Manfred calls up three separate groups of spirits, each apparently more powerful and awesome than the preceding. But he finds, disappointingly, that he is equal to them all and that they can tell him nothing that he doesn't already know, because they are of the mind's creation — that is the tragic limitation of the creature cooped in clay. Of the first group of spirits, drawn from the natural elements that inspire awe and that were the foundations of men's first religions — "Earth, ocean, air, night, mountains, winds, thy star" (the personal star under whose influence he was born, i.e., his own nature) — of these he asks only forgetfulness or oblivion. But they answer evasively: they are immortal and know not death and consequently know not whether death could grant his boon. They only echo his own words. Then he asks them to appear in some visible form, and the spirit of his star appears in the form of a beautiful female figure — the ideal that he still hopes in desperate and self-deluding moments to grasp in reality. But of course the spirit vanishes as he tries to seize it, and he falls senseless.

At this point Byron inserted the "incantation" or curse pronounced upon Manfred, ostensibly in the voice of one of the spirits, probably his own "star." It had been written during the summer of his bitterness against Lady Byron and her advisers, and there are lines that seem so obviously directed against her as to be inappropriate in the context of the drama:[4]

> From thy false tears I did distil
> An essence which hath strength to kill. . . .
>
> By the cold breast and serpent smile,
> By thy unfathomed gulfs of guile,
> By that most seeming virtuous eye,
> By thy shut soul's hypocrisy. . . .
> (*Manfred*, I, i, 232–233, 242–245)

[4] The "incantation" was first published as a separate poem in *The Prisoner of Chillon and Other Poems*, Dec. 5, 1816. While it was supposedly written during the summer, it seems to embody some of the bitterness which he felt on hearing in October of his wife's cold replies through intermediaries to Mme. de Staël's attempts to effect a reconciliation.

But in the depth of his remorse and the conviction of his own "delinquencies" Byron felt that it fitted his alter ego Manfred well enough:

> There are shades which will not vanish,
> There are thoughts thou canst not banish.
>
> * * * * * * * *
>
> In proving every poison known,
> I found the strongest was thine own.
>
> * * * * * * * *
>
> I call upon thee! and compel
> Thyself to be thy proper Hell!
>   (*Manfred*, I, i, 204–205, 240–241, 250–251)

The last lines quoted are a premonition of the conclusion of the drama.

The next scene is on the Jungfrau, and we see more clearly that Manfred is really Childe Harold in his most uncompromising mood and essence, Harold no longer capable of the sad tranquillity beyond tragedy, no longer capable of living with the imperfections of human nature or of finding solace in "the pathless woods" or the wild Alpine crags and waterfalls. Unable to get superhuman aid from the spirits he had conjured up, he is contemplating suicide, but

> There is a power upon me which withholds,
> And makes it my fatality to live. . . .
>   (*Manfred*, I, ii, 23–24)

At this point he sees an eagle and is reminded again of the disparity between his soaring aspirations and his earth-bound condition.

> How beautiful is all this visible world!
> How glorious in its action and itself!
> But we, who name ourselves its sovereigns, we,
> Half dust, half deity, alike unfit
> To sink or soar, with our mixed essence make
> A conflict of its elements, and breathe
> The breath of degradation and of pride,
> Contending with low wants and lofty will,
> Till our Mortality predominates,
> And men are — what they name not to themselves,
> And trust not to each other.   (*Manfred*, I, ii, 37–47)

The sound of the shepherd's pipe heightens his sense of imprisonment in the flesh and his desire for escape.

> Oh, that I were
> The viewless spirit of a lovely sound,
> A living voice, a breathing harmony,
> A bodiless enjoyment.   (*Manfred*, I, ii, 52–55)

Here is the quintessence of the Byronic-Romantic quandary: the final indignity to the intransigent romantic is that the "half-deity" of the spirit is linked with the "half-dust" of humanity and can never soar freely. The romantic who will settle for nothing less than being all deity has come to the logical end of his rope. And so Manfred, crying "Earth! take these atoms!" starts his plunge over the precipice, but is saved by a chamois hunter who takes him to his hut. Manfred envies the hunter his humble virtues and simple pleasures but cannot emulate them. He has gone beyond the point where common human satisfactions, even those of an idealized Noble Savage, can substitute for his immortal longings.

Manfred has hinted in his conversation with the chamois hunter at the immediate cause of the oppressive sense of guilt that weighs upon him. He sees blood on the brim of the wine cup offered him:

> . . . my blood! the pure warm stream
> Which ran in the veins of my fathers, and in ours
> When we were in our youth, and had one heart,
> And loved each other as we should not love. . . .
> (*Manfred*, II, i, 24–27)

Later, alone by a cataract, he calls up the Witch of the Alps, merely to look upon her beauty. Her serenity and understanding elicit more confessions. She recognizes him for "a man of many thoughts, / And deeds of good and ill, extreme in both, / Fatal and fated in thy sufferings."

Manfred then launches an autobiographic statement that offers a clear subjective summary of Childe Harold-Byron's romantic career.

> My pang shall find a voice. From my youth upwards
> My spirit walked not with the souls of men . . .
> The thirst of their ambition was not mine,

> The aim of their existence was not mine. . . .
> My joy was in the wilderness, to breathe
> The difficult air of the iced mountain's top. . . .
>   (*Manfred*, II, ii, 50–51, 53–54, 62–63)

Then he approaches "the core of my heart's grief." There was only one with whom he "wore the chain of human ties":

> She was like me in lineaments . . .
> She had the same lone thoughts and wanderings,
> The quest of hidden knowledge, and a mind
> To comprehend the Universe: nor these
> Alone, but with them gentler powers than mine,
> Pity, and smiles, and tears — which I had not;
> And tenderness — but that I had for her;
> Humility — and that I never had.
> Her faults were mine — her virtues were her own —
> I loved her, and destroyed her! . . .
> Not with my hand, but heart — which broke her heart;
> It gazed on mine, and withered.[5]
>   (*Manfred*, II, ii, 105, 109–119)

Guilt in this narcissistic love (the only kind that could satisfy the engulfing ego of the self-centered romantic) makes Manfred seek forgetfulness by plunging amidst mankind and finally by seeking death. The Witch of the Alps offers her aid, on condition that Manfred swear obedience to her will (to the will of Nature?), but his reply is the same as before:

> Obey! and whom? the Spirits
> Whose presence I command, and be the slave
> Of those who served me — Never!
>   (*Manfred*, II, ii, 158–160)

Manfred finally decides to call the dead "And ask them what it is we dread to be," and for that purpose he seeks the most powerful of the spirits in their own haunts, on the summit of the Jungfrau. First we see the Destinies, with Nemesis at their head

---

[5] This passage was recognized by Byron's contemporaries as a clear reference to the incest with his half-sister Augusta. Of course it was an idealization of Augusta, who had scarcely "a mind / To comprehend the Universe," but the narcissistic projection of romantic love saw in the mirror what it wanted to see, a reflection of its imagined self. Byron had not literally destroyed his sister, but he had perhaps a guilty sense of having destroyed her reputation.

— a favorite of Byron, often invoked against his enemies. In introducing these spirits Byron cannot resist putting some political overtones in the conversation. Nemesis says,

> I was detained repairing shattered thrones —
> Marrying fools, restoring dynasties —
> Avenging men upon their enemies,
> And making them repent their own revenge;
> Goading the wise to madness; from the dull
> Shaping out oracles to rule the world
> Afresh — for they were waxing out of date,
> And mortals dared to ponder for themselves,
> To weigh kings in the balance — and to speak
> Of Freedom, the forbidden fruit.
>   (*Manfred*, II, iii, 62–71)

When Manfred confronts Arimanes, king of all the Destinies, and the spirits bid this child of the earth prostrate himself, he replies:

> Bid *him* bow down to that which is above him,
> The overruling Infinite — the Maker
> Who made him not for worship — let him kneel,
> And we will kneel together.
>   (*Manfred*, II, iv, 46–49)

This seems to indicate that Byron — like Shelley in *Prometheus Unbound*, who conceived a power above Jupiter, the man-made god who enslaved mankind — recognized a force in the universe more powerful than and independent of the spirits created by man's mind. But that is no solution for Manfred's problem, for such a force is inaccessible to him and deaf to his pleas. If Manfred had hoped to find spirits above him, he was disappointed. His magic science had succeeded in conjuring only spirits like his own. The Destinies themselves recognize him for their equal. One says:

> This man
> Is of no common order, as his port
> And presence here denote: his sufferings
> Have been of an immortal nature — like
> Our own . . .
>   his aspirations
> Have been beyond the dwellers of the earth,

> And they have only taught him what we know —
> That knowledge is not happiness, and science
> But an exchange of ignorance for that
> Which is another kind of ignorance.
> (*Manfred*, II, iv, 51–55, 58–63)

At Manfred's request Nemesis calls up the phantom of Astarte, the loved one whom he had destroyed. He asks her to speak to him. But even Arimanes is unable to make her break her silence. "She is not of our order, but belongs / To the other powers." Manfred pleads again:

> speak to me. . . .
> Thou lovedst me
> Too much, as I loved thee: we were not made
> To torture thus each other — though it were
> The deadliest sin to love as we have loved.
> (*Manfred*, II, iv, 117, 120–123)

Finally she utters his name, prophesies his death on the morrow, and says farewell. He cannot elicit any words of forgiveness from her for the very reason that she too is the creation of his mind and he cannot forgive himself. As the spirit of Astarte disappears Manfred is overcome. But the spirits he has conjured still find him their equal:

> He is convulsed — This is to be a mortal,
> And seek the things beyond mortality. . . .
> Yet, see, he mastereth himself, and makes
> His torture tributary to his will.
> Had he been one of us, he would have made
> An awful Spirit.   (*Manfred*, II, iv, 157–162)

Byron had difficulty with the third act, for he had created an impasse in the drama, as he had in his life, that he did not know how to end. He was rightly dissatisfied with the first draft in which he had made the Abbot a ridiculous figure who threatened Manfred if he did not repent and give all his lands to the Monastery, and whom he conjured the demon Ashtaroth to carry away to the accompaniment of a devilish mocking song. The denouement was melodramatic and equally out of tone with the earlier acts: Manfred died from fire, presumably demonic lightning, in his tower without any attempt to justify his defiance of the spirits. When Byron rewrote the third act in Rome in May,

1817, he made the Abbot a more sympathetic character and a sounding board for Manfred's final justification and defiant end.

In a passage which is a remarkably clear apologia for the failure of Byron's own political ambitions, Manfred confesses that he "had those earthly visions / And noble aspirations in my youth, / To make my own the mind of other men, / The enlightener of nations." But he soon discovered that his uncompromising nature made success impossible:

> I could not tame my nature down; for he
> Must serve who fain would sway; and soothe, and sue,
> And watch all time, and pry into all place,
> And be a living Lie, who would become
> A mighty thing amongst the mean — and such
> The mass are; I disdained to mingle with
> A herd, though to be leader — and of wolves.
> The lion is alone, and so am I.
>
> *(Manfred,* III, i, 116–123)

After hearing him the Abbot summed up what may have been Byron's own self-appraisal:

> This should have been a noble creature: he
> Hath all the energy which would have made
> A goodly frame of glorious elements,
> Had they been wisely mingled; as it is,
> It is an awful chaos — Light and Darkness —
> And mind and dust — and passions and pure thoughts
> Mixed, and contending without end or order, —
> All dormant, or destructive.
>
> *(Manfred,* III, i, 160–167)

The Byronic "Promethean spark" illuminates Manfred's reply to the demons who have come to claim his soul. It is the final transcendence of the indomitable mind. We see how far Manfred is from Faust:

> I stand
> Upon my strength — I do defy — deny —
> Spurn back, and scorn ye![6]
>
> *(Manfred,* III, iv, 119–121)

---

[6] This is no doubt the passage that Southey referred to when he said that "Byron's *Manfred* met the Devil and bullied him."

When the spirit refers to Manfred's many crimes, he replies:

> What I have done is done; I bear within
> A torture which could nothing gain from thine:
> The Mind which is immortal makes itself
> Requital for its good or evil thoughts, —
> Is its own origin of ill and end —
> And its own place and time. . . .
>
> (*Manfred*, III, iv, 127–132)

Instead of a deathbed repentance, we have Manfred's simple statement to the Abbot before he expires: "Old man! 't is not so difficult to die."

The average non-romantic reaction to *Manfred*, in Byron's day, as in this, might well be summed up in the words of the chamois hunter: "This is convulsion, and no healthful life." It is easy to ridicule the fevered sufferings of the hero and his self-inflation to equality with immortal spirits. Unless one is willing to enter the Byronic world with full sympathy and understanding, such phrases as "This man / Is of no common order. . . . His sufferings / Have been of an immortal nature, like / Our own," and "Had he been one of us, he would have made / An awful spirit" seem almost a burlesque of the self-aggrandizement of the romantic ego. But from another point of view Byron's statement of intransigent human longings and despair must remain a poetic landmark of the romantic agony. And its bold recognition of the mind's limitations as well as the affirmation of its invincibility and integrity lend the poem an abiding interest beyond what may be attached to the personal problems of the poet.

Cain was an outpouring, not wholly coherent or consistent, of Byron's revolt against conventional religious orthodoxy coupled with speculations on free will and man's destiny, and a questioning of "the politics of Paradise." Since childhood he had been fascinated by the Old Testament, as much by its poetry (he had drawn freely on its themes and its phrasing in *Hebrew Melodies*) as by its grim picture of man's relations with his stern Maker. From his Cambridge days, when he had first read widely in eighteenth century rationalist and deistic literature, he had taken delight in arguing about the inconsistencies of orthodox dogmas, but he continued to have a genuine interest in and curiosity concerning religious subjects. Goethe, who was much impressed by *Cain*, later said that Byron should have lived "to execute his vocation. . . . To dramatise the *Old* Testament. What a subject, under his hands, would the Tower of Babel have been!"[7] But Byron was not so much interested in dramatizing it as in using it as the basis for his frankest challenge to generally accepted religious views. E. H. Coleridge remarked when he was editing Byron's poetry at the turn of the present century: "It is all but impossible for the modern reader to appreciate the audacity of *Cain*, or to realize the alarm and indignation which it aroused by its appearance."[8] It is even more difficult today, when what we now call "Fundamentalism," or the literal interpretation of the Bible, is fighting a losing rearguard action, to realize what a bombshell *Cain* was when it struck England in 1821.

Byron knew that the drama was daring and tried to shore up his defenses in the preface. He had given as subtitle "A Mystery" and maintained that he had not taken the same liberties with his subject as had "those very profane productions," the Mystery or Morality plays of the Middle Ages. The author had, he said, "endeavoured to preserve the language adapted to his characters; and where it is (and this is but rarely) taken from actual *Scripture*, he has made as little alteration, even of words, as the rhythm would permit. . . . With regard to the language of Lucifer, it was difficult for me to make him talk like a clergyman upon the same subjects; but I have done what I could to restrain him within the bounds of spiritual politeness."

But it was too obvious that Byron had made Cain an intellectual rebel and iconoclast, questioning traditional beliefs in the justice of the divine governance of the universe, measured in human and utilitarian terms. When Cain says he has nothing to be thankful for, Adam, who is a strict Evangelical and talks like one, asks: "Dost thou not *live?*" Cain replies: "Must I not die?" And Cain "blasphemes" further by saying:

> The snake spoke *truth;* it *was* the Tree of Knowledge;
> It *was* the Tree of Life: knowledge is good,
> And Life is good; and how can both be evil?
>
> (*Cain*, I, i, 36–38)

[7] Henry Crabb Robinson, *On Books and Their Writers*, ed. Edith J. Morley, I, 372.

[8] *Poetry*, V, 202.

Eve joins Adam in counselling: "Content thee with what *is*." But Cain will not be silenced:

> They have but
> One answer to all questions, " 'T was *his* will,
> And *he* is good." How know I that? Because
> He is all-powerful, must all-good, too, follow?
> I judge but by the fruits — and they are bitter....
> (Cain, I, i, 74–78)

In a sense Byron made his own theology. He had long admired Milton's Satan as an arch-rebel, and in his defense of *Cain* he referred again and again to the precedent set by Milton: "If *Cain* be 'blasphemous,' *Paradise Lost* is blasphemous." But Byron's Lucifer has the hauteur without the grandeur of Milton's Satan, and at times he is tinged with the Mephistophelian tendency to stoop to grim ironic mockery, which is more Byronic than Satanic. Moreover, it is obvious that Milton was on the side of the angels (the good angels), whereas Byron conceived of Lucifer not as the "Arch-Fiend" and enemy of mankind, but as their defender. If Lucifer is, like Satan, aware of his angelic origin, he does not recognize his "fall" as anything but unjust, and he boasts a superior morality. He too takes on a Promethean character and is a champion of humanity against an authoritarian and arbitrary deity. He links Cain with himself as

> Souls who dare look the Omnipotent tyrant in
> His everlasting face, and tell him that
> His evil is not good!   (*Cain*, I, i, 138–140)

Byron's strong leaning to Manicheanism, the belief in the struggle of equal forces of good and evil within the universe (and within himself), has caused him to attempt to make Lucifer a rival of God, but the confusions and doubts in his own mind are reflected in the drama. In the first place, the roles of god and devil are reversed, for Lucifer is a champion of the "good principle," whereas God by his deeds is shown as "evil." But Byron's haunting sense of sin disturbed the picture and left him without full conviction in his own skepticism. It is significant that Cain in the end is remorseful and repentant and does not cry out against a tyrant god but accepts his judgment of exile.

Cain's conversations with Lucifer furnish a dialogue between two halves of Byron's mind, on the one hand a groping skepticism and disillusionment with the inexorable conditions of life in the

world in which he was forced to live, and on the other hand a
Shelleyan reaching out for an ideal world which Byron never
quite believed in. With all his boast that he has adhered strictly
to Scripture, Byron took even more liberties than Milton with the
story in Genesis. Cain the intellectual rebel is wholly Byron's
invention. Encouraged by Lucifer he bares his mind:

> I never could
> Reconcile what I saw with what I heard. . . .
> I look
> Around a world where I seem nothing, with
> Thoughts which arise within me, as if they
> Could master all things — but I thought alone
> This misery was *mine*. My father is
> Tamed down; my mother has forgot the mind
> Which made her thirst for knowledge at the risk
> Of an eternal curse. . . .   (*Cain*, I, i, 168–169, 175–182)

Lucifer urges him to resistance: "Nothing can / Quench the mind,
if the mind will be itself / And centre of surrounding things —
't is made / To sway." Cain is a willing pupil, for he thirsts for
knowledge, but he is disappointed by the evasive answer to his
first question: "What is death?" Like the spirits raised by Manfred, Lucifer is immortal and knows not death. It is obvious to the
reader, though not yet to Cain (for dramatic purposes), that
Lucifer can raise speculative questions but can answer only those
to which Cain himself knows the answers, for he too is a creation
of the mind of man.

Lucifer has promised to show Cain a pictorial history of past,
present, and future worlds. In the second act Cain flies with
Lucifer through the "Abyss of Space" and they discuss some of
the things suggested to Byron's imagination by his reading of
Cuvier: the idea that the world was destroyed several times before
the creation of man, and that the pre-Adamite world was peopled
by rational beings more intelligent than man. But these speculations are always linked to the basic Byronic problems. What
absorbs him is that these intelligent beings should be "all doomed
to death — and wretched." Lucifer himself puts the damper on
the ennobling thought of those greater beings:

> But if that high thought were
> Linked to a servile mass of matter — and,
> Knowing such things, aspiring to such things,

> And science still beyond them, were chained down
> To the most gross and petty paltry wants,
> All foul and fulsome — and the very best
> Of thine enjoyments a sweet degradation,
> A most enervating and filthy cheat
> To lure thee on to the renewal of
> Fresh souls and bodies, all foredoomed to be
> As frail and few so happy.   (*Cain*, II, i, 50–60)

At the beginning of the journey Cain pays tribute to Lucifer, whom we may here equate with the speculative mind of man — a tribute qualified in the expected Byronic way:

> I know not what thou art: I see thy power,
> And see thou show'st me things beyond *my* power,
> Beyond all power of my born faculties,
> Although inferior still to my desires
> And my conceptions.   (*Cain*, II, i, 79–83)

Cain is overwhelmed with the view of the "unimaginable ether" and the "aerial universe of endless expansion." He is "Intoxicated with eternity" and exclaims:

> Oh God! Oh Gods! or whatsoe'er ye are!
> How beautiful ye are! how beautiful
> Your works, or accidents, or whatsoe'er
> They may be! Let me die, as atoms die
> (If that they die), or know ye in your might
> And knowledge! My thoughts are not in this hour
> Unworthy what I see, though my dust is. . . .
>   (*Cain*, II, i, 110–116)

The cosmic voyage has more of philosophy and science than of theology in it. And in the end Cain is frustrated in his search for knowledge, for Lucifer only answers his questions by asking further ones. Even Lucifer's conducted tour through Hades has taught him no more of the mystery of death. He is forced to conclude:

> It was a lying tree — for we *know* nothing.
> At least it *promised knowledge* at the *price*
> Of death — but *knowledge* still: but what *knows* man?
>   (*Cain*, II, ii, 61–63)

Lucifer's poor consolation is:

> And this should be the human sum
> Of knowledge, to know mortal nature's nothingness. . . .
> (*Cain*, II, ii, 421–422)

Lucifer's final advice is an echo of the "indomitable mind" passages in *Childe Harold* and *Manfred*. Lucifer is a Utilitarian:

>   judge
> Not by words, though of Spirits, but the fruits
> Of your existence, such as it must be.
> *One good* gift has the fatal apple given, —
> Your *reason:* — let it not be overswayed
> By tyrannous threats to force you into faith
> 'Gainst all external sense and inward feeling:
> Think and endure, — and form an inner world
> In your own bosom — where the outward fails. . . .
> (*Cain*, II, ii, 456–464)

The third act comes back to earth and ostensibly to the Biblical story, though the elaboration of the characters and the motive for the murder are all Byron's invention. It is inevitable that Cain, naturally skeptical and strengthened in his rebelliousness by his conversations with Lucifer, should take a dim view of the docile attitude and humble sacrifices of Abel. Byron has made the tragic irony hinge upon Cain's sudden fit of anger at Abel's insistence on a blood sacrifice. But after he has spilled his brother's blood, Cain subsides into a remorse that is deeper and more agonizing than any punishment that could be inflicted upon him. He does not protest the angel's mark on his brow, which is "nought to that which is within it." He accepts the justness of his fate with tragic rather than Biblical acquiescence.

> Eastward from Eden will we take our way;
> 'T is the most desolate, and suits my steps.
> (*Cain*, III, i, 552–553)

Whatever merit *Cain* may have as a drama, aside from the clear and often pungent statement of familiar Byronic ideas about the disparity between man's limited condition and the infinite reach of his aspirations, rests in the characters. Cain is something more than a mere puppet voicing Byron's revolt against the reigning orthodoxy. Byron has converted him from the jealous villain of Biblical story and tradition into a character with some subtlety and human warmth. "I thirst for good," he tells Lucifer.

His normal nature is gentle and noble. Even when exasperated by the complacent acceptance of their lot by his brother and sister, he says: "Your gentleness must not be harshly met." His love for Adah, his sister (and wife), is deep and sincere, and is not undermined by the cold logic of Lucifer himself. When Lucifer says, "I pity thee who lovest what must perish," Cain replies: "And I thee who lov'st nothing." He has a sharp sensitivity to the beauty of the visible world. The setting sun or Adah's face can fill his eyes "with pleasant tears." His savage indignation at cosmic wrongs scarcely disturbs his gentleness in dealing with those he loves even in face of their bland acceptance of the world as it is. Only once, when his brother goads him beyond endurance by his insistence on a bloody sacrifice, is he seized by a momentary rage — itself an evidence of the fleshly tyranny against which he has rebelled. Then he subsides into the tragic gentleness of a broken spirit. None of the rebellious feeling but all of the fight has left him.

Adah, though a typical Byronic heroine, passive and utterly devoted to Cain, has moments of sad tolerance and understanding that lift her into a three-dimensional character. Adam, Eve, and Abel are only voices of traditional attitudes against which Byron was battling, and he made little effort to endow them with independent characters.

It has been pointed out that in the scenes involving Lucifer there is no drama because there is no conflict. Cain even before he met Lucifer was in Satanic revolt and did not need convincing. But though they may have the same beliefs, there is a temperamental difference in their reaction to the cosmic picture. They represent conflicting moods rather than ideas. Lucifer could adhere to strict and cold logic, for he was a detached and immortal spirit, whereas Cain with the coils of life and the sentence of death upon him had all the human feelings to complicate his philosophic view of the universe. He felt keenly the degradation of the human state, and Lucifer's tour and tutoring only heightened his sense of the littleness of man while whetting his appetite for infinite beauty and knowledge which were unattainable. In this sense the conversation of the two characters did dramatize an inner conflict of the author.

In *Manfred* the romantic complaint is that man is "half dust, half deity." The assumption is (and this offered hope, at least to the transcendental romantic) that if one could escape the dust and become "a bodiless spirit" he would find happiness. *Cain* opened the way to a blacker despair, for the journey through the spirit world suggests that even deities may not be happy. All knowledge does not bring all happiness, and though Cain had seen things "Beyond all power of my born faculties," they were "inferior still to my desires / And my conceptions." Romantic intransigence could go no further.

Though Byron protested that it was "less speculative than *Cain*, and very pious," *Heaven and Earth*, suggested by a verse in Genesis (6:2) recording the love of "sons of God" (which Byron took to be angels) for "the daughters of men," was as likely to shock the British reading public. But one of the women, Aholibamah, a lineal and spiritual descendant of Cain, and one of the angels, Azaziel, voice Byron's iconoclastic views as clearly as does Cain or Lucifer. In fact, the drama flew in the face of British mores more directly than did *Cain*, whose speculations were generalized and in the cosmic sphere, whereas the illicit love with angels was both immoral and sacrilegious. Byron should have seen this, but after his exile he was either blind to British prejudices or contemptuous of them. He told Medwin: "Kinnaird tells me that he can get no bookseller to publish it. It was offered to Murray, but he is the most timid of God's booksellers, and starts at the title."[9] It was finally published by John Hunt in the second number of *The Liberal* in 1823.

Parallel with the defiance of conventional beliefs and overshadowing it in large measure is the familiar Byronic theme of the ineffable longing for a celestial life and love free from the imperfections of the earthly state. To her weaker sister Anah, Aholibamah, Byron's chief spokesman, says:

> And where is the impiety of loving
> Celestial natures? . . .
>   Then wed thee
> Unto some son of clay, and toil and spin!
> There's Japhet loves thee well, hath loved thee long:
> Marry, and bring forth dust!
>   (*H. and E.*, I, i, 10–11, 15–18)

Though formed of clay she has the pride in her immortal part that gives her equality with her angel:

[9] Medwin, *Conversations of Lord Byron*, Paris, 1824, I, 189.

> There is a ray
> In me, which, though forbidden yet to shine,
> I feel was lighted at thy God's and thine.
>   (*H. and E.*, I, i, 103–105)

Anah, swept on by her love for Azaziel but troubled with a conviction of sin, is perhaps a more tragic figure. Her plight is presented with sympathy. She says:

> Great is their love who love in sin and fear . . .
>   to an Adamite
> Forgive, my Seraph! that such thoughts appear,
> For sorrow is our element. . . .
>   (*H. and E.*, I, i, 67, 69–71)

Japhet too, the rejected earthly lover of Anah, is endowed with the dignity of his tragic mortality. He too can admire "The eternal beauty of undying things." A son of Noah, he is torn between his duty to be saved for the sake of future generations and his desire to save the "loveliest of earth's daughters" from a doom that even the serpent is to escape on the ark. His half-questioning the purposes of an unjust fate, his compassion, and his hopeless love make him a not unsympathetic character. He pities his brother "For being happy, / Deprived of that which makes my misery." Byron has ennobled him further by making him a defender of the human lot against the spirits who rejoice at the coming destruction of the race of mankind in the flood — "The abhorred race / Which could not keep in Eden their high place, / But listened to the voice / Of knowledge without power." The spirits taunt him:

> When the great barrier of the deep is rent,
> Shall thou and thine be good or happy? — No!
> Thy new world and new race shall be of woe — . . .
>   And art thou not ashamed
>   Thus to survive. . . .
>   Who would outlive their kind,
>   Except the base and blind?
>   (*H. and E.*, I, iii, 127–129, 135–136, 144–145)

But when they picture the "New beings — years, diseases, sorrow, crime — / With all companionship of hate and toil," Japhet replies:

The eternal Will
Shall deign to expound this dream
Of good and evil; and redeem
    Unto himself all times, all things;
      And gathered under his almighty wings,
        Abolish Hell!
And to the expiated Earth
Restore the beauty of her birth,
    Her Eden in an endless paradise,
Where man no more can fall as once he fell,
And even the very demons shall do well!
        (*H. and E.*, I, iii, 193–203)

When will this take place? "When the Redeemer cometh; first in pain, / And then in glory." It was a prophecy Byron would have liked to believe, but the spirits have the last word:

Meantime still struggle in the mortal chain,
    Till Earth wax hoary;
War with yourselves, and Hell, and Heaven, in vain,
    Until the clouds look gory
With the blood reeking from each battle-plain;
New times, new climes, new arts, new men; but still,
The same old tears, old crimes, and oldest ill,
Shall be amongst your race in different forms. . . .
        (*H. and E.*, I, iii, 207–214)

As for Noah, he combines all the platitudes of a stern father and an Evangelical parson. E. H. Coleridge remarked: "Byron said that it was difficult to make Lucifer talk 'like a clergyman.' He contrived to make Noah talk like a street-preacher."[10] The scene ends melodramatically with the sisters in sadness rather than joy, being carried off from their drowning families by their angel lovers, while women and children plead hopelessly for safety in the ark. Japhet mourns: "Why, when all perish, why must I remain?"

Though Medwin quoted Byron as saying that he had plans for a second part of the drama, which he outlined (the erring angels, driven out of all the celestial abodes, are forced to return the sisters to the earth where they perish while Japhet pleads vainly to have them taken aboard the ark), he had really said all he wanted to say and any continuation would have been an

---

[10] *Poetry*, V, 309n.

anticlimax. It would have been equally unsatisfactory to picture his lovers escaping to some haven among the stars and there living happily. It would have made the tale seem even more impious, and, what is more important, would have violated Byron's own sense of the inexorable fate of all who try to go against the current in life and love.

Although there is less exposition and logical argument than in *Cain*, the same questions are raised: "Then why is evil — he being good?" and "where is the impiety of loving / Celestial natures?" (That is, of aspiring to the ideal.) There was no answer to the first question. As for the second, Byron had already shown in *Childe Harold* and in *Manfred*, as well as in *Cain*, that, whether impious or not, the aspiration "Beyond the fitting medium of desire" for the "things beyond mortality" carried its own punishment of frustration. But the bitter defiance and skepticism of the chief characters, who share with Cain a divine discontent with "the inadequacy of his state to his conceptions," gives a passionate vibrancy to the drama. Byron told Murray that it was "more lyrical and Greek" than he had at first intended. The soaring poetical flights in rhyme relieve the monotony of the blank verse.

The Deformed Transformed is, as Byron acknowledged in the preface, founded partly on the story of a novel called *The Three Brothers* (by Joshua Pickersgill, 1803) and partly on the *Faust* "of the great Goethe." The drama has many faults: it is planless, the development of what little plot there is is inconsistent, and it has little poetry to redeem it. But Byron has seized the opportunity to make the lame hunchback, Arnold, sensitive, hungry for beauty and compensating power; while the Stranger or Caesar (the devil) is cynical, witty, truthful, and sardonic. They are the malleable spokesmen of two sides of his own nature.

The dramatic opening grew out of Byron's unforgettable memory of his mother in a fit of rage calling him "a lame brat." Finding his deformity intolerable, Arnold is about to end his existence by falling on his knife when a tall dark stranger appears out of the mist of the fountain, and at once reveals his Mephistophelian character. When Arnold asks whether he is spirit or man, he replies: "As man is both, why not / Say both in one?" The devil's sarcastic wit is not the poet's best, but Byron is more interested in the self-debate which the dialogue chiefly is. Arnold

says, "Do you — dare *you* / To taunt me with my born deformity?" The Stranger replies:

> Were I to taunt a buffalo with this
> Cloven foot of thine, or the swift dromedary
> With thy Sublime of Humps, the animals
> Would revel in the compliment.
>
> (*D. T.*, I, i, 105–108)

The Stranger then offers to change Arnold into any shape he
wishes; he will show him the "brightest which the world e'er
bore" and he can take his choice. Arnold, who seems already
aware of the Faustian tradition, asks on what condition: "Must it
be signed in blood?" But the Stranger says, "You shall have no
bond / But your own will, no contract save your deeds," a suggestive variation which Byron did not take the trouble to follow
up in the later scenes.

The Stranger then calls up in succession the phantoms of
historical and legendary figures, which Arnold rejects one by
one. He will not fight as a mock Caesar. He rejects Alcibiades,
and also Socrates, "that low, swarthy, short-nosed, round-eyed
satyr," for "I was not born for philosophy, / Though I have that
about me which has need on't." Antony is well enough, but he
wants to see more heroes before deciding. Arnold finally settles
for the beauty and strength of Achilles, but the Stranger dis-
suades him from taking on the twelve cubits of the marble
statue he had shown him, for "by being / A little less removed
from present men / In figure, thou canst sway them more."
Arnold himself indulges in some astute psychological analysis
which shows that Byron was fully aware of the effect of his
lameness on his character and ambitions.

> I ask not
> For Valour, since Deformity is daring.
> It is its essence to o'ertake mankind
> By heart and soul, and make itself the equal —
> Aye, the superior of the rest. There is
> A spur in its halt movements, to become
> All that the others cannot, in such things
> As still are free to both, to compensate
> For stepdame Nature's avarice at first.
>
> (*D. T.*, I, i, 313–321)

The Stranger having transformed Arnold takes on his discarded form: "I will be as you were, and you shall see / Yourself for ever by you, as your shadow." This is another subtle turn, the implications of which appear in the final fragment of a third part. Arnold is ready for adventures, and asked where he would like to go, he says, "Where the World / Is thickest, that I may behold it in / Its workings." The Stranger replies, "That's to say, where there is War / And Woman in activity." And so they set out on coal-black horses for Rome. The Stranger has taken the name of Caesar, a name that belongs to Empire, and "therefore fittest for / The Devil in disguise."

And so the devil and his pupil enter into the carnage of the sack of Rome, Caesar making his sardonic comments along the way. Arnold has a pointless encounter with Benvenuto Cellini. Caesar makes sport of the bloodthirstiness of some Lutheran soldiers trying to kill the Pope, who escapes, to his delight: "I would not have his bulls abolished — / 'T were worth one half our empire: his indulgences / Demand some in return." Arnold saves the life of a beautiful patrician, Olimpia, and falls in love with her. A lyric chorus of the first scene of a third part celebrates the happiness of the lovers in their country retreat. But Byron had a second thought and wrote a fragment of a third part that returned to realism and irony. He summed up his intentions for the ending in a memorandum at the beginning: "Jealous — Arnold of Caesar. Olympia [sic] at first not liking Caesar — then? — Arnold jealous of himself under his former figure, owing to the power of intellect, etc., etc., etc." It would have been a fitting end if Byron could have carried it off poetically and dramatically, but he contented himself with a few bright remarks from Caesar.

Despite occasional cleverness and shrewd insight displayed in the dialogue, the drama fails to come off the ground. It has no structural tightness and it lacks the passionate depth of feeling and conviction that carried the other speculative dramas into occasional poetry and dramatic intensity.

8

Historical Dramas

A CURIOUS COMBINATION of circumstances and interests
turned Byron's pen to the composition of historical tragedies in
1820, and in the course of a year he had produced three dramas in
this genre, two of them, *Marino Faliero* and *The Two Foscari*,
taken from episodes in Venetian history, and one, *Sardanapalus*,
founded on the life and character of an Assyrian king. Byron's
interest in dramatic writing had been lively since his Harrow days
when he declaimed dramatic pieces on Speech Days and attended
the London theater frequently. This interest grew during his
years of fame and while he was searching for suitable manuscripts
for the Committee of Drury Lane, despite his having to wade
through dozens of dreary historical tragedies.

He recognized *Manfred* as a dramatic poem rather than a drama
in the stricter sense. Besides, it belonged to that secondary category which he associated in his mind with the "lava of the
imagination," a personal catharsis, and he wanted to demonstrate
to himself and to the world that he could write something more
regular and more ambitious than he had attempted thus far. The
critical shafts leveled at *Manfred*, the outcry against *Don Juan*,
and the urging of Shelley as well as his friends in England that
he do something worthy of his talents, all combined with his
absorbing interest in drama and in history to stimulate him to the
task. If he had failed in his ambition to equal his master Pope in
moral satire in the heroic couplet, here was another opportunity
to demonstrate that he could do something more "classical" than
he had done before or than his contemporaries were producing.
Hence his insistence on following the unities and his eschewing
the romantic irregularities of poetic dramas modeled after the

Elizabethans. In several letters to Murray he outlined his aims, and his formula for producing a great tragedy. ". . . this is not to be done by following the old dramatists, who are full of gross faults, pardoned only for the beauty of their language; but by writing naturally and *regularly*, and producing *regular* tragedies, like the *Greeks;* but not in *imitation*. . . . as I think that *love* is not the principal passion for tragedy (and yet most of ours turn upon it), you will not find me a popular writer. Unless it is Love, *furious, criminal*, and *hapless*, it ought not to make a tragic subject: when it is melting and maudlin, it *does*, but it ought not to do; it is then for the Gallery and second price boxes."[1] His aim was to write something "simple and severe." "And there are neither rings, nor mistakes, nor starts, nor outrageous ranting villains, nor melodrame, in it."[2]

He had seen enough of the preference of London audiences for "ranting villains" and melodrama not to want to be judged by them. Despite his great desire for dramatic success, his sensitive fear of being at the mercy of actors and galleries made him willing to let his reputation rest on the reading.[3] He confessed his feelings frankly in the preface to *Marino Faliero*: "I have had no view to the stage; in its present state it is, perhaps, not a very exalted object of ambition; besides, I have been too much behind the scenes to have thought it so at any time. And I cannot conceive any man of irritable feeling putting himself at the mercies of an audience. . . . Were I capable of writing a play which could be deemed stage-worthy, success would give me no pleasure, and failure great pain."[4]

Byron had early been attracted to the picturesque aspects of Venetian history. "Every thing about Venice," he wrote in this same preface, "is, or was, extraordinary — her aspect is like a dream, and her history is like a romance." And in the Palace, he

[1] *Letters and Journals*, V, 217–218. Letter of Jan. 4, 1821.

[2] *Letters and Journals*, V, 243. Letter of Feb. 16, 1821.

[3] For an interesting study of Byron's ambivalence about the theater, see David V. Erdman, "Byron's Stage Fright: the History of His Ambition and Fear of Writing for the Stage," *ELH*, VI (1939), 219–243.

[4] When *Marino Faliero* was, against his wishes and after strenuous efforts to stop it, put on at Drury Lane, Byron was in an agony of distress and anxiety until he learned that it was a moderate success. It is ironic that Byron's greatest stage success came after his death, when his plays were presented by Macready and others in the 1830's and 1840's in the most melodramatic fashion. *Manfred, Marino Faliero*, and *Sardanapalus* appeared many times, with marvelous stage effects — the background of the Alps for *Manfred*, and the conflagration of the palace for *Sardanapalus*.

continued, "The black veil which is painted over the place of Marino Faliero amongst the Doges, and the Giants' Staircase,[5] where he was crowned, and discrowned, and decapitated, struck forcibly upon my imagination; as did his fiery character, and strange story." Byron delved into Venetian histories for background and details of the character. He prided himself on the accuracy of his account and his faithfulness to his sources, chiefly Marin Sanudo's *Vite dei Doge* (1733), a translation of which he included in an appendix. It was in line with his general devotion to truth, the compulsion that made him quote the words of Scripture in *Cain,* and whole phrases from travelers' accounts of shipwreck in *Don Juan.* But his researches, like those of many amateurs, though diligent, did not take into consideration the evaluation of sources, the necessity of comparing Sanudo's eighteenth century narrative with contemporary sources of the fourteenth century events.

But if the story is not historically true it does not greatly matter, for the characters and many of the circumstances are inevitably creations of a very Byronic sort, and should be judged not as history but as products of the literary imagination. The Doge Faliero easily takes on the coloring of a high-minded though choleric patrician, filled with noble zeal for the liberty of the people but inhibited in the conspiracy by considerations of pride and humanitarian reluctance to shed the blood of the Forty who had been his friends. Byron rejected jealousy as "an exhausted passion in the drama," but has made Faliero's motive for joining the conspirators the offense to his pride in the light sentence given by the high tribunal of the Forty to Michel Steno, a haughty young noble who had written on the walls ribald aspersions on the faithfulness of the Doge's young wife. And he has made the wife, Angiolina, as innocent as Desdemona but insipidly faultless, while the passionate Doge's purely "friendly" interest in her strains credulity. One can imagine Byron's cynical reaction to this passage if it had been written by another:

> A pride not in your beauty, but your conduct;
> A trust in you; a patriarchal love,
> And not a doting homage; friendship, faith, —
> Such estimation in your eyes as these
> Might claim, I hoped for.   (*M. F.,* II, i, 362–366)

---

[5] Byron was unaware that the original staircase had been torn down in the fifteenth century and the new one erected in another place.

We get a more believable, and more Byronic, picture of
Faliero in the words of one of the conspirators:

> he is one
> Who would become a throne, or overthrow one —
> One who has done great deeds, and seen great changes;
> No tyrant, though bred up to tyranny . . .
> noble
> In nature, although haughty; quick, yet wary:
> Yet for all this, so full of certain passions,
> That if once stirred and baffled, as he has been
> Upon the tenderest points, there is no Fury
> In Grecian story like to that which wrings
> His vitals with her burning hands, till he
> Grows capable of all things for revenge;
> And add too, that his mind is liberal,
> He sees and feels the people are oppressed,
> And shares their sufferings.   (*M. F.*, II, ii, 162–176)

Faliero has some qualms from the beginning concerning his
ability to participate in the blood bath necessary to free the state
from tyranny. Yet he assures the conspirators that the feeling of
his own wrongs and his "pity for the people" will be security for
his not betraying them. But the dramatic intensity of the play
builds up to the point where the Doge is forced into a torturing
struggle with his own feelings when the question arises as to
whether any of the patricians among the Forty can be spared.
Byron has made the most of the inner conflict in this novel situation, when a "Prince has plotted for his people's freedom."
Faliero asks, "And is it then decided! Must they die? /. . . . My
own friends by blood and courtesy, / And many deeds and days
— the Senators?" Bertuccio replies, "You passed their sentence,
and it is a just one." Then the Doge:

> Aye, so it seems, and so it is to *you;*
> You are a patriot, a plebeian Gracchus —
> The rebel's oracle, the people's tribune —
> I blame you not — you act in your vocation;
> They smote you, and oppressed you, and despised you;
> So they have *me*: but *you* ne'er spake with them;
> You never broke their bread, nor shared their salt;
> You never had their wine-cup at your lips:
> You grew not up with them, nor laughed, nor wept,
> Nor held a revel in their company. . . .
> (*M. F.*, III, ii, 453–462)

It is not difficult to see here a parallel with the conflict that complicated Byron's revolutionary activities and sympathies though it did not dampen his hatred of tyranny nor his zeal for the cause of freedom. It is the same battle of humane and patrician instincts with the ruthless singleness of purpose often necessary for revolutionary accomplishments that may be seen in Byron's risking the alienation of the Carbonari by taking a wounded commandant of the hated soldiery into his own house in Ravenna, his sending Turkish prisoners home in Greece, and his ambivalence with regard to English Radicalism because of his personal friendship with many of the nobility who would inevitably be on the other side in the event of a revolution about which he talked frequently of joining.[6]

But Faliero made his hard decision and did not betray the conspirators; it was the hesitation and delay, however, coupled with the weakness of one of the underlings who tried to save a patrician which caused the plot to fail and Faliero to be seized.

The last act stretches out the unreality of the angelic Angiolina and the self-justification of the condemned Doge into something of an anticlimax. Faliero accepts his doom as the work of fate, but lectures his judges on their injustice to the people, and prophesies the future degradation of Venice, pronouncing a curse on her, "Thou den of drunkards with the blood of Princes! / Gehenna of the waters! thou Sea-Sodom," before his "Gory head rolls down the Giants' Steps!"

It is fair to say that Byron was not in his element in the "regular" drama which he attempted in *Marino Faliero*. The blank verse encouraged a kind of prosiness which he tried to overcome by a rhetorical elevation of style that leaves the taste of artificiality even when he is writing with sincerity and feeling. The best touches are deviations from the grand style he essayed, and the greatest interest attaches not to the evocation of objective history or tragic character but to occasional flashes of Byronic insight or personal revelation.

The Two Foscari, Byron's second Venetian drama, composed shortly after *Marino Faliero*, and in less than a month, has even fewer virtues. The author was less concerned with faithfulness

[6] The extent to which Byron's own political ideas and feelings entered into the character of Faliero is discussed by E. D. H. Johnson in "A Political Interpretation of Byron's *Marino Faliero*," *Modern Language Quarterly*, III, No. 3 (Sept., 1942).

to historical events and authentic characters, and the lack of subtlety in the depiction of the "humours" of the chief figures is matched only by the artificial rhetoric of their speeches. The erring son of the Doge Francesco Foscari, Jacobo, thrice exiled for plotting against the state and suspected of complicity in murder, has been distorted into a noble youth whose sole motive was the desire to return to the Venice he loved. The stoical devotion to duty of the Doge, who is forced (contrary to the historical record) to sit in judgment with the Council of Ten on his own son, the relentlessness of Loredano in his feud with the Foscari, and the outspoken devotion and defiance of Marina, wife of the young Foscari, make it almost a drama of "humours," for every reaction and every speech of the characters is predictable.

In the background is the assumption of the oppression of the people by the usurped tyranny of the patrician rulers, but the interest centers on the persecution of the Doge and his family by an oligarchy under the sway of the revenge-seeking Loredano. Aside from this, two themes appear, both with a Byronic coloring. One is the love of Venice, embodied in the young Foscari, who would risk any hardship, even torture, to return to her. A corollary of this is the devotion to the state on the part of the Doge, who can gently reprimand his daughter-in-law when she, indignant at her husband's suffering, says she would be glad to escape from such a land: "That is not a Venetian thought, my daughter." The other theme is the freedom of the mind, for which Marina becomes Byron's chief spokesman. Unlike the passive Angiolina of *Marino Faliero*, she is the voice of rebellion that is never silenced by timidity or considerations of policy.

Byron has succeeded even less well than in *Marino Faliero* in producing the sense of strong and basic passions leading to inevitable doom that is at the core of the "regular" or Greek tragedy he was emulating. And aside from purple passages on Venice and the rebellious speeches of Marina, there is little to redeem the play in either dramatic force or language. It only demonstrates again Byron's failure when he ventured far outside his own experience and feelings.

It is precisely because *Sardanapalus* is a more interesting self-revelation that it is a more interesting drama. Here Byron abandoned both the notion that he was writing a "regular" tragedy (except for adherence to the unities) and the conception of historical accuracy. Fortunately there was little historical fact to work with. His imagination was captured by an account in Diodorus Siculus (*The Historical Library of Diodorus the Sicilian*) of Sardanapalus, last king of the Assyrians, immersed "in Sloth and Luxury," who "led a most effeminate life . . . wallowing in Pleasure and wanton Dalliances." With this he combined an account by Ctesias of Cnidos, one of Diodorus's sources, of another king, Asurbanipal, who, though debauched and effeminate, was roused to battle by circumstances and avoided capture by burning himself in his palace. From these slight suggestions Byron created the character of Sardanapalus, voluptuous but not effeminate, refraining from war and conquest for humane reasons, faithful to a mistress who urges him on to heroic action, recognizing the bond to the wife he has abandoned, trusting those who betray him, capable of noble and chivalric battle when forced to fight and of stoic denial and sacrifice at the end. His occasional outbursts of Byronic sarcasm and skepticism lend spice to the character.

Sardanapalus was begun in Ravenna in January, 1821, when Byron was going out nightly to make love to the Countess Guiccioli, dangerously harboring the arms of the Carbonari, and hoping for an opportunity to free himself from his "sloth" and engage in some heroic action. "It is no great matter, supposing that Italy could be liberated, who or what is sacrificed. It is a grand object — the very *poetry* of politics."[7] The opening lines, spoken by Salemenes, the faithful brother-in-law who serves as the conscience of Sardanapalus, give a clue to the problem of the play and to the author's own conflict clearly reflected in it:

> He must be roused. In his effeminate heart
> There is a careless courage which Corruption
> Has not all quenched, and latent energies,
> Repressed by circumstance, but not destroyed —
> Steeped, but not drowned, in deep voluptuousness. . . .
>   he may redeem
> His sloth and shame, by only being that
> Which he should be. . . .   (*Sard.*, I, i, 9–13, 18–20)

But Sardanapalus is only roused to indignation at the demand that he lead his people in new conquests.

> I understand thee — thou wouldst have me go
> Forth as a conqueror. By all the stars

[7] *Letters and Journals*, V, 205. Diary, Feb. 18, 1821.

> Which the Chaldeans read — the restless slaves
> Deserve that I should curse them with their wishes,
> And lead them forth to glory.   (*Sard.*, I, i, 121–125)

Bacchus, he says, is nobler than all the warriors "because he turned a fruit to an enchantment, / Which cheers the sad, revives the old, inspires / The young, makes Weariness forget his toil, / And Fear her danger; opens a new world / When this, the present, palls." When further urged to act as a monarch, that is, to be a warrior king, Sardanapalus replies:

> The ungrateful and ungracious slaves! they murmur
> Because I have not shed their blood, nor led them
> To dry into the desert's dust by myriads,
> Or whiten with their bones the banks of Ganges. . . .
> (*Sard.*, I, ii, 226–229)

Instead he has founded cities — "what could that blood-loving beldame, / My martial grandam, chaste Semiramis, / Do more, except destroy them? . . . enough / For me, if I can make my subjects feel / The weight of human misery less, and glide / Ungroaning to the tomb." When Salemenes says, "Thy Sires have been revered as Gods — ," he replies (borrowing from Hamlet):

> Talk not of such to me! the worms are Gods;
> At least they banqueted upon your Gods. . . .
> Those Gods were merely men; look to their issue —
> I feel a thousand mortal things about me,
> But nothing godlike, — unless it may be
> The thing which you condemn, a disposition
> To love and to be merciful, to pardon
> The follies of my species, and (that's human)
> To be indulgent to my own.
> (*Sard.*, I, ii, 269–270, 272–278)

Myrrha, the Ionian slave girl, Sardanapalus's noble-hearted mistress, was modeled on an idealized Teresa Guiccioli, and was brought in because Teresa had urged Byron to put more love into the drama. Even more than Salemenes she becomes the conscience of the king, using all her charms and persuasion to put steel into his soft nature.

The leaders of the revolt against his throne, about whom Sardanapalus had been warned, are Arbaces, a soldier, and Beleses, a priest. When Salemenes accuses them before the king, "factious priest, and faithless soldier! thou / Unit'st in thy own person the

worst vices / Of the most dangerous orders of mankind,"
Sardanapalus will not have them seized. He gives them back their
swords and their freedom, but not without flaunting his agnos-
ticism before the priest.

Sardanapalus was right in mistrusting the priest more than the
soldier, for the latter is touched by his clemency and repents,
whereas the former pursues his relentless purpose to overthrow
the soft king. But the monarch is "soft, not fearful," and when
the time comes for him to defend his palace and the people who
are loyal to him, he is careless of danger and does not spare himself. He is all steel in action, and in battle he drinks water, not
wine. Myrrha urges the soldiers on like a raging lioness, "with
floating hair and flashing eyes." This sudden transformation of
the pleasure-softened, effeminate king into a man of action and
self-effacing courage gives an unreality to the character which
has been remarked by many critics. But as a projection of idealized Byronic qualities Sardanapalus becomes more understandable
and more interesting.

It is obvious that in *Sardanapalus* Byron had abandoned the
ambition to write an objective historical tragedy, which as serious
poetry he conceived to be the best substitute for the Popean
satire he had earlier aspired to compose. He had fallen back into
the familiar vein of the poetry which is "the lava of the imagination." It is as such that the poem must be judged. We see the
subtle fluctuations but basic honesty of the poet's mobile temperament in the confession, more revealing than anything in Byron's
letters, of his feeling for his wife in the interview with Zarina:
"My gentle, wronged Zarina! / I am the very slave of Circumstance / And Impulse. . . ." And again in the end, when Sardanapalus no longer defends his self-indulgence but bows to fate
and is self-accusing, we see variations of recognizable Byronic
moods, though here somewhat spoiled by melodrama.

One might say that its failure as an historical tragedy in the
grand style is the measure of its success as a self-revelatory romantic poem. When Byron wrote of himself he wrote well.
There is a fiery flow in the blank verse that often lifts it to poetry,
and there is less of the artificial rhetoric that mars the Venetian
dramas.

Little need be said about *Werner* as a dramatic production or
as poetry, though it was posthumously the most popular of his

poetic dramas and the one most often on the stage. Byron confessed in the preface that it was a dramatization of a story he had read as a boy, *The German's Tale*. It was a melodrama by Harriet Lee, published in the fourth of a series of volumes called *The Canterbury Tales*. Although he claimed no originality ("I have adopted the characters, plan, and even the language of many parts of this story"), he departed from the model at many points, and the Byronic warping of the characters is obvious. The action takes place against the grim background of fate and circumstance in the semi-Gothic setting of castles in Silesia and Prague at the end of the Thirty Years' War. Werner's son Ulric becomes in Byron's hands a sort of "poetical Zeluco," corrupted into crime in an effort to protect the name and inheritance of his father, whose character in turn had been bruised and misshapen by the hardships he had endured when *his* father disinherited him for marrying a poor Italian girl. The brooding melancholy and paranoiac suspicion of Werner, the steely and fated pride of Ulric, the Gothic and unrealistic nature of the other characters add up to little more than the crudest melodrama unrelieved by occasional wit or wisdom such as leaven the other dramas. One critic has suggested that Byron wrote the play with his tongue in his cheek to achieve the stage success that had been denied to his other dramas.[8] But the popularity of *Werner* on the Victorian stage might better be ascribed to the bathetic taste of the age.

[8] See T. H. Vail Motter, "Byron's *Werner* Re-estimated: A Neglected Chapter in Nineteenth Century Stage History," in *Essays in Dramatic Literature*: The Parrott Presentation Volume, ed. Hardin Craig, Princeton, 1935.

9

Italian Poems

BYRON'S ITALIAN POEMS include *The Lament of Tasso, Ode on Venice, The Prophecy of Dante, The Morgante Maggiore,* and *Francesca of Rimini,* the last two rather close translations, one of the first canto of Pulci's poem and the other of the famous episode from the fifth canto of Dante's *Inferno. Beppo* should also logically be included in this group, but since its style and manner are far different from that of the other Italian poems and since it marked the beginning of Byron's free and original use of the ottava rima for satiric narrative and commentary, it will be considered separately. These poems on Italian themes and persons were all written in the first years of his residence in Italy, most of them before he had left Venice permanently to live in Ravenna. His enthusiasm for Italian literature, history, and life was still glowing. It was a time when he had practically cut his ties with England and had resigned himself to living the life of an exile in his adopted country. He loved the language, "that soft bastard Latin, / Which melts like kisses from a female mouth," as he said in *Beppo,* and he at one time toyed with the idea of writing his major work in that tongue, though he was sobered in time by the reflection that, however fluently he might speak it (with the Venetian dialect he had learned from his mistresses), it would take years of laborious effort to master it to the point where he could make it his literary vehicle. By the time he wrote the fourth canto of *Childe Harold* in the summer of 1817 he had resigned himself to the thought that even as an exile, "I twine / My hopes of being remembered in my line / With my land's language."

The Lament of Tasso was written while Byron still retained vivid impressions of "the inkstand and chair, the tomb and the house" of the poet at Ferrara and particularly of the cell in the hospital of St. Anna where Tasso was incarcerated for supposed insanity. The poem was an outpouring of strong feeling for the "eagle-spirit of a Child of Song" with whom he shared a sense of identification. He saw Tasso as one who, like himself, had suffered "Long years of outrage — calumny — and wrong," but who would not stoop to despair:

> For I have battled with mine agony,
> And made me wings wherewith to overfly
> The narrow circus of my dungeon wall.
>
> (*Tasso*, 21–23)

Byron chose to view Tasso's plight and his long-suffering fortitude as another example of the "chainless mind."

> For I have anguish yet to bear — and how?
> I know not that — but in the innate force
> Of my own spirit shall be found resource.
>
> (*Tasso*, 44–46)

Without any authority in the biographical record, he has ascribed Tasso's suffering and persecution to his love for Lèonora d'Este, "Sister of my Sovereign." This apparently had nothing to do with his confinement, but Byron has based Tasso's burning indignation and despairing protests on the assumption that it was so. The most glowing passages are built on the parallel he sees in his own life:

> It is no marvel — from my very birth
> My soul was drunk with Love, — which did pervade
> And mingle with whate'er I saw on earth. . . .
>
> (*Tasso*, 149–151)

Byron has imagined feelingly Tasso's recognition of his own wanderings of mind and hallucinations.

But Tasso was obsessed with time's revenge, a favorite Byronic theme soon to be incorporated in the fourth canto of *Childe Harold*. Though he is no longer "quick in feeling," he is sustained by the thought that his poetic fame will last longer than the Duke or his sister or Ferrara itself. And his fate and that of Leonora will be "entwined for ever."

Byron has endowed Tasso with the romantic ego and romantic sensibilities. It is on this basis that the poem must be judged. The pentameter couplet, varied with unrhymed lines or alternate rhyme, handled with an almost Keatsian freedom from end-stopped lines, gives the impression of blank verse. The fervor of the feeling casts an incandescent glow over lines that, detached from the context, may seem undistinguished. Tasso's pang has found a voice, though it may not be exactly his own.

The theme of the *Ode on Venice* is one that Byron had already handled better in the fourth canto of *Childe Harold*: the decay and degradation of Venice and particularly her thralldom to Austria,

> Thirteen hundred years
> Of wealth and glory turned to dust and tears....
>
> (*Ode*, 15–16)

One passage stands out almost as vividly as the famous description of Greece in *The Giaour* beginning "He who hath bent him o'er the dead." Hope for Venice is only a "false delay,"

> The sick man's lightning half an hour ere Death ...
> And then he talks of Life, and how again
> He feels his spirit soaring — albeit weak,
> And of the fresher air, which he would seek;
> And as he whispers knows not that he gasps,
> That his thin finger feels not what it clasps,
> And so the film comes o'er him. ...
>
> (*Ode*, 37, 45–50)

The pageant of history offers little but despair to mankind. "There is no hope for nations! ... For 't is our nature strikes us down." When we look back we see only "A blindfold bondage" and men who pour their "blood for kings as water." Yet "a few spirits" could see more clearly than the dumb crowd who were able only to "trample on each other to obtain / The cup which brings oblivion of a chain / Heavy and sore, — in which long yoked they ploughed / The sand," and it is they who may overthrow tyranny and let "Freedom's Fountains" flow again. As for the populace, "their necks were too much bowed, / And their dead palates chewed the cud of pain." But these "few spirits," "despite of deeds / Which they abhor, confound not with the cause / Those momentary starts from Nature's laws." This is one of the clearest statements in poetry of Byron's revolutionary philosophy: a few choice spirits (presumably aristocrats, but in any event above the necessitous blind grabbing of the dumb masses) will lead the revolt and will not be too much dismayed by "deeds which they abhor," such as the "Reign of Terror" in the French Revolution, which they "confound not with the cause" but recognize as the understandable excesses of a people long oppressed.

It is an easy step, though one that takes Byron away from Venice, to the eloquent praise of America which ends the poem. Here was a people who had won their freedom "in full and free defiance." Then follows a kind of prophetic statement of Byron's own dedication to the cause and his burning desire to free himself from his lethargy and engage in some heroic action. It was the "red-hot earnest" sentiment that was to fill his Ravenna journal when a revolution in the Romagna seemed imminent, and that was to carry him to Greece on his last journey.

The *Ode on Venice*, like *The Lament of Tasso*, was written in the tetrameter couplets and alternate rhymes that Byron found most serviceable for rhetorical grandeur, but in *The Prophecy of Dante* he boldly tried a metrical experiment, Dante's own terza rima, which had rarely been used in English poetry. Byron's admiration for the Italian poet was not slight. Though he had a liking for other Italian writers, he recognized Dante's pre-eminence. He wrote in his diary on January 29, 1821: "Why, they talk Dante — write Dante — and think and dream Dante at this moment . . . to an excess, which would be ridiculous, but that he deserves it." The old and bitter truths and the uncompromising acerbity as well as the sharp poetic eloquence of the *Inferno* appealed to him more than did the sentimental sonnets of Petrarch. But in his poem he has made Dante the spokesman for his own revolutionary ideas.

The Countess Guiccioli had suggested that he write a poem on Dante, as he acknowledged in a dedicatory sonnet, but once he had embarked on it his interest centered less on Dante the poet than on Dante the exile and the political prophet. In the preface he says: "The reader is requested to suppose that Dante addresses him in the interval between the conclusion of the *Divina Commedia* and his death, and shortly before the latter event, fore-

telling the fortunes of Italy in general in the ensuing centuries."
Although he apologized for his attempt to use the terza rima
("Harsh Runic copy of the South's sublime," as he said in the
Dedication), he sometimes achieved a remarkable imitation of the
tone and spirit of his model, as in the first lines, wherein he
imagines Dante's reaction to the completion of his great work:

> Once more in Man's frail world! which I had left
>   So long that 'twas forgotten; and I feel
>   The weight of clay again, — too soon bereft
> Of the Immortal Vision which could heal
>   My earthly sorrows, and to God's own skies
>   Lift me from that deep Gulf without repeal,
> Where late my ears rung with the damned cries
>   Of Souls in hopeless bale. . . .   (*Dante*, I, 1–8)

No longer guided by Beatrice, who had been his companion in
the Vision, cut off from his native soil where she is buried, he
must find his way in the "savage wood" of this world and adjust
himself to his unhappy situation. He starts with the integrity of
his own fame: "The World hath left me, what it found me, pure
/ And if I have not gathered yet its praise, / I sought it not
by any baser lure." He would not "dabble in the pettiness of
fame" by catering to "men's fickle breath." He would have had
his Florence, his native city, "great and free," but the wrong she
has done him grates on his spirit.

> No, — she denied me what was mine — my roof,
> And shall not have what is not hers — my tomb.
> (*Dante*, I, 83–84)

His first thought of revenge is tempered by the reflection that the
dust of Beatrice rests there, but his renunciation only shifts the
burden to God — "to thy hands I yield / My many wrongs, and
thine Almighty rod / Will fall on those who smote me." But it
is only a recognition that he cannot cope with the problem and
he falls again into despair.

> The sense of earth and earthly things come back,
>   Corrosive passions, feelings dull and low,
> The heart's quick throb upon the mental wrack,
>   Long day, and dreary night. . . .
>   to die
> Is nothing; but to wither thus — to tame

> My mind down from its own infinity —
>   To live in narrow ways with little men,
>   A common sight to every common eye,
>   A wanderer, while even wolves can find a den. . . .
>   (*Dante*, I, 131–134, 158–163)

But in the second canto Dante is shown in quite a different frame of mind. He has become the champion of Italian nationalism, and the seer-prophet of the future of that country with which he now identifies himself:

> my bones shall be within thy breast,
>   My Soul within thy language.   (*Dante*, II, 20–21)

His prophecy encompasses the past as well as the future and ends with the Italy that Byron knew, oppressed and divided. The vultures are more humane than the nations that will come to prey on Italy: "these but gorge the flesh, and lap the gore / Of the departed, and then go their way; / But those, the human savages, explore / All paths of torture, and insatiate yet, / With Ugolino hunger prowl for more." Before the canto ends, Dante is so absorbed in the plight of the Italians in the nineteenth century that he forgets his role as prophet and exhorts them as contemporaries to put aside their doubt and discord, which alone prevents them from throwing off the oppressors, and to unite.

In the third canto Dante turns his prophetic eyes from the "mass of never-dying ill," which the future centuries present to his vision, to some of the stars that will shine through the night of gloom and give his country honor and the world delight, artists and men of mind, "The gay, the learned, the generous, and the brave, / Native to thee as Summer to thy skies." And especially, "Poets shall follow in the path I show, / And make it broader." Many will sing of Love and some of Liberty. But few will soar on eagle's wing, and many will bow in sycophancy "to some small prince."

Of the free spirits who come into his vision he singles out three. Petrarch, the prince of sonneteers, "shall rank among my peers, / And Love shall be his torment; but his grief / Shall make an immortality of tears, / And Italy shall hail him as the Chief / Of Poet-lovers, and his higher song / Of Freedom wreathe him with as green a leaf." But to Dante (and to Byron) there would be two poets greater still. One was to be Ariosto, whose lyre would "fill the earth with feats of Chivalry: / His Fancy like a rainbow." The other, Tasso, "of a tenderer, sadder mood, / Shall pour his soul out o'er Jerusalem" (*Gerusalemme Liberata*).

In the fourth and last canto Dante reflects on the function and fate of the poet and artist.

> For what is Poesy but to create
> From overfeeling Good or Ill; and aim
> At an external life beyond our fate,
> And be the new Prometheus of new men,
> Bestowing fire from Heaven, and then, too late,
> Finding the pleasure given repaid with pain. . . .
>
> (*Dante*, IV, 11–16)

With his own example before him he exclaims: "Alas! / Despair and Genius are too oft connected," and in the ages that pass before his prophetic eye he sees Michel Angelo, who would bring new wonders to the world — the dome of St. Peter's, the statue of Moses — but who was not appreciated by his patrons. And then he turns to the artists who prostitute their gifts to tyrants and to the powerful who "Tread on the universal necks that bow." And this leads him back to his own plight and to the same thoughts of revenge and despair.

Byron's reading in the Italian originals of Frere's *Whistlecraft*, which had given him the happy inspiration for using the ottava rima in the mock-heroic style in *Beppo* and the early cantos of *Don Juan*, was responsible for his attempt to translate Luigi Pulci's *Il Morgante Maggiore*. Though he was satisfied with rendering only the first of twenty-eight cantos with as much literal faithfulness as the use of the original verse form would allow, the whole poem appealed to him because of its light and irreverent handling of sacred subjects. Byron wrote to Murray: "I think my translation of Pulci will make you stare: it must be put by the original, stanza for stanza, and verse for verse; and you will see what was permitted in a Catholic country and a bigotted age to a Churchman, on the score of religion: — and so tell those buffoons who accuse me of attacking the liturgy."[1] This was at a time when Byron was futilely trying to demonstrate to the English that his own free handling of such subjects in *Don Juan* had its counterpart in some of the best literature of the past. E. H. Coleridge has well summarized the characteristics of Pulci which attracted

[1] *Letters and Journals*, IV, 402. Letter of Feb. 7, 1820.

Byron: ". . . the co-presence of faith, a certain *simplicity* of faith, with an audacious and even outrageous handling of the objects of faith, combined with a facile and wanton alternation of romantic passion with a cynical mockery of whatsoever things are sober and venerable."[2]

As it happens, however, there is less evidence of this in the first canto, which Byron translated, than in the rest of Pulci. The only passage that might greatly shock a pious reader is the account in stanzas 66 and 67 of the gormandizing of the monks, which he has rendered *con amore*:

> As though they wished to burst at once, they ate;
> And gorged so that, as if the bones had been
> In water, sorely grieved the dog and cat,
> Perceiving that they were all picked too clean.
>
> (*M. M.*, I, 67)

Byron already had the practice of writing several cantos of *Don Juan* to give him facility and colloquial ease in the use of the ottava rima. In the *Morgante* preface he said he was "induced to make the experiment partly by his love for, and partial intercourse with, the Italian language, of which it is so easy to acquire a slight knowledge, and with which it is nearly impossible for a foreigner to become accurately conversant. The Italian language is like a capricious beauty, who accords her smiles to all, her favours to few, and sometimes least to those who have courted her longest." Despite the modesty of this pronouncement, he took great pride in his translation. He boasted again and again of his accomplishment. Several months after it was completed he wrote: ". . . the *Pulci* I am proud of: it is superb; you have no such translation. It is the best thing I ever did in my life."[3] He wanted Murray to publish the original Italian on the facing page so that the faithfulness of the translation could be judged. But a candid appraisal of the translation hardly justifies Byron's pride in it either as literal translation or as a poetic achievement. The effort to be literal and to keep the meter and rhyme often makes for awkwardness either through inversion or choice of words that will approximate the Italian in sense rather than in poetic smoothness. But Byron was anxious to demonstrate that the

[2] *Poetry*, IV, 280.
[3] *Letters and Journals*, V, 83. Letter of Sept. 28, 1820, to Murray.

colloquial undress of his translation was not a liberty but had its counterpart in the original. It was as a tour de force rather than as a literary production that he was proud of it.

Byron's translation of the episode of Paolo and Francesca from the *Inferno* of Dante which he titled "Francesca of Rimini" was a further attempt to show what he could do with the terza rima. The existing variants indicate that he had great difficulty, much more than with the *Morgante*, in fitting the literal sense into the rhyme and meter of the original. It was different from expressing his own thoughts in the terza rima as he had done in *The Prophecy of Dante*. When he sent it to Murray in March, 1820, he confessed, "I have done it into *cramp* English, line for line, and rhyme for rhyme, to try the possibility." Except for a few felicitous lines it is indeed in "cramp English," with awkward inversions ("But Caina waits for him our life who ended"), long drawn out equivalents for Dante's starkly simple phrases ("non vi leggemmo avante" becomes "no further leaf did we uncover"), and weak rhymes ("seated nigh" — "unsuspiciously").

But it was no doubt the episode in the *Inferno* itself that intrigued Byron and made him anxious to put it into English. Living dangerously in the Palazzo of Count Guiccioli in Ravenna while engaged in a passionate love affair with the Countess, he entered feelingly into the parallel situation described by Dante. But greater still was his admiration for Dante's compassionate account of the inevitable tragedy of hapless passion, "How many sweet thoughts, what strong ecstasies, / Led these their evil fortune to fulfill!"

It is understandable that Byron was eager for his version of this episode to be published even in "cramp English," but it is also understandable that Murray's advisers should have wisely cautioned against putting it in competition with Cary's excellent blank verse translation then in eager demand. The "Francesca of Rimini" was not published until 1830, when Moore included it in his *Letters and Journals of Lord Byron*.

Byron's Italian poems as a whole (with the exception of *Beppo*, hereafter to be considered) were only partially successful. Like his historical dramas they were best when they were subjective rather than objective. When they wrested from their subjects something of immediate import to the author like the "innate force / Of my own spirit" and the Byronic concept of "Time's revenge" superimposed on the paranoia of Tasso, or the need for Italian unity against the oppressors which rouses the greatest eloquence in *The Prophecy of Dante*, the Italian poems achieved their maximum force. But as in the dramas the attempt to present objectively a heroic theme encouraged a stilted rhetorical style which was not natural to Byron and in which he felt somewhat ill at ease.

10

Shorter Romantic Poems

BY FAR THE GREATER NUMBER of Byron's shorter romantic poems are direct expressions of his feelings for individuals. They might be described as troubled love poems, voicing the agony of love itself or the melancholy of loss or betrayal. And that description might apply as well to a number of the lyrics among the *Hebrew Melodies,* the one group of shorter poems not written to relieve personal feelings. The themes and attitudes are nothing new but only varying adaptations of moods and feelings already observed in the early poems and in *Childe Harold.* The idealization of innocence seen in the stanzas to Ianthe prefixed to the seventh edition of the first *Childe Harold* finds its counterpart in "Maid of Athens," and the theme of "the unpossessed is sweetest" is expressed most clearly in some of the "Thyrza" poems. It reaches its logical extreme in "And Thou Art Dead, As Young and Fair":

> The love where Death has set his seal,
> Nor age can chill, nor rival steal,
>   Nor falsehood disavow:
> And, what were worse, thou canst not see
> Or wrong, or change, or fault in me.

But the majority of these poems illustrate and emphasize the self-portraiture in the account of Rousseau in the third canto of *Childe Harold*: "with ethereal flame / Kindled he was, and blasted." They range from a direct statement of agonized loss and despair as in the Thyrza poems to the more detached melancholy of the *Hebrew Melodies.* Typical of the first are the cries of pain on the marriage of Mary Chaworth and later on seeing her with her child, "The babe which ought to have been mine."

117

("Epistle to a Friend") The earliest of these, "Hills of Annesley! bleak and barren," recording the desolation of an adolescent love, has the greatest poetic and personal impact. The others seem whining and artificial in comparison.[1]

The so-called Thyrza poems, now known to have been addressed to John Edleston, a choir boy at Cambridge to whom Byron became passionately attached and whose death in 1811 was perhaps the greatest emotional shock of his life, have never been considered as a whole nor given their proper evaluation as poetry.[2] His attachment to Edleston, probably the deepest, sincerest, and most unqualified of any in his life, inspired some of his most poignant lines among the shorter romantic poems. One of his finest lyrics may well have sprung from his early association with Edleston, for he was first attracted by the chorister's voice:[3]

> There be none of Beauty's daughters
>   With a magic like thee;
> And like music on the waters
>   Is thy sweet voice to me:
> When, as if its sound were causing
> The charmèd Ocean's pausing,
> The waves lie still and gleaming,
> And the lulled winds seem dreaming:
>
> And the midnight Moon is weaving
>   Her bright chain o'er the deep;
> Whose breast is gently heaving,
>   As an infant's asleep:
> So the spirit bows before thee,
> To listen and adore thee;
> With a full but soft emotion,
> Like the swell of Summer's ocean.

[1] In addition to the "Hills of Annesley!" the poems to Mary Chaworth include "Well! Thou Art Happy" and "To a Lady on Being Asked My Reason for Quitting England in the Spring," both written in 1808 after a visit to her at Annesley after her marriage. In 1811 his "Epistle to a Friend" (Rev. Francis Hodgson) refers to the same episode. "The Dream," written at Geneva in 1816, describes his adolescent love affair with Mary Chaworth in detail.

[2] For evidence of the identity of Thyrza and of the biographical background of the Edleston attachment, see Marchand, *Byron* (indexed under Edleston).

[3] Reasons for ascribing the inspiration of the poem to Edleston are given in Marchand, *Byron*, I, 313n.

There is another reference to the sweetness of Edleston's voice in the "Stanzas to Jessy": "I would not hear a Seraph Choir, / Unless that voice could join the rest." The poem "To E. — ," the second piece in *Fugitive Pieces*, though dated "November, 1802," perhaps for camouflage, is probably also addressed to Edleston, "though unequal is *thy* fate, / Since title deck'd my higher birth." Another early poem, "The Cornelian," acknowledging a gift from Edleston ("He offer'd it with downcast look, / As *fearful* that I might refuse it"), makes similar mention of their unequal station.[4]

But the "lava of the imagination" flowed most searingly after he learned that Edleston had died in May, 1811. Byron was abroad and did not hear of it until October. He wrote to Hodgson, "I heard of a death the other day that shocked me more than any of the preceding [his mother and two close friends had died within a few weeks of each other], of one whom I loved more than I ever loved a living thing, and one who, I believe, loved me to the last. . . ."[5] The next day he poured out his feelings in the first Thyrza poem:

> Ours too the glance none saw beside;
>   The smile none else might understand;
>   The whispered thought of hearts allied,
>   The pressure of the thrilling hand. . . .

There is evidence here and throughout the Thyrza poems that the relationship was what Byron called it years later in his diary of 1821, "a violent, though *pure*, love and passion" and that it was a romance that held him in "the most romantic period of my life." It was precisely because Byron could look back on the

---

[4] G. Wilson Knight (*Lord Byron's Marriage*, p. 30) suggests, probably rightly, that two other early poems refer to Edleston. "Pignus Amoris" recalls "a Friend I know, / Who loved me for myself alone," and mentions a "simple toy" (the Cornelian?) which that friend had given him. More significantly it voices a view that Byron ever held of his relations with Edleston:

> For Both were open, Both were young.

> And Youth is sure the only time,
>   When Pleasure blends no base alloy;
>   When Life is blest without a crime,
>   And Innocence resides with Joy.

"The Adieu" refers again to the gift and proclaims "Our souls were equal, and our lot / In that dear moment quite forgot."

[5] Marchand, *Byron*, I, 295n.

experience as an idealized vision of innocence and purity combined with a guileless and unselfish attachment on both sides that
the sense of loss grew into immitigable grief, and in the end the
grief is for the loss of his own innocence and is compounded with
his whole melancholy view of life as inadequate to the ideal conceptions of human longing. This first poem "To Thyrza" records
the memory of pleasures past:

> The kiss, so guiltless and refined,
>   That Love each warmer wish forbore;
> Those eyes proclaimed so pure a mind,
>   Ev'n passion blushed to plead for more.

But there followed a surge of anguish which found utterance first
in some new stanzas[6] for *Childe Harold:*

> There, Thou! — whose Love and Life, together fled,
> Have left me here to love and live in vain. . . .
>
> (II, 9)

> Oh! ever loving, lovely, and beloved!
> How selfish Sorrow ponders on the past,
> And clings to thoughts now better far removed!
> But Time shall tear thy shadow from me last.
>
> (II, 96)

The passage of time only increased his feeling of desolation.
After visiting Cambridge he wrote "Away, Away, Ye Notes of
Woe!" He struggled to escape the obsession with his loss ("One
Struggle More, and I Am Free"), "One last long sigh to Love
and thee, / Then back to busy life again." But he comes back to
the same conclusion:

> Time tempers Love, but not removes,
>   More hallowed when its Hope is fled:
> Oh! what are thousand living loves
>   To that which cannot quit the dead?

Then he thought of escape through "Oblivion," the "dreamless
sleep that lulls the dead" ("Euthanasia"). Finally, the best that
he could do was to take consolation in the thought that death has
set his seal on a perfection that cannot fade ("And Thou Art
Dead, As Young and Fair"):

---

[6] Stanzas 9, 95–98 in the second canto.

I know not if I could have borne
　To see thy beauties fade . . .
Thy day without a cloud hath passed,
And thou wert lovely to the last;
　Extinguished, not decayed;
As stars that shoot along the sky
Shine brightest as they fall from high.

The memory of Edleston haunted Byron for years, though the
need for poetic outpouring of his grief subsided after a few
months. The last two Thyrza poems were written in March,
1812. The first is a kind of regret and apology for the natural
subsidence of his grief that permits him to mingle with men once
more and not pass the goblet "unquaff'd." It is at bottom the
romantic complaint that the frailty of man will not permit a
constancy of grief. The last Thyrza poem ("On a Cornelian
Heart Which Was Broken") declares that he who wears it feels
it to be "A fitter emblem of *his own*." The Thyrza poems would
perhaps have been better had the author written when he had
achieved more detachment, or if he had perfected them over a
period of years as Tennyson did the lyrics of *In Memoriam*. And
yet the "unpremeditated art" of a genuine feeling of loss does
come through, if not with the sheer metrical beauty of Tennyson's first poetic expression of his agony in "Break, break, break,"
at least with a conviction of sincerity more moving at its best
than much of the agonized egoism of Byron's other romantic love
poems.

Equally sincere is the expression of "the ethereal flame" with
which he was "kindled" and "blasted" in his love for his half-
sister Augusta. The poems to Augusta display more technical
skill, more sure feeling for the harmonious blending of sound
and sense, and less purely conventional phrasing than do the
Thyrza poems. The first one, sent in a letter to Moore on May 4,
1814, was meant as "Stanzas for Music." Byron said that it had cost
him "something more than trouble," and the manuscript indicates
a good deal of revision. The flowing anapests give a ringing
earnestness to the lines and make them seem "passion's essence."

I speak not, I trace not, I breathe not thy name,
There is grief in the sound, there is guilt in the fame:
But the tear which now burns on my cheek may impart
The deep thoughts that dwell in that silence of heart.

> Too brief for our passion, too long for our peace,
> Were those hours — can their joy or their bitterness cease?
> We repent, we abjure, we will break from our chain, —
> We will part, we will fly to — unite it again![7]

Byron's next poem addressed to Augusta was his tribute to her constancy and consolation during the separation proceedings. It was probably the last poem he wrote before leaving England forever in April, 1816. There is less of agonized passion and more of gentle tenderness in the tone:

> When Fortune changed — and Love fled far,
> And Hatred's shafts flew thick and fast,
> Thou wert the solitary star
> Which rose and set not to the last.

This same tender mood pervades the stanzas in the third canto of *Childe Harold* (with an added liberated defiance of convention in the statement):

> And there was one soft breast, as hath been said,
> Which unto his was bound by stronger ties
> Than the church links withal; and — though unwed,
> *That* love was pure. . . .   (III, 55)

During the summer of 1816, while he was battling with the melancholy and remorse that brought into being "Darkness," "The Dream," the third canto of *Childe Harold*, and *Manfred*, Byron wrote two more poems to his sister, both embodying the ideal of love and constancy which he saw in her. The galloping anapests and the drumming of the alternate rhyme in the octets of the "Stanzas to Augusta" beginning "Though the day of my Destiny's over" tend to belie the sentiment to a degree. The temptation to overstatement in this form was so great that, however genuine the feelings that prompted it may have been, it seemed to verge on burlesque and satire:

---

[7] A facsimile of the original manuscript is given in the appendix to Lord Lovelace's privately printed *Astarte* (1905). Byron crossed out many words, phrases, and lines and rewrote them. The principal variants are given in E. H. Coleridge's edition (*Poetry*, III, 413–414). In the revised edition of *Astarte*, edited by Mary Countess of Lovelace (1921), are printed some opening lines intended for *Lara*, written about the same time as the "I speak not" verses and expressing similar feelings, though even more convulsive.

> Though the rock of my last Hope is shivered,
>   And its fragments are sunk in the wave,
> Though I feel that my soul is delivered
>   To Pain — it shall not be its slave.

And certainly in the fourth stanza he ran into irony:

> Though human, thou didst not deceive me,
>   Though woman, thou didst not forsake,
> Though loved, thou forborest to grieve me . . .
> Though trusted, thou didst not disclaim me . . .
> Though watchful, 'twas not to defame me. . . .

It is not surprising that John Cam Hobhouse, who never quite understood or sympathized with Byron's melancholy moods, was moved to parody this poem. His version has much of the realistic-satiric spirit of Byron in it — the facetious Byron that Hobhouse knew so well:

> Dear *Byron* this humbug give over;
>   Never talk of decay or decline.
> No mortal alive can discover
>   The cause of so causeless a whine. . . .
>
> Though a poet, you should not abuse us;
>   Though a wit, have a truce with your jokes;
> Though you govern us all, yet excuse us
>   If we think there's enough of this hoax.
> Though trusted, no creditors touch thee;
>   Though parted, 'tis but from thy wife;
> Though wakeful, with Molly to much thee
>   'Tis not such a damnable life.[8]

The "Epistle to Augusta" echoes many of the moods of the third canto of *Childe Harold* with a somewhat less feverish resignation and despair sustained by the thought of that sister in whose heart "I know myself secure, as thou in mine." There is the familiar lament of the "lonely soul," the feeling that he has lived through all of life at an early age and has nothing but memories and regrets. But there is a ring of greater calmness, and sincerity, than in the hectic moanings of the Childe.

Byron wrote nothing that could properly be called a love poem to Annabella Milbanke, either before or after her marriage to him, unless the "Love and Gold" lines (posthumously pub-

---

[8] *Letters and Journals,* IV, 73–74n.

lished — the title was furnished by E. H. Coleridge) were really addressed to her. Those lines are not very flattering; they suggest that the many suitors around her were after her fortune and they end with the doubtful compliment: "But thou deserv'st a better heart, / Than they or I can give for thine." The mood of the poems that grew out of the separation was compounded of bitterness, frustration, and self-pity. There is little reason to doubt that they rose from genuine feeling. It is likely that Byron was speaking the literal truth when he wrote in his Memoirs (as Moore recalled it) that the tears fell over the verses of "Fare Thee Well" as he wrote them. This does not make it a better poem, but it probably gives a truer account of his feelings at the time than anything he wrote in letters or uttered in conversations that were recorded. The swinging rhythm may have made it seem insincere to the callous world, though Madame de Staël is said to have remarked on reading it that "if her husband had bade her such a farewell she could not have avoided running into his arms, and being reconciled immediately — 'Je n'aurois pu m'y tenir un instant.' "[9] The interest for us lies rather in the completeness of the self-revelation of his volatile feelings, even to the sentimentality which he usually turned off before it overflowed.

Byron's "Lines on Hearing That Lady Byron Was Ill," written in a maddened mood after he had heard of his wife's cold rebuff of an offer of reconciliation made through Madame de Staël, is a brutally savage attack on her "implacability." It is effective as a statement of his sense of frustration, but it seldom ascends to poetic evocation except in the line "The moral Clytemnestra of thy lord," which Byron himself repeated again and again in letters.[10]

Some of Byron's most memorable lyrics, "Most musical, most melancholy," were the product of his Eastern travels. "If I am a poet," he told Trelawny, ". . . the air of Greece has made me one." One thinks first of that glorification of sweet innocence in the rippling rhythms of the "Maid of Athens":

[9] *Poetry*, III, 534.

[10] "A Sketch," usually included among the "Poems of the Separation," is so different in tone and manner from the others that it is better considered under another heading. I have chosen to discuss it with the "*Jeux d'Esprit*" (Chapter 11), though it might equally be thought of as a Popean satire.

> By those tresses unconfined,
> Wooed by each Ægean wind;
> By those lids whose jetty fringe
> Kiss thy soft cheeks' blooming tinge;
> By those wild eyes like the roe,
> Ζωή μου, σᾶς ἀγαπῶ.

The judgment of this poem has been so closely associated with the mingled emotions of romantic Byronism, Philhellenism, and sentimental love that even Byron scholars have been prone to accept it with the uncritical faith accorded to nursery rhymes. A critical eye, however, detects its weaknesses as poetry. Aside from the Greek refrain, which has musical and exotic connotations for the English reader, it has all the faults of singsong rhythm, well-worn poetic diction, and forced imagery.

Also to be considered under the head of lyrics inspired by the Greek experience are the many purple passages incorporated in longer poems but really embodying independent moods, picturesque and melancholy. Some of these have already been discussed in connection with the Oriental tales.

The justly famous "Isles of Greece" was fitted with considerable strain into the third canto of *Don Juan*. It should be considered on its own merit as one of the finest lyrics springing from Byron's Greek experience. The mood and theme are both closely akin to those of the second canto of *Childe Harold:* the melancholy of a people living in slavery in the shadow and with the mementos of their glorious past, and the admonition that the Greeks themselves must strike the blow for freedom — "Trust not for freedom to the Franks —" The theme is the same but there is a finer touch, a smoother blending of harmony with sense. With all its histrionic qualities it has lines which bear associations that are fixed in the memory by their music, not subtle but strong enough to overcome critical reservations. Again Byron is at his best in this kind of magnetic charming of the commonplace by sheer personality into something rich and strange.

> The Isles of Greece, the Isles of Greece!
>   Where burning Sappho loved and sung,
> Where grew the arts of War and Peace,
>   Where Delos rose, and Phoebus sprung!
> Eternal summer gilds them yet,
> But all, except their Sun, is set. . . .

Place me on Sunium's marbled steep,
   Where nothing, save the waves and I,
May hear our mutual murmurs sweep;
   There, swan-like, let me sing and die:
A land of slaves shall ne'er be mine —
   Dash down yon cup of Samian wine!

Of other lyrics that grew out of his Eastern travels, those inspired by his brief love for Mrs. Constance Spencer Smith whom he had met at Malta, deserve passing mention. The "Stanzas Written in Passing the Ambracian Gulf" equate his own feelings with those of Antony at the battle of Actium, "Where stern Ambition once forsook / His wavering crown to follow *Woman*." It concludes with the gallant if somewhat insincere lines, "I cannot *lose* a *world* for thee, / But would not lose *thee* for a *World*." The sentiment seems characteristically more authentic in the lines commemorating the end of the affair:

The spell is broke, the charm is flown!
   Thus is it with Life's fitful fever:
We madly smile when we should groan;
   Delirium is our best deceiver.[11]

It is significant that Byron's successful love affairs inspired the least poetry. Caroline Lamb preserved in her own handwriting a sentimental poem which she said Byron wrote to her,[12] but she will be remembered chiefly for the bitter lines he penned when exasperated by her invasion of his privacy after the affair had ended, the famous "Remember Thee" verses. Byron wrote more sentimental lines to Lady Frances Webster, the woman who got away, or whom he "spared." After composing the sonnets "To Genevra" he wrote in his diary: "I never wrote but one sonnet before, and that was not in earnest, and many years ago, as an exercise — and I will never write another. They are the most puling, petrifying, stupidly platonic compositions. I detest the Petrarch so much, that I would not be the man even to have obtained his Laura, which the metaphysical, whining dotard never

[11] The poems to Mrs. Spencer Smith include two written at Malta: "Lines Written in an Album, at Malta" and "To Florence," and the lady came into his thoughts when he was lost in a storm near Zitsa in Albania ("Stanzas Composed During a Thunder-Storm"). Byron's feelings on the passing of the spell are most elaborately described in the stanzas to "Florence" in *Childe Harold* (II, 30–35).

[12] See Marchand, *Byron*, I, 335n.

could."[13] Byron's sadly ironic reflections poured forth more freely when he learned in 1816 that she whose innocence had inspired his sentimental verses had become involved scandalously with the Duke of Wellington, the hero of Waterloo.

> When we two parted
>   In silence and tears,
> Half broken-hearted
>   To sever for years,
> Pale grew thy cheek and cold,
>   Colder thy kiss;
> Truly that hour foretold
>   Sorrow to this. . . .
>
> Thy vows are all broken,
>   And light is thy fame;
> I hear thy name spoken,
>   And share in its shame. . . .
> They knew not I knew thee,
>   Who knew thee too well: —
> Long, long shall I rue thee,
>   Too deeply to tell.[14]

Byron's "Stanzas for Music" written on the death of his Harrow friend the Duke of Dorset has the ring of deep and unalloyed feeling equaled only by some of the Thyrza poems. It was a dirge to his own decay of feeling. He called it "the *truest*, though the most melancholy" poem he ever wrote. Though composed in 1815 it anticipated the mood of the third canto of *Childe Harold:*

> There's not a joy the world can give like that it
>   takes away,
> When the glow of early thought declines in Feeling's
>   dull decay. . . .

[13] *Letters and Journals*, II, 379. Byron later wrote two sonnets on more congenial themes that may without apology take their place among his best lyrics: the "Sonnet on Chillon" and the "Sonnet to Lake Leman."

[14] For the circumstances of the composition and a final stanza not included in the published poem, see Marchand, *Byron*, II, 580–581, and the accompanying notes. Byron's other poems to Lady Frances Webster include "Remember Him Whom Passion's Power" and the two sonnets "To Genevra." E. H. Coleridge was no doubt wrong in his assumption that the stanzas beginning "I speak not, I trace not, I breathe not thy name" were addressed to Lady Frances Webster. See Marchand, *Byron*, I, 449n.

The same brooding dark humor that produced the third *Childe
Harold* and *Manfred* engendered also several notable short poems
during the summer of 1816. "Darkness" pictures with immitigable
cynicism and despair the unheroic end of the last men on a dying
planet. The blank verse reinforced with a vocabulary of gloom
creates an intolerable atmosphere in which humanity has returned
to the bestiality whence it sprang. "The brows of men by the
despairing light / Wore an unearthly aspect." They looked
"With mad disquietude on the dull sky" and "With curses cast
them down upon the dust, / And gnashed their teeth and howled."
It is characteristic that Byron, a lover of dogs, ascribed the one
altruistic instinct to a canine rather than a human actor. One dog
"sought out no food, / But with a piteous and perpetual moan, /
And a quick desolate cry, licking the hand / Which answered not
with a caress — he died."

In "Churchill's Grave" Byron brooded over "Obscurity and
Fame, — / The Glory and the Nothing of a Name." It is a reflection on those who "rip / The veil of Immortality, and crave / I
know not what of honour and of light / Through unborn ages,"
to be rewarded only with a forgotten grave.

"Prometheus" gives tribute to Byron's perpetual hero and pre-
sages the complaint of Manfred that man is "half dust, half deity":

> Thou art a symbol and a sign
>   To Mortals of their fate and force;
> Like thee, Man is in part divine,
>   A troubled stream from a pure source. . . .

But as in *Manfred* the conclusion is that the Spirit, the indomitable
mind of man, may achieve "Its own concentered recompense, /
Triumphant where it dares defy, / And making Death a Victory."

The "Fragment" beginning "Could I remount the river of my
years" is a speculation on "The under-earth inhabitants." It starts
with the thought that "The absent are the dead . . . equal must it
be / If the deep barrier be of earth, or sea; / It may be both —
but one day end it must / In the dark union of insensate dust."
Are the dead "But mingled millions decomposed to clay?" "Or
do they in their silent cities dwell / Each in his incommunicative
cell?" But these are unanswered questions, and the key of Earth's
"profundity is in the Grave." Whatever merit the poem may have,
however, does not rest in its "profundity" but in the lyrical
release of a mood that transcends the commonplace reflections
out of which it sprang:

Could I remount the river of my years
To the first fountain of our smiles and tears,
I would not trace again the stream of hours
Between their outworn banks of withered flowers,
But bid it flow as now — until it glides
Into the number of the nameless tides.

During that same dark summer Byron wrote "The Dream," a strange autobiographic outpouring that traced with photographic realism the moments of exaltation and despair in his love for Mary Chaworth. Although it is written in blank verse, it reads like romantic prose charged with feeling. After a prologue on sleep, "A boundary between the things misnamed / Death and existence," and the dream, "A slumbering thought" that "curdles a long life into one hour," he imagines with the vivid reality of a dream the crucial moments in his relationship with Mary that had seared themselves indelibly into his memory. The first was when they stood on a hill "crowned with a peculiar diadem / Of trees," and he "trembled on her words." He "had ceased / To live within himself; she was his life / . . . upon a tone, / A touch of hers, his blood would ebb and flow / And his cheek change tempestuously." Then he realized that she loved another and looked on him only as a brother. Their leave-taking he describes with circumstantial detail. He "shook as 'twere / With a convulsion," but would not show his feelings to her. Successive "dreams" give kaleidoscopic pictures of the boy grown up and on his travels, of Mary wedded and unhappy, of Byron's own wedding day when he was seized by "unutterable thoughts," and finally of Mary's wandering mind. The conclusion reveals the Wanderer finding consolation in communing with "the quick Spirit of the Universe" and seeking its mysteries. The poem has interest chiefly as a poetized diary of his private feelings, more patently autobiographical in detail than *Childe Harold*. He found outlet here for emotions too sensitive and sentimental to be confided in letters to his friends or in conversation with those who, though intimates, expected him to be the "facetious companion." Byron found that he could be more truthful in verse than in prose. "The Dream" is the logical extreme of his theory that one kind of poetry is the safety-valve of the imagination.

Byron's attachment to the Countess Guiccioli, in many respects the strongest of all his ties with women, gave rise to four poems, only two of which could be said to be unequivocally flattering, though all of them were honest expressions of feeling. The first, "Stanzas to the Po," composed soon after their meeting in 1819, leaves no doubt of the sincerity of his passion (Byron told his friend Hobhouse that the verses "were written in *red-hot* earnest and that makes them good"), but he has injected a note of frank realism that verges on cynicism:

> My heart is all meridian, were it not
>   I had not suffered now, nor should I be
> Despite old tortures ne'er to be forgot
>   The slave again — Oh! Love! at least of thee!
> 'Tis vain to struggle, I have struggled long
>   To love again no more as once I loved,
> Oh! Time! why leave this ~~worst of~~ earliest passion strong?
> To tear a heart which pants to be unmoved?[15]

When Byron wrote the dedicatory sonnet to his *Prophecy of Dante* he was glowing with his attachment and with the reading of the Italian love sonneteers, and his critical sense was in abeyance:

> Thou, in the pride of Beauty and of Youth,
>   Spakest; and for thee to speak and be obeyed
> Are one; but only in the sunny South
>   Such sounds are uttered, and such charms displayed,
> So sweet a language from so fair a mouth —
> Ah! to what effort would it not persuade?

The next poem has no direct reference to the Guiccioli, but it was written when Byron was considering breaking the tie and returning to England before love could be killed by habit or gradual cooling:

> Could Love for ever
> Run like a river,
> And Time's endeavour
>   Be tried in vain —
> No other pleasure
> With this could measure;
> And like a treasure
>   We'd hug the chain.

[15] This is the ending of the poem as it stands in an autograph manuscript in the Berg Collection in the New York Public Library. Note the change in the next to the last line from "worst of passions" to "earliest passion." For a discussion of the difference between this version and the text as first printed, see Marchand, "Lord Byron and Count Alborghetti," *PMLA*, LXIV (Dec., 1949), 977–978.

> But since our sighing
> Ends not in dying,
> And, formed for flying,
>   Love plumes his wing;
> Then for this reason
> Let's love a season;
> But let that season be only Spring.

The lyrical melancholy alone distinguishes this poem from the harsher mockery of the main stream of Byron's realistic-satiric vein. It illustrates very well the delicate balance between the two moods in Byron's life and poetry.

The "Stanzas Written on the Road Between Florence and Pisa" constitute a glowing, though indirect, tribute to Teresa Guiccioli. It was the anticipation of seeing her again after a separation of several months that no doubt inspired this light-hearted song celebrating a romantic ardor that had not grown colder with time and distance.

> Oh Fame! — if I e'er took delight in thy praises,
> 'Twas less for the sake of thy high-sounding phrases,
> Than to see the bright eyes of the dear One discover
> She thought that I was not unworthy to love her.

Byron's last three poems, the only extant ones written during his last sojourn in Greece, returned to themes of love and glory, and particularly of a hapless love that added to the poignancy of the tragedy of his last days — his hopeless unrequited attachment to the page boy Loukas Chalandritsanos. He had threatened to write more cantos of *Don Juan* if the occasion arose, but in the tightening vise of circumstances in Missolonghi, in ill health and disappointment, his poetic impulses found vent not in irony and humor but in the romantic agony once more. The first of these pieces was the poem written on his thirty-sixth birthday:

> My days are in the yellow leaf;
>   The flowers and fruits of Love are gone;
> The worm, the canker, and the grief
>   Are mine alone!
>
> The fire that on my bosom preys
>   Is lone as some volcanic isle;
> No torch is kindled at its blaze —
>   A funeral pile.

> The hope, the fear, the jealous care,
> The exalted portion of the pain
> And power of love, I cannot share,
> But wear the chain.

Though his days were "in the yellow leaf," the fire in his bosom was still capable of striking a poetic spark equal to anything he had written before in this vein. His pang found a voice that was lyrically memorable:

> Tread those reviving passions down,
> Unworthy manhood! — unto thee
> Indifferent should the smile or frown
> Of Beauty be.

> If thou regret'st thy youth, *why live?*
> The land of honourable death
> Is here: — up to the Field, and give
> Away thy breath![16]

But he could not tread those reviving passions down, nor could the thought of honor and glory quench the flame. In the "Last Words on Greece" (E. H. Coleridge's title) he admits defeat:

> What are to me those honours or renown
> Past or to come, a new-born people's cry?
> Albeit for such I could despise a crown
> Of aught save laurel, or for such could die.
> I am a fool of passion, and a frown
> Of thine to me is as an adder's eye.

Byron's last extant poem beginning "I watched thee when the foe was at our side" (titled by E. H. Coleridge "[Love and Death]") recounted his tender care for Loukas in various crises and ended:

> And when convulsive throes denied my breath
> The faintest utterance to my fading thought,
> To thee — to thee — e'en in the gasp of death
> My spirit turned, oh! oftener than it ought.

---

[16] Though it has not been mentioned in print, the passion referred to in this poem was undoubtedly his frustrated love for Loukas Chalandritsanos. For details see the index of Marchand, *Byron.* See also Doris Langley Moore, *The Late Lord Byron.*

Thus much and more; and yet thou lov'st me not,
   And never wilt! Love dwells not in our will.
Nor can I blame thee, though it be my lot
   To strongly, wrongly, vainly love thee still.[17]

However much detachment Byron occasionally achieved, and however successful he may have been in portraying the other side of the romantic coin in his satires in which he could laugh at even his own tangled emotions, it is significant that he ended as he began with the poetry which is the "lava of the imagination."

The *Hebrew Melodies* constitute a group of Byron's lyrics that are finely executed, rich in tone, and unified in mood, and for the most part have their origins in human sympathies not directly and immediately related to the author's own emotional quandaries. They were written in compliance with the request of Byron's friend Douglas Kinnaird that he supply lyrics for some authentic Hebrew airs that Isaac Nathan had adapted from the music of the synagogues. Once embarked Byron entered upon the task with some enthusiasm, for the poetry and music of the Old Testament, coupled with its poignant melancholy, had long appealed to him. When it came to the publication of the volume, however, Byron could not resist inserting other lyrics which were neither Hebrew nor Christian in theme but which Nathan, flattered by the attentions of the most popular poet of the day, was willing enough to set to music and to publish. The result was that, as one critic has noted, "Pious persons who bought the *Hebrew Melodies* in the expectation of finding sacred poetry by Lord Byron found instead a book almost as secular as *The Bride of Abydos*. Nine of the poems are Biblical in subject but Byronic in treatment; two are love songs; five are reflective lyrics, neither Jewish nor Christian; and five are expressions of what might be called proto-Zionism."[18] Some of the harps and minstrels and waters may also have been unconscious imitations of Thomas Moore's *Irish Melodies*.

[17] Reference to his illness of February 15 and the earthquake of February 21 indicate that the poem was written after the one on his thirty-sixth birthday (Jan. 22). See Marchand, *Byron*, III, 1207–8n.

[18] Joseph Slater, "Byron's Hebrew Melodies," *Studies in Philology*, XLIX (Jan., 1952), 86. Nathan set to music and published eleven other poems or portions of poems by Byron, in addition to the lyrics in the *Hebrew Melodies*, including the "Maid of Athens" and sections of *The Giaour* and *The Bride of Abydos*. See Slater, p. 87.

The volume opened with the now well-known lyric inspired by Byron's seeing the beautiful Mrs. Wilmot in a dress of mourning with spangles on it: "She walks in Beauty, like the night / Of cloudless climes and starry skies." Not unexpectedly Byron saw in her "A heart whose love is innocent!" But this poem is the only one that is really out of tone with the Hebrew melodies proper, for even the love songs have much of the haunting sadness and the sense of desolation which inform the poems voicing a wild lament for the lost Jewish homeland. The lyric "Oh! Snatched Away in Beauty's Bloom" is reminiscent of the Thyrza theme and mood but with less of the hectic coloring of the poems born of the immediate grief. And of the poems with Biblical subjects one is a love poem with a Byronic cast, "Herod's Lament for Mariamne": "Revenge is lost in Agony / And wild remorse to rage succeeding."

Two themes that were congenial to Byron's spirit dominate the lyrics derived from Old Testament sources: one is the deep pathos of the loss of Eden, the wail of a wandering and homeless people, and the other the battle cry of Jewish Nationalism. The lost Eden was easily identified in Byron's feelings with the general romantic lament for lost innocence and beauty. "The Wild Gazelle" is typical:

> The cedars wave on Lebanon,
> But Judah's statelier maids are gone!

They "must wander witheringly, / In other lands to die." The theme is repeated in "Oh! Weep for Those." Byron displayed considerable dexterity and skill in adapting the Biblical language to his purposes:

> Tribes of the wandering foot and weary breast,
> How shall ye flee away and be at rest!

"On Jordan's Banks" reiterates the first theme and introduces the second, the militant spirit that will conquer at last:

> On Jordan's banks the Arab's camels stray,
> On Sion's hill the False One's votaries pray....
> How long by tyrants shall thy land be trod?
> How long thy temple worshipless, Oh God?

The battle cry is raised in "On the Day of the Destruction of Jerusalem by Titus" and again in "By the Waters of Babylon": "Our hands may be fettered — our tears still are free."

Byron easily identified himself with an oppressed people reaching for freedom. This militant theme found its finest expression in the ringing lines of "The Destruction of Sennacherib," rightly admired as one of Byron's most musical lyrics. It is a tour de force but a brilliant one with perfect blending of mood and meter. As with most of Byron's successful lyrics it transcends the alliterative and anapestic and sound-association devices and even the commonplace melodramatic theme and captures the imagination and feelings of anyone sensitive to music and poetry.

> The Assyrian came down like the wolf on the fold,
> And his cohorts were gleaming in purple and gold;
> And the sheen of their spears was like stars on the sea,
> When the blue wave rolls nightly on deep Galilee. . . .
>
> And there lay the steed with his nostril all wide,
> But through it there rolled not the breath of his pride;
> And the foam of his gasping lay white on the turf,
> And cold as the spray of the rock-beating surf. . . .
>
> And the widows of Ashur are loud in their wail,
> And the idols are broke in the temple of Baal;
> And the might of the Gentile, unsmote by the sword,
> Hath melted like snow in the glance of the Lord!

That Byron associated the militant Zionism of the *Hebrew Melodies* with the struggles for freedom with which he later allied himself is evident in a letter he wrote to John Murray from Ravenna when the Austrians were poised to quench the fires of freedom then burning among the Neapolitans: " 'Oh Jerusalem, Jerusalem!' The Huns are on the Po; but if once they pass it on their march to Naples, all Italy will rise behind them: The Dogs — the Wolves — may they perish like the Host of Sennacherib!"[19]

[19] *Letters and Journals*, V, 72. Letter of Sept. 7, 1820.

11

Jeux d'Esprit and Occasional Poems

ANY CONSIDERATION of Byron's poetry which did not take account of his *jeux d'esprit* and occasional poems would do him less than justice, for the spontaneous ebullience of his mind sometimes produced sparks of wit and wisdom which were peculiar to his genius. Though few of these pieces could be called poetry in the highest sense — some critics would make an exception for "So We'll Go No More A-Roving" — they are filled with an effervescent spirit and with phrases that the world would not willingly let die, and has not. They take on added interest from the fact that they display a facility and an agility of mind such as produced many of the bons mots and bantering lines in *Don Juan*. In fact, many of the stanzas in that poem were born of the same impulses that filled Byron's letters with bubbling *jeux d'esprit* of this kind. One thinks of the fragment written on the back of the manuscript of the first canto, or the now often quoted stanza in the second canto ending:

> Let us have Wine and Woman, Mirth and Laughter,
> Sermons and soda-water the day after.   (II, 178)

For convenience in discussing these occasional poems, I shall divide them into three not always distinguishable groups. First there are those which arise from overflowing high spirits, or from a humorous observation of the little ironies of life and character. Generally these are written without malice though they may ridicule individuals. One of the best examples is to be found in the "Lines to Mr. Hodgson," written ostensibly on board the Lisbon packet as Byron was leaving England for his pilgrimage to the East. The blustering tone is all tongue-in-cheek, for it is only his high spirits at parting overflowing into burlesque.

In the same spirit of banter is the "Farewell Petition to J. C. H., Esqre" written at Constantinople after Hobhouse had announced his intention of returning to England. Hobhouse's companionship encouraged this kind of facetiousness. They had agreed to take as their motto Swift's phrase, "Vive la Bagatelle." Byron twitted his friend on the publication of his "Miscellany" and made sport of his valet Fletcher's complaints about

> The *chicken's toughness*, and the *lack* of *ale*
> The *stoney mountain* and the *miry vale*
> The Garlick steams, which *half* his meals enrich,
> The *impending vermin*, and the threatened *Itch*. . . .

These were merely themes from his letters transferred into rhyme. This kind of nonsense verse, filled with punning and play on words, sometimes had a critical point as in his "Epitaph for Joseph Blacket, Late Poet and Shoemaker." Byron did not share the romantic taste for the poetry of "rustic and humble life," nor did he believe that the best poetry came from the spontaneous overflow of the powerful feelings of peasants or shoemakers.

> Stranger! behold, interred together,
> The *souls* of learning and of leather.
> Poor Joe is gone, but left his *all:*
> You'll find his relics in a *stall*.
> His works were neat, and often found
> Well stitched, and with *morocco* bound.
> Tread lightly — where the bard is laid —
> He cannot mend the shoe he made;
> Yet he is happy in his hole,
> With verse immortal as his *sole*.

But Byron could laugh at his own pretensions too, even when he was boasting of having swum the Hellespont ("Written After Swimming from Sestos to Abydos"). Comparing himself to Leander, he could turn both feats to a jest:

> 'Twere hard to say who fared the best:
> Sad mortals! thus the Gods still plague you!
> He lost his labour, I my jest:
> For he was drowned, and I've the ague.

Byron's letters from Italy contain some of the most clever and amusing verses in this genre, ranging from the delicate "So We'll Go No More A-Roving" to the raucous and ribald "My Dear Mr. Murray." Nothing Byron ever wrote quite equals the former in its lightness of touch in dealing with the keenly felt romantic theme of jaded pleasures. It is a theme much labored in *Childe Harold*. But the fine balance of irony, regret, and acceptance coupled with the music of the lines lifts it to a height of poetic grace seldom achieved by Byron.

> So we'll go no more a-roving
>   So late into the night,
> Though the heart be still as loving,
>   And the moon be still as bright.
>
> For the sword outwears its sheath,
>   And the soul wears out the breast,
> And the heart must pause to breathe,
>   And Love itself have rest.
>
> Though the night was made for loving,
>   And the day returns too soon,
> Yet we'll go no more a-roving
>   By the light of the moon.

Another poetic epistle to Thomas Moore was written after an hour's swim in the Adriatic, "with a black-eyed Venetian girl before me, reading Boccaccio." It displays a pleasing facility without the perfection of form or depth of feeling of the earlier poem.

> My boat is on the shore,
>   And my bark is on the sea; . . .
>
> Here's a sigh to those who love me,
>   And a smile to those who hate. . . .

Byron's letters to his publisher John Murray from Venice were full of good-natured quizzing, sometimes at Murray's publishing list as in "To Hook the Reader, You, John Murray," or the "Ballad to the Tune of 'Sally in Our Alley,'" ridiculing Gally Knight's poems.[1] One of the cleverest of the pieces in this vein is Byron's "*delicate* declension" of Dr. Polidori's tragedy. Murray was embarrassed by having to decline a play offered by Byron's one-time physician and asked the poet to frame the reply, which he did in verse:

---

[1] Gally Knight, whom Byron had met in Spain and Greece, had written *Phrosyne, a Grecian Tale* (1817). His "drivel" was a favorite butt for Byron's wit. He mentioned him in "Another Simple Ballat," in "My Dear Mr. Murray," and in "You Ask for a 'Volume of Nonsense.'"

> Dear Doctor, I have read your play,
> Which is a good one in its way, —
> Purges the eyes, and moves the bowels,
> And drenches handkerchiefs like towels. . . .

But "plays / Are drugs," he says, and then lists some of those Murray had already published, softening the criticism with a reference to himself:

> There's Byron, too, who once did better,
> Has sent me, folded in a letter,
> A sort of — it's no more a drama
> Than *Darnley, Ivan,* or *Kehama;*[2]
> So altered since last year his pen is,
> I think he's lost his wits at Venice,
> Or drained his brains away as stallion
> To some dark-eyed and warm Italian. . . .[3]

There is equal gusto in the rollicking "My Dear Mr. Murray," the verses written when he was sending home by Hobhouse the manuscript of the fourth canto of *Childe Harold.*

> My dear Mr. Murray,
> You're in a damned hurry
>   To set up this ultimate Canto;
> But (if they don't rob us)
> You'll see Mr. Hobhouse
>   Will bring it safe in his portmanteau.

And he ended with three stanzas of ribaldry concerning his Italian mistress.[4]

There were a few barbs along with the compliments in another versified epistle to Murray:

> Strahan, Tonson, Lintot of the times,
> Patron and publisher of rhymes,
> For thee the bard up Pindus climbs,
>   My Murray.

---

[2] *The Death of Darnley* and *Ivan* were tragedies by William Sotheby; *The Curse of Kehama* was a poetic drama with an Eastern setting by Robert Southey. Byron's own drama, about the reception of which he was a little uncertain and consequently defensive, was *Manfred.*

[3] The last two lines quoted here, omitted in Coleridge's editions, were first published by Peter Quennell in *Byron: A Self-Portrait,* II, 416. Letter of Aug. 21, 1817.

[4] See Marchand, *Byron,* II, 722.

> To thee, with hope and terror dumb,
> The unfledged MS. authors come;
> Thou printest all — and sellest some —
>   My Murray.

More malicious are the poems in a second group of *jeux d'esprit*, born of anger, pique, or prejudice, but never devoid of humor. The malice ranges from light to intense. Some of the lighter ones verge closely in tone upon those just discussed. Such is the "Farewell to Malta":

> Adieu, ye joys of La Valette!
> Adieu, Sirocco, sun, and sweat! . . .
> Adieu, ye curséd streets of stairs!
> (How surely he who mounts them swears!) . . . .
> Adieu, the supercilious air
> Of all that strut *en militaire!*

Then there are the literary gibes that have a certain bite though nonsensically humorous, such as "I read the Christabel," "Who Killed John Keats?", and the references to "Wordsworth, the grand metaquizzical poet" (in the lines beginning "The braziers, it seems, are preparing to pass"). The best of these literary sallies, however, are to be found in the sprightly attacks on the Lake Poets in *Don Juan*, which may better be discussed as a part of that poem.

As Byron's patience with Murray grew shorter preceding his final break with his publisher, his poetical epistles, though still humorous, became more frankly biting, as in "For Orford and for Waldegrave," which accuses Murray of paying him less than he paid his other authors. Byron's ribbing of his friends usually had a basis in a real pique, however good-humored the attack. Such was his ridicule of Hobhouse for the "seditionary" activities and associations that had caused him to be sent to Newgate. He felt that his friend had sullied himself by his alliance with the "Radical mob."

> How came you in Hob's pound to cool,
>   My boy Hobbie O?
> Because I bade the people pull
>   The House into the Lobby O.

It is not surprising that Hobhouse did not see the humor of this and felt that Byron had stabbed him in the back while he was suffering as a martyr for the cause of liberty, but he forgave his friend on the grounds that he was out of touch with English politics. When Hobhouse was released and elected to Parliament from Westminster Byron continued his banter, but sent his verses to Murray and not Hobhouse:

> Would you go to the house by the true gate,
>   Much faster than ever Whig Charley went;
> Let Parliament send you to Newgate,
>   And Newgate will send you to Parliament.

Byron's fondness for Martial led him to write a number of epigrams with a Byronic flavor:

> The world is a bundle of hay,
>   Mankind are the asses who pull;
> Each tugs it in a different way, —
>   And the greatest of all is John Bull!

He found the form effective too for political satire. His epigrams on Pitt, on Cobbett, and particularly on Castlereagh display acerbity rather than humor.

But the mordant qualities of Byron's satire were most evident where he was personally involved. The most savage of his occasional pieces are "A Sketch," directed against Mrs. Clermont, who strengthened Lady Byron's "implacability" during the separation proceedings, and "Question and Answer," his brutal dissection of Sam Rogers. In his attack on Mrs. Clermont Byron outdoes his master Pope in personal invective, but he was too angry to be clever and the pure acid of the satire is diluted considerably with bilge water. And in his anger he fell into the eighteenth century habit in personal satire, quite contrary to his own convictions, of smearing the character by pointing up her lowly origins: "Born in the garret, in the kitchen bred, / Promoted thence to deck her mistress' head. . . . " His reference to her as a snake whose "black slime" betrays her as she crawls is a far cry from Pope's subtle and poetic but at the same time blistering "What? that thing of silk, / Sporus, that mere white curd of Ass's milk?" Byron's attempt to break the butterfly upon a wheel was disastrous both to his humor and to his satiric purpose, and it added nothing to his poetic achievement.

The satire on Samuel Rogers, on the other hand, though no less bitter, is both clever and humorous. The suspicion that Rogers was gossiping about him behind his back, despite his seeming friendliness, caused Byron's gorge to rise, but left him with enough detachment to write tellingly. Though given to criticizing his friends caustically in their absence, Byron was acutely sensitive to rumors of criticism about himself. Such rumors gave rise to his undying hatred of Southey. Though he continued to be outwardly friendly with Rogers, he suspected him, and his suspicion led to a malicious analysis of the cadaverous banker poet. Rogers' corpse-like appearance was a common subject of jest, and Byron made the most of it.[5] The caricature in the "Question" had enough likeness to be recognized:

> Nose and Chin that make a knocker,
> Mouth that marks the envious Scorner,
> With a Scorpion in each corner
> Curling up his tail to sting you,
> In the place that most may wring you;
> Eyes of lead-like hue, and gummy,
> Carcass stolen from some mummy,
> Bowels — (but they were forgotten,
> Save the Liver, and that's rotten),
> Skin all sallow, flesh all sodden,
> Form the Devil would frighten G–d in.

The "Answer" accumulates a devastating bill of particulars on Rogers' character:

> That's the Bard, and Beau, and Banker:
> Yet, if you could bring about
> Just to turn him inside out,
> Satan's self would seem less sooty. . . .
> Chastened bow, and mock humility,
> Almost sickened to Servility:
> Hear his tone (which is to talking
> That which creeping is to walking —
> Now on all fours, now on tip toe):
> Hear the tales he lends his lip to. . . .

[5] One story of Rogers was that when he visited the catacombs near Rome he was mistaken for one of the skeletons. Byron wrote to Murray on Feb. 20, 1818, after hearing of some of Rogers' backbiting: "He cannot say that I have not been a sincere and warm friend to him, till the black drop of his liver oozed through. . . . Now, if I once catch him at any of his jugglery with me or mine, let him look to it. . . . the more that I have been deceived . . . the more will I pay off the balance; and so, if he values his quiet, let him look to it; in three months I could restore him to the Catacombs." (*Letters and Journals*, IV, 202–203.) Byron's "Question and Answer" was probably written soon after this. He sent it to Murray to show to certain friends but not to publish. It was first published in *Fraser's Magazine,* Jan., 1833, while Rogers was still living, but he took no notice of it, and his generous tribute to Byron in his *Italy* remained in all editions of his published poems.

Considering Byron's rather exaggerated, though sincere, admiration for the poetry of Rogers, the final lines indicate the intensity of his pique:

> For his merits — don't you know 'em?
> Once he wrote a pretty Poem.

Byron's occasional poems, personal and political, may entice our attention, as they captured the interest of his contemporaries, by their subject matter and occasional pungency of statement, rather than by any poetic qualities. Some of the topical poems written on the spur of the moment, like the "Lines to a Lady Weeping," and better yet the "Windsor Poetics" and "When a Man Hath No Freedom to Fight for at Home," ring a genuine note. The frank *lèse majesté* of the "Windsor Poetics" was such as had put Leigh Hunt in jail, but Byron was safely abroad when the poem was published in 1819. The lines were composed "on the occasion of his Royal Highness the Prince Regent being seen standing between the coffins of Henry VIII and Charles I, in the Royal Vault at Windsor."

> Famed for contemptuous breach of sacred ties,
> By headless Charles see heartless Henry lies:
> Between them stands another sceptered thing —
> It moves, it reigns — in all but name, a king:
>
> Charles to his people, Henry to his wife,
> — In him the double tyrant starts to life. . . .

Byron renewed the attack on George IV in "The Irish Avatar," which is as bitter in its denunciation of the servility of the Irish, who welcomed George to Dublin only ten days after the death of Queen Caroline (to whom the liberals had rallied in her disputes with the king). The poem is full of strong feeling and has some good lines. But the abdication of Napoleon, the "little Pagod" whom Byron had long admired as statesman and soldier, roused him to compose some more memorable stanzas in the "Ode to Napoleon Buonaparte." Here was admirable illustration of his favorite *sic transit* theme:

> But thou forsooth must be a King
>   And don the purple vest,
> As if that foolish robe could wring
>   Remembrance from thy breast.

But this did not reach the poetic intensity of the stanzas on Napoleon in the third canto of *Childe Harold*.

Two occasional pieces, written at the request of friends for recital at Drury Lane, were as forced and stilted as anything Byron ever wrote. The "Address" which Lord Holland asked Byron to write for the opening of the new theater gave him infinite trouble. Attempting to emulate the neo-classical writers in this genre, he fell into the worst clichés and poetic jargon of the eighteenth century. His couplets have neither the Popean bite nor the Johnsonian sonority, and what is worse they have nothing of the usual Byronic flavor. Byron was stage-struck into dullness in the same way in his "Monody on the Death of the Right Hon. R. B. Sheridan." Although he told Lady Blessington that his feelings were directly involved and that "every word that I wrote came direct from the heart," for he was a sincere admirer of Sheridan, Byron later confessed to Murray: "I did as well as I could; but where I have not my choice I pretend to answer for nothing."[6] How much more effective were Byron's prose tributes to Sheridan in his "Detached Thoughts," reminiscences of his years of fame written in Ravenna in 1821.

One poem composed in December, 1813, gives evidence that the satiric spirit was not dead in Byron during that time when he was most absorbed in the romantic agony which produced *Childe Harold* and the Oriental tales. It is significant too that "The Devil's Drive" was written, not in the heroic couplet, the verse form of his serious efforts at satire, but in irregular rhymed stanzas, ranging in length from six to twelve or more lines but resembling both in metrics (alternate rhymes and a couplet at the end) and in idiom and manner, the ottava rima of *Beppo* and *Don Juan*. On his cynical drive the devil encounters the ravages of the Napoleonic wars and the hypocrisies of English society. He is delighted when he hears a psalm from a Methodist chapel:

> When *Faith* is all, 'tis an excellent sign,
> That the *Works* and Workmen both are mine.

Byron savored the topical references of the devil in the Houses of Parliament, but many of the lines are rather clumsy and lack the agility of his later satiric thrusts in the ottava rima. It is as well that the poem was not published during Byron's life. Its chief interest lies in its foreshadowing of the greater satires.

6 *Letters and Journals*, III, 366. Letter of Sept. 27, 1816.

12

Beppo

BYRON'S FIRST MENTION of *Beppo* is in a letter of October 12, 1817, to John Murray, written after he had finished the first draft of the fourth canto of *Childe Harold* but was still working on additional stanzas: "I have since written a poem (of 84 octave stanzas [99 as finally published]), humourous, in or after the excellent manner of Mr. Whistlecraft (whom I take to be Frere), on a Venetian anecdote which amused me."[1] The happy accident of his having seen John Hookham Frere's adaptation of the Pulcian ottava rima and mock-heroic style in the *Prospectus and Specimen of an Intended National Work*, supposedly "by the brothers Whistlecraft" and "intended to comprise the most interesting particulars relating to King Arthur and his Round Table," no doubt gave Byron the idea for the verse form and the waggish colloquial style of the poem, but the materials and the "*estro*," as he called it (the psychological urge), had long been growing in his mind. He was ripe for a change of style and poetical mood. Since his arrival in Venice in November of 1816 his spirits had experienced a "rebound" and the gloom and despair of the summer gradually passed away, or at least appeared at less frequent intervals and was interspersed with lighter and livelier feelings which found outlet in the exuberance and wit of his letters, sometimes bursting into versified *jeux d'esprit*. But the habit of the melancholy voice which he had so long cultivated in poetry was hard to break. With some difficulty he completed a new third act of *Manfred* and distilled his Roman voyage into the fourth canto of *Childe Harold*, but there is evidence that he was growing tired of that vein, and that it no longer satisfied his

[1] *Letters and Journals*, IV, 172–173.

deepest convictions about poetry nor tallied with his current moods. His letters to Murray and Moore during 1817 reflect something of his dissatisfaction with the style that had become his trademark in the eyes of the public. On March 9th he wrote Murray: "The thing I have sent you [*Manfred*], you will see at a glimpse, could never be attempted or thought of for the stage; I much doubt it for publication even. It is too much in my old style. . . . I certainly am a devil of a mannerist, and must leave off. . . ."[2] And the roots of his misgivings were revealed more clearly in that passage already quoted (in Chapter 1) wherein he proclaimed that he and his contemporaries were "upon a wrong revolutionary poetical system" and that they were all at an "ineffable distance" from Pope.[3] This was written only a month before he had finished *Beppo*. Although in the same letter he said that he believed the fourth canto of *Childe Harold* was his best, he added that he thought of "concluding with it," that is, ending his writing career, the implication being that he had written himself out in that vein. In March he had complained to Moore: "I suppose now I shall never be able to shake off my sables in public imagination," and he urged Moore to assure Jeffrey that he was not "the misanthropical and gloomy gentleman he takes me for."[4]

So that by the time he finished *Childe Harold* he was ready for another manner and another idiom that would reflect more clearly and more honestly the totality of his view of the world and not just one facet of it. He did not quite find it in *Beppo*, for the episode itself was too slight and the emotional gamut too limited to give full scope to his powers, but the flood gates were opened to a freedom of expression that was to give full vent to Byron's peculiar genius.

The anecdote which amused him and which formed the basis of the tale on which he hung his comments on Venetian life and morals was told to Byron and his friend Hobhouse on the evening of August 29, 1817, in his summer palace at La Mira just outside Venice where Marianna Segati, "pretty as an antelope," with

---

[2] *Letters and Journals*, IV, 71–72. On March 25, 1818, after advising Murray to "consult the knowing ones" as to the advisability of putting his name to *Beppo*, Byron added: "It will, at any rate, show them that I can write cheerfully, and repel the charge of monotony and mannerism." (*Letters and Journals*, IV, 218.)

[3] *Letters and Journals*, IV, 169.

[4] *Letters and Journals*, IV, 73–74. Letter of March 10, 1817.

"large black, Oriental eyes," and no doubt possessing other qualities which found embodiment in the Laura of the tale, had established herself in Byron's house as his *amica*. It is ironically appropriate to the spirit of *Beppo* that the story was told by the husband of Marianna, who, Hobhouse says, used to spend the weekends at La Mira courting another lady.

This was the anecdote as Hobhouse recorded it in his diary: "A Turk arrived at the Regina di Ungheria [*sic*] inn at Venice and lodged there — he asked to speak to the mistress of the inn a buxom lady of 40 in keeping with certain children & who had lost her husband many years before at sea — after some preliminaries my hostess went to the Turk who immediately shut the door & began questioning her about her family & her late husband — she told her loss — when the Turk asked if her husband had any particular mark about him she said — yes he had a scar on his shoulder. Something like this said the Turk pulling down his robe — I am your husband — I have been to Turkey — I have made a large fortune and I make you three offers — either to quit your amoroso and come with me — or to stay with your amoroso or to accept a pension and live alone." Hobhouse added: "The lady has not yet given an answer, but Me Zagati [*sic*] said I'm sure I would not leave my amoroso for any husband — looking at B. this is too gross even for me."[5]

There is little doubt that this was the spark that ignited Byron's already eager desire to record in verse some of the amusing facets of Italian life which had been overflowing in his letters to his friends in England. The happy circumstance of his discovery of Frere fixed the form of the new poem.[6] The deliberate colloquial ease of the ottava rima in that poem appealed to him, for it seemed a healthy antidote to the heavy pomposities of the con-

[5] Marchand, *Byron*, II, 708. Another contemporary account of the incident was recorded in the diary of Emanuele Cicogna (the MS. is now in the Museo Correr in Venice) under date of Aug. 25, 1817. In this account the lady was married to the proprietor of the inn when her husband returned. But Segati's version of the story, which had the woman living with her *"amoroso,"* suited Byron's purposes much better, for it accorded much more closely with what he had observed of Italian society. It did not matter too much that Byron learned, after the mock-heroic version was recorded in *Beppo*, that the story was not true. His account was much truer to the realities of Italian manners than either of the originals.

[6] The poem by Frere was probably brought to Byron's attention either by W. S. Rose or by Douglas Kinnaird. See Marchand, *Byron*, II, 708–709.

ventional language of English poetry, even after Wordsworth.
He was not then familiar with Frere's original sources in the
Italian mock-heroic writers, though he had read and admired
Casti's *Novelle Galanti*, Boccaccian tales in ottava rima, and also
the *Animali Parlanti*, translated anonymously by W. S. Rose, who
paid him a visit about the time he began *Beppo*.[7] But the possibilities of the style for the deflation of both the stilted language
and the pretentious sentiments of English poetry struck him when
he read Frere's defense of a colloquial vocabulary:

> Preserve with care your noble parts of speech
>   And take it as a maxim to endeavour
> To talk as your good mother used to teach,
>   And then these lines of mine may last for ever;
> And don't confound the language of the nation
> With long-tailed words in *osity* and *ation*.[8]

And so he was fortunately diverted from the Popean couplets,
to which he had usually turned to express his sense of the ironies
or absurdities of life. With one stroke he freed himself not only
from the restrictions of the *Childe Harold* manner, but also from
the artificial voice which he too frequently assumed when he self-
consciously attempted to follow the footsteps of his great master.
This was the freedom that he needed to express both the honest
vagaries of his mobile personality and the most serious observations of his agile mind. The immensely adaptable ottava rima
could be used to express a genuine sentiment, built up by the
alternate rhyme and reinforced by the couplet at the end, or to
blow a burlesque bubble to be pricked by a ludicrous rhyme.
Byron had found a medium in which he could be relaxed and
honest, or bantering and witty, as in his letters. He could rise to
poetry when he wished and return to prose without apology.
And since he believed that no poetry was more than half good,
why worry about the descent from Pegasus. Let the critics
cavil at the careless ease of his style:

> I've half a mind to tumble down to prose,
>   But verse is more in fashion — so here goes!   (St. 52)

---

[7] R. D. Waller in the introduction to his edition of Frere's "Whistlecraft," which he calls *The Monks and the Giants*, gives an excellent survey
of Frere's (and Byron's) predecessors, Pulci, Berni, Casti, in the use of
the ottava rima for mock-heroic purposes. Elizabeth F. Boyd's *Byron's
Don Juan* (Chapter IV) also discusses in some detail Byron's debt to these
sources.

[8] Frere, *Whistlecraft*, I, 6.

The lack of unity either in subject or in tone, the digressions, the ironic deflation of commonly accepted attitudes and sentiments, the conversational idiom, the unheroic, or mock-heroic, portraits of the characters, the epigrammatic wit, the comic rhymes used to emphasize the punch lines of the couplets, the realism of the interpretation of life — all contributed to endow his verse with the disarming quality of his most amusing letters.

The obvious attraction of this style of writing to Byron was its flexibility with respect to both matter and mood. Impatient of restraint and formalism of all kinds, he found it infinitely pleasing to digress at will and let the story wait. Yet two themes emerge eventually, though not to the exclusion of a welter of impressions and comments on whatever struck his fancy. One is the "moral" of the story, the tolerance of the Italians in matters of love and marriage, and the other is the contrast between Italian and English attitudes and manners, though the satire on things English goes beyond the single theme. But the greater interest attaches to the amusing pageant of Venetian life and morals as Byron had seen them during his months of residence in that sea-born city. Though pleased with Italy, he was not sentimentally uncritical. His opening description of the Carnival is amiable but spiced with ridicule of that "farewell to flesh," when

> The People take their fill of recreation,
> And buy repentance, ere they grow devout,
>   However high their rank or low their station,
> With fiddling, feasting, dancing, drinking, masquing,
> And other things which may be had for asking.
>
> (St. 1)

Then they say "farewell to carnal dishes," "To live for forty days on ill-dressed fishes."

He turns next to praise of the pretty faces and black eyes of the Venetian women. Here as elsewhere in the poem Byron made use of associational digression. The women when leaning over a balcony look as if they had stepped out from a painting by Giorgione, and that leads to a description of a portrait he had admired in the Manfrini Palace: "*such* a woman! love in life!"

> Love in full life and length, not love ideal,
>   No, nor ideal beauty, that fine name,
> But something better still, so very real,
>   That the sweet Model must have been the same;
> A thing that you would purchase, beg, or steal,
>   Wer't not impossible, besides a shame. . . .

Then instead of ending with the expected facetious couplet, Byron turned serious:

> The face recalls some face, as 't were with pain,
> You once have seen, but ne'er will see again. . . .
>
> (St. 13)

And he slips back wholly into one of the lost-innocence moods of *Childe Harold*:

> One of those forms which flit by us, when we
>   Are young, and fix our eyes on every face;
> And, oh! the Loveliness at times we see
>   In momentary gliding, the soft grace,
> The Youth, the Bloom, the Beauty which agree,
>   In many a nameless being we retrace,
> Whose course and home we knew not, nor shall know,
> Like the lost Pleiad seen no more below.   (St. 14)

But there is a quick transition back to banter:

> Shakespeare described the sex in Desdemona
>   As very fair, but yet suspect in fame,
> And to this day from Venice to Verona
>   Such matters may be probably the same,
> Except that since those times was never known a
>   Husband whom mere suspicion could inflame
> To suffocate a wife no more than twenty,
> Because she had a "Cavalier Servente."
>
> Their jealousy (if they are ever jealous)
>   Is of a fair complexion altogether,
> Not like that sooty devil of Othello's
>   Which smothers women in a bed of feather,
> But worthier of these much more jolly fellows;
>   When weary of the matrimonial tether
> His head for such a wife no mortal bothers,
> But takes at once another, or *another's*.[9]   (St. 17–18)

And thus the theme was presaged in a seeming casual aside. But the meat of the poem was in the digressions, and Byron would postpone the story for more than thirty stanzas. Next it seemed fit to describe the gondola, so convenient for assignations:

[9] Byron had an example ready at hand in Sr. Segati, Marianna's husband, who amicably accepted Byron's hospitality while he courted another lady.

> It glides along the water looking blackly,
> Just like a coffin clapt in a canoe,
> Where none can make out what you say or do.
> * * * * * * * * * *
> But not to them do woeful things belong,
> For sometimes they contain a deal of fun,
> Like mourning coaches when the funeral's done.
>
> (St. 19–20)

Then he introduces his heroine, drawn from the life no doubt, probably a composite of Marianna and other women he had met in or out of the Carnival, with perhaps a dash of his new "*amica,*" the "fornarina" or baker's wife. One may suspect that the selection of his heroine's name was not as casual as he made it appear:

> Her real name I know not, nor can guess,
> And so we'll call her Laura, if you please,
> Because it slips into my verse with ease.   (St. 21)

It is not far-fetched to suppose, in view of Byron's often-expressed cynical contempt for the Platonic ideal, that he chose the name of Petrarch's sentimentally veiled love with ironic tongue-in-cheek, for his heroine was one who might inspire ogles rather than sonnets.

> Indeed, she shone all smiles, and seemed to flatter
> Mankind with her black eyes for looking at her.
>
> (St. 23)

And Laura's husband's name, which gives the title to the poem, ("His name Guiseppe, called more briefly, Beppo") may well have been chosen with a roguish eye on the Guiseppe (called Beppe) who was the notoriously devoted *cavalier servente* of the aging Countess Benzone, at whose "*conversazione*" Byron later met the Countess Guiccioli.

Laura was a married woman "'tis convenient, / Because in Christian countries 'tis a rule / To view their little slips with eyes more lenient." We are thus prepared for Laura's defection quite in accord with the easygoing Italian acceptance of the extramarital relationship, after Beppo had sailed away and was long overdue.

> And so she thought it prudent to connect her
> With a vice-husband, *chiefly* to *protect her*.   (St. 29)

The Count, her "*cavalier servente,*" Byron pictured as a coxcomb, who knew "Music, and dancing, fiddling, French and

Tuscan," and who was a critic and connoisseur of the Opera. The Count's virtue was that he was faithful. "He was a lover of the good old school, / Who still become more constant as they cool." This leads to a discussion of the function of "*serventismo*." Byron had thus far resisted that kind of service (not having yet succumbed to the charms of the Countess Guiccioli), and could therefore voice, if not a moral disapproval, at least a superior British disdain for such male subservience.[10] At the same time he was glad to seize the opportunity to compare the Italian laxity and tolerance with the moral rigidity of the English. But his praise of married women was not limited to the Italians. They should

> preserve the preference
> In *tête à tête* or general conversation. . .
> Because they know the world, and are at ease,
> And being natural, naturally please.
>
> 'Tis true, your budding Miss is very charming,
>   But shy and awkward at first coming out . . .
> The Nursery still lisps out in all they utter —
> Besides, they always smell of bread and butter.
>
> (St. 38–39)

Then he was off full tilt in his comparison of Italy and England:

> With all its sinful doing, I must say,
>   That Italy's a pleasant place to me,
> Who love to see the Sun shine every day. . . .
>   *   *   *   *   *   *   *   *   *   *   *
> Not through a misty morning twinkling weak as
>   A drunken man's dead eye in maudlin sorrow,
> But with all Heaven t'himself; that day will break as
>   Beauteous as cloudless, nor be forced to borrow
> That sort of farthing candlelight which glimmers
> Where reeking London's smoky caldron simmers.

10 Even after he had become the acknowledged *cavalier servente* of the Countess Guiccioli, Byron chafed under the system. He wrote to Hobhouse on Oct. 3, 1819: "I am not tired of Italy, but a man must be a Cicisbeo [slang for *cavalier servente*] and a Singer in duets, and a connoisseur of Operas — or nothing — here. I have made some progress in all these accomplishments, but I can't say that I don't feel the degradation. Better be . . . anything, than a flatterer of fiddlers, and fan carrier of a woman. I like women — God he knows — but the more their system here developes upon me, the worse it seems, after Turkey too; here the *polygamy* is all on the female side." (*Letters and Journals*, IV, 357.) But when he wrote *Beppo* he was still amused at the custom, and thought it less vicious than the clandestine intrigues and hypocrisy of the English.

> I love the language, that soft bastard Latin,
>   Which melts like kisses from a female mouth,
> And sounds as if it should be writ on satin,
>   With syllables which breathe of the sweet South,
> And gentle liquids gliding all so pat in,
>   That not a single accent seems uncouth,
> Like our harsh northern whistling, grunting guttural,
> Which we're obliged to hiss, and spit, and sputter all.
>   (St. 41, 43–44)

Again the strain becomes serious, with an idealization of Italian beauty portrayed by Raphael and Canova. Then he is off on another digression — an ironic praise of England:

> "England! with all thy faults I love thee still,"
>   I said at Calais, and have not forgot it;
> I like to speak and lucubrate my fill;
>   I like the government (but that is not it);
> I like the freedom of the press and quill;
>   I like the Habeas Corpus (when we've got it) . . .
>
> I like the taxes, when they're not too many;
>   I like a seacoal fire, when not too dear;
> I like a beef-steak, too, as well as any;
>   Have no objection to a pot of beer;
> I like the weather, — when it is not rainy,
>   That is, I like two months of every year. . . .
>
> Our standing army, and disbanded seamen,
>   Poor's rate, Reform, my own, the nation's debt . . .
> Our cloudy climate, and our chilly women,
>   All these I can forgive, and those forget,
> And greatly venerate our recent glories,
> And wish they were not owing to the Tories.
>   (St. 47–49)

Then the author with mock-apology pretends to get on with the story (in the fiftieth stanza):

> But to my tale of Laura, — for I find
>   Digression is a sin. . . .

But he gets little further than saying that the Count and Laura "made their new arrangement" and were "As happy as unlawful love could make them," before he is wandering again, on youth and love, on the Carnival, the Ridotto and the fashionable world, which reminds him of the "dynasty of Dandies" in England, and

how the world is lost by love or war. This in turn brings reflections on the fate of Napoleon and on Fortune who rules the lives of men. He brings himself up once more with the exclamation —
"the Devil take it! / This story slips for ever through my fingers."

But Byron had found his métier in the easy conversational digressions, one thing leading to another as naturally and unapologetically as in a letter. He follows Laura through the crowd, but stops to comment on whatever interests or amuses him. Laura observing a Turk staring at her sets the narrator off on the attitudes toward women among the Mussulmans, and this opens up the whole question of women's education, with a pointed satire on the English learned ladies or "Bluestockings." Then Byron voices his contempt for literary coxcombs.

> One hates an author that's *all author* — fellows
>   In foolscap uniforms turned up with ink,
> So very anxious, clever, fine, and jealous,
>   One don't know what to say to them, or think,
> Unless to puff them with a pair of bellows;
>   Of Coxcombry's worst coxcombs e'en the pink
> Are preferable to these shreds of paper,
> These unquenched snuffings of the midnight taper.
>   (St. 75)

Continuing with the ironic account of the deprivations of the Turkish women, he keeps the focus still on England, and ends with a sly gibe at his mathematical wife:

> They stare not on the stars from out their attics,
> Nor deal (thank God for that!) in Mathematics.
>   (St. 78)

Then he confesses with candor:

> I fear I have a little turn for Satire,
>   And yet methinks the older that one grows
> Inclines us more to laugh than scold, though Laughter
> Leaves us doubly serious shortly after.   (St. 79)

When Byron finally returned to the narrative he brought it to a natural conclusion deftly and with little digression. Laura and the Count invite the husband in for coffee, Laura immediately puts her husband in the wrong and returns to henpecking him, but receives him back quite calmly, while he and the Count remain good friends.

In *Beppo* Byron was aware that he had found a congenial medium at last, in that it seemed to give freedom for the expression of all the facets of his mind and emotions. He had some premonitions that, if the public would accept it, he could expand his creative activity immeasurably, though he was probably not completely aware, nor would he have admitted, that it was for him a form more satisfactory than the heroic couplet in which to express his serious views of life as well as his lighter observations of human frailty. The measure of that blindness is that, as we have already observed (Chapter 3, "Popean Satires"), he continued to the end of his writing career to attempt to "moralize his song" in the style of Pope. Later, after he had written several cantos of *Don Juan* and had begun to consider that poem an outlet not only for buffoonery and waggish wit but also for serious satire on modern society, he had the instinctive feeling that this was the style best suited to his talents, in which he could produce his most original contributions to literature, and possibly to poetry. But still he did not abandon his critical allegiance to and emulation of Pope. *Beppo*, however, he never regarded as anything more than a playful satire, designed to shock and amuse like one of his *jeux d'esprit* in his letters to Murray or Moore. And it was a relief from the heavy "sables" that had become his trademark in the minds of the reading public.

Though *Beppo* was written with apparent ease and colloquial abandon, Byron took exceeding care with the phrasing of every line, as is evident in the revisions in the manuscript.[11] The informal style was the result of an art that conceals art. What seemed purely spontaneous in this poem was carefully considered for tone and connotation and exact nuance of phrasing. His revisions show how carefully and almost unerringly he settled after many trial efforts on phrases with apt balance and harmony of sound and meaning, and how often his happiest lines were not achieved on the "first spring." For example, the line "Our cloudy climate — and our chilly women" (stanza 49) had first

[11] For a detailed discussion and analysis of the manuscript revisions of *Beppo*, see "The Devil a Bit of Our *Beppo*," by Truman Guy Steffan, *Philological Quarterly*, XXXII, (1953), 154-171. Steffan has shown that Byron made the most telling changes in the final couplets, which were designed to give a forceful ironic turn or amusing twist to the thought developed in each stanza.

started with the less euphonious "Our smoky chimnies." And the finely balanced line on the Italian Dama's eyes, "Soft as her clime, and sunny as her skies" (stanza 45), began with the less smooth "Like her own Clime — all Sun and fruit — and skies."

While Byron abandoned the Popean couplet in *Beppo*, he employed many of the master's devices in addition to balance in the line. One of the most frequently used, and subtly Byronic in its use, is the satiric juxtaposition of the lofty or sentimentally pretentious with the trivial or prosaically absurd. And Byron adds his own device of facetious rhyme to heighten the effect. We will see even more of Byron's modifications of Pope's technique in *Don Juan*.

13

Don Juan, "A Versified Aurora Borealis"

EARLY IN 1818 Byron was already contemplating another poem in the spirit of *Beppo*.[1] On April 23 he wrote to Murray: "If *Beppo* pleases, you shall have more in a year or two in the same mood."[2] But with the news of that poem's success (it had been published on February 28) he was eager to continue and had begun something in that vein by the middle of the summer. The first hint that he was at work on *Don Juan* comes in a letter of July 10 to Murray: "I have . . . two Stories, one serious and one ludicrous (*à la Beppo*), not yet finished, and in no hurry to be so."[3] But by September 19 he could announce to Moore: "I have finished the first canto (a long one, of about 180 octaves) of a poem in the style and manner of *Beppo*, encouraged by the good success of the same. It is called *Don Juan*, and is meant to be a little quietly facetious upon every thing. But I doubt whether it is not — at least, as far as it has yet gone — too free for these very modest days. However, I shall try the experiment, anonymously; and if it don't take, it will be discontinued."[4]

[1] A large part of this chapter is borrowed or adapted from my Introduction to *Don Juan* in the Riverside Edition (Houghton Mifflin).

[2] *Letters and Journals*, IV, 231.

[3] *Letters and Journals*, IV, 245. Actually the manuscript of what he apparently intended for the beginning of the first canto but which he later labeled the "Dedication" is dated July 3, 1818. (See Steffan and Pratt, *Byron's Don Juan, A Variorum Edition*, II, 8, where a facsimile of the first page of the manuscript is given.)

[4] *Letters and Journals*, IV, 260. As usual he continued adding more stanzas as ideas occurred to him. For Byron a poem was never completed until it was printed, for he was always sending in additional stanzas for

How far Byron had at this time worked out the plan of the poem is indicated partly by what he says in the first canto and partly by the letters he wrote before and after its publication. He makes it clear from the beginning that he had designed it to be a mock-epic. From the first line ("I want a hero . . .") through many a digressive stanza he proclaims his purpose. "Most epic poets plunge *'in medias res'*" but that will not be his method. "My way is to begin with the beginning," he says, and then indicates his tongue-in-cheek attitude by adding, "The regularity of my design / Forbids all wandering as the worst of sinning." And more directly in some added stanzas near the end of the canto he states his pretended epic intentions:

> My poem's epic, and is meant to be
>   Divided in twelve books; each book containing,
> With Love, and War, a heavy gale at sea,
>   A list of ships, and captains, and kings reigning,
> New characters; the episodes are three:
>   A panoramic view of Hell's in training,
> After the style of Virgil and of Homer,
> So that my name of Epic's no misnomer.
>
> All these things will be specified in time,
>   With strict regard to Aristotle's rules,
> The *Vade Mecum* of the true sublime,
>   Which makes so many poets, and some fools:
> Prose poets like blank-verse, I'm fond of rhyme,
>   Good workmen never quarrel with their tools;
> I've got new mythological machinery,
> And very handsome supernatural scenery.
>
> There's only one slight difference between
>   Me and my epic brethren gone before,
> And here the advantage is my own, I ween
>   (Not that I have not several merits more,
> But this will more peculiarly be seen);
>   They so embellish that 't is quite a bore
> Their labyrinth of fables to thread through,
> Whereas this story's actually true.   (I, 200–202)

---

insertion. He had considered the poem completed with 163 stanzas when he dated the manuscript Sept. 6, 1818. (See Steffan and Pratt, II, 148, facsimile.) The first canto finally ran to 222 stanzas, and the Variorum gives eight "rejected" ones.

Byron's insistence on the truth of his story was not wholly facetious. Although the narrative episode which is the basis of the first canto, like that in *Beppo*, was second hand — it was not drawn from his own experience but from that of an acquaintance[5] — the characters, the attitudes, and the feelings were faithfully extracted from his own most poignant memories, almost photographically reproduced. There can be no doubt that the romantic adolescent love of Juan, the self-deceiving Platonism of Julia (who in this bears a striking resemblance to Lady Frances Webster), the character of the learned Donna Inez, an obvious satiric portrait of his wife (with traits of his mother thrown in), to say nothing of the author's own comments in the numerous digressions, were all drawn from the life Byron himself had known most intimately. In fact, he could write effectively no other way. The new poem appealed to him as a medium for telling the truth in poetry in a more transparent way than he had ever attempted before. He insisted on that again and again, both in the poem and in his conversation and letters. "But I hate things *all fiction*," he wrote John Murray. "There should always be some foundation of fact for the most airy fabric, and pure invention is but the talent of a liar."[6] And he told Lady Blessington: ". . . I always write best when truth inspires me, and my satires, which are founded on truth, have more spirit than all my other productions, for they were written *con amore*."[7] And again he wrote Murray: "Almost all *Don Juan* is *real* life, either my own, or from people I knew."[8]

Nor is it wise to dismiss as mere buffoonery Byron's statement of his plans for the poem. Although he obviously did not intend to limit himself to the twelve cantos of the conventional epic, he meant what he said about the episodes involving love and war and a heavy gale at sea, and as for the panoramic view of hell, he later told Murray that he had intended to have Juan end in hell or an unhappy marriage.

When his friends in England protested that, though clever, *Don Juan* could not be published because of its levity in dealing

[5] Byron wrote Hobhouse: ". . . the Julian adventure detailed was none of mine; but one of an acquaintance of mine (*Parolini* by name), which happened some years ago at Bassano, with the Prefect's wife when he was a boy." (*Lord Byron's Correspondence*, II, 101. Letter of Jan. 25, 1819.)

[6] *Letters and Journals*, IV, 93. Letter of April 2, 1817.

[7] Blessington, *Conversations of Lord Byron*, pp. 266–267.

[8] *Letters and Journals*, V, 346. Letter of Aug. 23, 1821.

with serious matters (they were particularly frightened by his references to "the intellectual eunuch Castlereagh" and feared that his satire on Lady Byron would revive the scandals of the separation), Byron replied sometimes apologetically and sometimes truculently. He wrote of it lightly at first as "a work never intended to be serious. Do you suppose that I could have any intention but to giggle and make giggle? — a playful satire, with as little poetry as could be helped, was what I meant. . . ." But at the same time he wrote: "You ask me for the plan of Donny Johnny: I *have* no plan — I *had* no plan; but I had or have materials; though if, like Tony Lumpkin, I am 'to be snubbed so when I am in spirits,' the poem will be naught, and the poet turn serious again . . . if continued, it must be in my own way. You might as well make Hamlet (or Diggory) 'act mad' in a strait waistcoat as trammel my buffoonery, if I am to be a buffoon: their gestures and my thoughts would only be pitiably absurd and ludicrously constrained. Why, Man, the Soul of such writing is its license. . . ."[9]

Though he later defended the poem as a serious satire on "abuses" in society, he continued to value it as an opportunity to voice his random thoughts and playful moods as in conversation. As late as the fifteenth canto he was still justifying his digressions in this manner (and in a style that, despite the rhyme, was strikingly conversational).

> And never straining hard to versify,
> I rattle on exactly as I'd talk
> With anybody in a ride or walk.
>
> I don't know that there may be much ability
>   Shown in this sort of desultory rhyme;
> But there's a conversational facility,
>   Which may round off an hour upon a time.
> Of this I'm sure at least, there's no servility
>   In mine irregularity of chime,
> Which rings what's uppermost of new or hoary,
> Just as I feel the *Improvvisatore*.   (XV, 19–20)

As he continued with the poem and saw the possibilities of its freedom of form, he grew fonder of it and more tenacious in defending it against the objections of his timorous friends in England. "If they had told me the poetry was bad, I would have

[9] *Letters and Journals*, IV, 342–343. Letter of Aug. 12, 1819, to Murray.

acquiesced; but they say the contrary, and then talk to me about morality. . . . I maintain that it is the most moral of poems; but if people won't discover the moral, that is their fault, not mine."[10] This may be taken as evidence that he had, subconsciously at least, accepted the fact that this was his nearest approach to and final substitute for the Popean ideal. That acceptance would go hand in hand with the gradual subsidence of the high and uncompromising Romantic ideal and with the contemplation of the comedy of imperfections which increasingly, though not exclusively, absorbed Byron's interest and literary concern during his Italian sojourn.[11] If circumstances had perforce brought him to compromise with life to the extent of accepting it on its own terms, though with wry and cynical qualifications, he could also compromise albeit with reluctance, with the literary ideal of Popean perfection which had so long been the will-o'-the-wisp of his ambition. He could finally acknowledge that his own natural and uninhibited style was an adequate substitute for the polished forms he had envied.

Perhaps because of his uneasy and slightly guilty feeling that he had abandoned his literary ideal Byron continued to defend *Don Juan* with a certain brash and even bawdy humor as though he was not quite sure of himself. Protesting against what he considered the false delicacy of his English readers, he wrote to Douglas Kinnaird: "As to 'Don Juan,' confess, confess — you dog and be candid — that it is the sublime of *that there* sort of writing — it may be bawdy but is it not good English? It may be profligate but is it not *life*, is it not *the thing*? Could any man have written it who has not lived in the world? — and tooled in a post-chaise? — in a hackney coach? — in a gondola? — against a wall? — in a court carriage? — in a vis à vis? — on a table? — and under it?"[12]

---

[10] *Letters and Journals*, IV, 279. Letter of Feb. 1, 1819, to Murray.

[11] William H. Marshall (*The Structure of Byron's Major Poems*, 1962, p. 23) has made an observation that deserves further exploration: "In the poems written in and after 1816, the poet demonstrated his growing acceptance of imperfection in man's capacities and of disorder in human affairs as the basis for sublimational order in art: in his major poems of the Middle Phase Byron dramatized the ironic situations of those who were essentially unable to reconcile themselves to imperfection." One might quarrel with so precise a date and suggest that Byron frequently slipped back into the earlier phase, but certainly the dominant tone of *Don Juan* is acceptance, sometimes reluctant, of imperfection in human affairs.

[12] *Byron: A Self-Portrait*, ed. Peter Quennell, II, 491. Letter of Oct. 26, 1819. (Corrected from the MS. in the British Museum.)

But his confidence in the poem increased. He wrote more seriously to Murray: "I read over the *Juans*, which are excellent. Your Synod was quite wrong; and so you will find by and bye. I regret that I do not go on with it, for I had all the plan for several cantos, and different countries and climes."[13] He began to consider his purpose as something more than "to giggle and make giggle." He wrote Murray again: "*Don Juan* will be known by and bye, for what it is intended, — a *Satire* on *abuses* of the present states of Society, and not an eulogy of vice: it may be now and then voluptuous: I can't help that. Ariosto is worse; Smollett . . . ten times worse; and Fielding no better. No Girl will ever be seduced by reading *D. J.:* — no, no; she will go to Little's poems and Rousseau's *romans* for that, or even to the immaculate De Stael: they will encourage her, and not the Don, who laughs at that, and — and — most other things."[14] And speaking of the Countess Guiccioli's objections to the poem, he wrote: "The truth is that *it is* TOO TRUE, and the women hate every thing which strips off the tinsel of *Sentiment.* . . ."[15]

And when Murray and others urged him to write a serious epic, some "great work" which would better employ his powers, he replied: "You have so many '*divine*' poems, is it nothing to have written a *Human* one? without any of your worn-out machinery. Why, man, I could have spun the thoughts of the four cantos of that poem into twenty, had I wanted to bookmake, and its passion into as many modern tragedies. Since you want *length*, you shall have enough of *Juan*, for I'll make 50 cantos."[16] His plan was simply to construct a picaresque tale upon which to hang the freest possible commentary on the manners and customs and absurdities of the countries with which he was familiar. "The 5th is so far from being the last of *D. J.*, that it is hardly the beginning," he wrote Murray in February, 1821. "To how many cantos this may extend, I know not, nor whether (even if I live) I shall complete it; but this was my notion: I meant to have made him a *Cavalier Servente* in Italy, and a cause for a divorce in England, and a Sentimental 'Werther-faced man' in Germany, so as to show the different ridicules of the society in each of those countries, and to have displayed him gradually

---

[13] *Letters and Journals*, V, 359. Letter of Sept. 4, 1821.

[14] *Letters and Journals*, VI, 155–156. Letter of Dec. 25, 1822.

[15] *Letters and Journals*, V, 97. Letter of Oct. 12, 1820.

[16] *Letters and Journals*, IV, 284. Letter of April 6, 1819.

gâté and *blasé* as he grew older, as is natural. But I had not quite fixed whether to make him end in Hell, or in an unhappy marriage, not knowing which would be the severest. The Spanish tradition says Hell: but it is probably only an Allegory of the other state."[17]

Glorying in his new freedom, Byron was jealous of any attempts on the part of his friends or his publisher in England to curb his frankness from moral squeamishness or fear for his reputation. "You sha'n't make *Canticles* of my Cantos," he wrote Murray. "The poem will please, if it is lively; if it is stupid, it will fail; but I will have none of your damned cutting and slashing."[18] "Come what may," he wrote again, "I never will flatter the million's canting in any shape. . . ."[19] And later: "*I* know what the World is in England, by my own proper experience of the best of it — at least of the loftiest. And I have described it every where as it is to be found in all places."[20]

Spontaneous as *Don Juan* was, Byron did, despite his protest that he could not furbish, do a considerable amount of polishing and verbal revision, as is apparent in first drafts and even in the printer's copies of his manuscripts. But the changes were fewer as he proceeded, whether from laziness or increased facility it is difficult to say. And often some of his best stanzas seem to have sprung whole from his pen, for they stood with only minor word changes.

He was aware of the uneven quality of his poem, for he wrote defensively: "You say that *one half* is very good: you are *wrong;* for, if it were, it would be the finest poem in existence. *Where* is the poetry of which *one half* is good? is it the Æneid? is it Milton's? is it Dryden's? is it any one's except *Pope's* and Goldsmith's, of which *all* is good? . . . But if *one half* of the two new Cantos be good in your opinion, what the devil would you have more? No — no: no poetry is *generally* good — only by fits and starts — and you are lucky to get a sparkle here and there. You might as well want a Midnight *all stars* as rhyme all perfect."[21]

By following his own genius with abandoned freedom, Byron hit with a crushing blow the poetic conventions, not only of the

[17] *Letters and Journals*, V, 242–243. Letter of Feb. 16, 1821.
[18] *Letters and Journals*, IV, 283. Letter of April 6, 1819.
[19] *Letters and Journals*, IV, 327. Letter of Aug. 1, 1819.
[20] *Letters and Journals*, IV, 427. Letter of March 29, 1820.
[21] *Letters and Journals*, V, 18. Letter of April 23, 1820, to Murray.

eighteenth century, as was the aim of Wordsworth and other Romantics, but also of the nineteenth century. In his break with poetic language Byron did not realize fully what he owed to Wordsworth directly or indirectly. Certainly in *Beppo* and in *Don Juan* he made little distinction between the language of poetry and that of prose. In serious poems, and particularly those using the heroic couplet, he naturally fell into clichés. But in *Don Juan* he found his unique vehicle for the expression of every facet of the Romantic ego in a poetic novel-satire, "a versified Aurora Borealis," that created its own rules and its own artistic unities.

It was inevitable that the kaleidoscopic poem which reflected so clearly every passing mood and thought of the author should be limited by the preoccupations of that one heart and mind. And it is a tribute to Byron's understanding of the general human situation that he so seldom deviated into boredom, even though the major themes are few and frequently repeated: the vanity of ambition (already well-worn in *Childe Harold*), the pretentiousness of poets, his distaste for Tory tyrants and the Holy Alliance, the absurdity of "ladies intellectual," the hypocrisy of "Platonism" in love, the paradoxes of love and marriage, the basic savagery of men striving for self-preservation (the shipwreck), the beauty of "natural love" (Haidée — "Half naked, loving, natural, and Greek"), the hollowness of glory and the brutality of war, the frailty of women and the inconstancy of men, the hypocrisy and boredom of English society, the prevalence of cant in religion, in politics, in education. The intensity and vigor of the satire and the wit, the directness and the honesty of the exposure of sham feelings and conventional poses give life to many episodes and themes hackneyed enough in themselves.

His choice of a hero was a fortunate one. Byron took delight in creating a Don Juan who was not a heartless pursuer and despoiler of women like the legendary character, but a gentle innocent, first seduced by the self-deluding Donna Julia, then engulfed in the "natural love" of the sinless Haidée, repelled and revolted by the imperious commands of the Sultan's favorite, Gulbeyez, who had bought him for her pleasure, passively accepting the caresses of the supple Dudù, essentially unchanged at being swept by circumstances into the position of favorite of Catherine the Great (though Byron allows us to assume that he was becoming more *gâté* and *blasé* as he grew in experience), and finally becoming a detached observer of the intrigues and hypocrisies of the English society into which he was thrown in the last cantos, but ending on the solid breast of "her frolic Grace," the Duchess of Fitz-Fulke.

In general this follows Byron's own concept of his relations with women. Reputed to be a rake and a seducer, he felt himself the most pursued of men. Replying to a distorted story of his abduction of the Countess Guiccioli, he wrote: "I should like to know *who* has been carried off — except poor dear *me*. I have been more ravished myself than any body since the Trojan war. . . ."[22] And to Murray he wrote in 1819: "Your Blackwood accuses me of treating women harshly: it may be so, but I have been their martyr. My whole life has been sacrificed *to* them and *by* them."[23] And in another less obvious sense Byron did identify with his hero: he himself had become a lurid legend, a legend that had been built partly on the facts of his life and partly on what he had written; but underneath Juan was himself, his rational and ideal self which in the exigencies and pressures of real life he could not always be. It is a self-portrait of the personality he believed himself at bottom to be, and this personality was not generally known by the world; at most only some aspects of it would be recognized by those who knew him best.

But Byron's identification with the character he had created for the poem was far from complete; in fact, Don Juan scarcely develops as a personality, for Byron was content to use him as a pawn, a kind of simple norm against which to view the irrationality of the world. So that as a character reflecting striking and recognizable Byronic traits he is much less revealing than the heroes of many of Byron's less realistic poems — the Corsair or Manfred, for example. Because by the conditions he had set for himself in the poem the author could step in to make his own comments in rambling digressions, he was not dependent upon Juan as a spokesman, and used him as such only occasionally. The result was a more detached and objective narrative than is to be found in any of his purely autobiographic poems. Even so Byronic a scene as the one in which Julia at once cuckolds and berates her husband was, as we have seen, not drawn from his own experience.

By creating in Juan a fictional character only slightly built in

[22] *Letters and Journals,* IV, 370. Letter of Oct. 29, 1819, to Richard Belgrave Hoppner.

[23] *Letters and Journals,* IV, 386. Letter of Dec. 10, 1819.

his own image, Byron succeeded in lifting his satire (even that which sprang from very personal concerns such as his preoccupation with that "Princess of Parallelograms," as he called his mathematical wife) to a plane of universality and a tone of good humor. At the same time the poem remains the most intensely personal of all Byron's productions in the direct author's comments of the digressive stanzas.

The poem thus conceived and executed was the most subtle instrument for the rendering of the diapason of Byronic emotions and ideas. The serious is evenly balanced with the facetious, the romantic with the realistic unmasking of sham and hypocrisy and self-deception. Byron did not, as has sometimes been said, abandon Childe Harold entirely when he took up Don Juan. Just as the facetious and satiric vein had continued to flow in his letters and his conversation when the world knew him only as Childe Harold, so now he carried with him into the new poem many of the moods that belonged to that gloomy egoist.

One soon perceives in reading *Don Juan* that many stanzas, save for the meter, might have come from *Childe Harold,* such as several at the end of the first canto beginning:

> No more — no more — Oh! never more on me
> The freshness of the heart can fall like dew.   (I, 214)

Nothing could be more idyllic and romantic, more sympathetic to the softer sentiments of love than the picture of Juan and Haidée, "Nature's bride." And nothing could be more roguishly cynical than the stanzas following the description of this island romance: "I hate inconstancy," etc. In rapid succession "The Isles of Greece" and the reflections following it ("But words are things, and a small drop of ink, / Falling like dew, upon a thought, produces / That which makes thousands, perhaps millions, think") are followed by the satire on Southey, Coleridge, and Wordsworth, which in turn gives way to the sweet and solemn "Ave Maria" digression. Boisterous effervescence stands side by side with the most serious castigation of war or intolerance, and in the main, once we have accepted the genre, though there is little transition, there seems to be no incongruity, for we recognize the voice here as we would in a letter or a conversation. The medley of emotions has enough variety to hold the interest of any reader even moderately sympathetic with Byron's satiric aims.

14

Don Juan, Dedication, Cantos I-IV

ON THE COMPLETION of the first canto of *Don Juan* Byron had written to Moore that the poem was "dedicated to Southey in good, simple, savage verse, upon the Laureat's [sic] politics, and the way he got them."[1] The immediate personal provocation he explained to Hobhouse a little later: "On his [Southey's] return from Switzerland, two years ago, he said that Shelley and I 'had formed a League of Incest, and practised our precepts with, etc.' He lied like a rascal, for they *were not sisters*. . . . The attack contains no allusion to the cause; but some good verses, and all political and poetical."[2]

The political and poetical grievance against Southey and his friends was adequate motivation, for Byron considered them renegades who had deserted their once ardent revolutionary principles to accept posts in the Tory government, and in his view they had grown arrogant in assuming "That Poesy has wreaths for you alone: / There is a narrowness in such a notion, / Which makes me wish you'd change your lakes for Ocean." (Ded., 5)

The satire on both counts is bitter in parts, but two things are remarkable in the "Dedication." The first is that Byron was not too angry to be clever and to have fun in the process of deflating

[1] *Letters and Journals*, IV, 260. Letter of Sept. 19, 1818.

[2] *Lord Byron's Correspondence*, II, 89. Letter of Nov. 11, 1818. In deference to his prudential friends in England Byron agreed to omit a ribald reference to Southey (the "a-dry, Bob" stanza) and the politically dangerous attack on the "intellectual eunuch Castlereagh," and he finally suppressed the "Dedication" altogether because the poem was to be published anonymously: ". . . in that case we will *omit* the dedication to Southey; I won't attack the dog so fiercely without putting my name. . . ." (*Letters and Journals*, IV, 294. Letter of May 6, 1819, to Murray.) The dedication was not published with the poem during Byron's lifetime.

the political and literary characters of the "Lakers." His rhyming "laureate" with "Tory at"; his sly linking of the "Epic Renegade" Southey with Henry James Pye, who had brought ridicule on the laureateship with his fawning bad verses to the royal family; the gibe at Coleridge, "Explaining Metaphysics to the nation — / I wish he would explain his Explanation" (Ded., 2); the reference to Wordsworth's "rather long 'Excursion' / . . . a sample from the vasty version / Of his new system to perplex the sages" (Ded., 4) — all indicate that his savage indignation had not nullified his wit but rather sharpened it. The second remarkable thing in the dedication is that as he went on, though he grew more serious and less witty, he kept a critical balance in his evaluation of the poets whose politics and "systems" he had found offensive:

> You're shabby fellows — true — but poets still,
> And duly seated on the Immortal Hill.   (Ded., 6)

Unlike many of his contemporaries Byron could separate politics and poetic theories from poetry itself; his innate compulsion to preserve the nuances of truth qualified his condemnation even when he was being outrageous, and the qualifications essentially strengthened rather than weakened his attack.

> For me, who, wandering with pedestrian Muses,
>   Contend not with you on the winged steed,
> I wish your fate may yield ye, when she chooses,
>   The fame you envy and the skill you need. . . .
>   (Ded., 8)

The first canto of *Don Juan* is in some respects the best of the cantos. Its gusto, its playful humor and facetious rhymes, the rapier-like satire on the mathematical Annabella in the person of Donna Inez and on the farcical aspects of Juan's education, the romantically tender seduction of Juan by the innocent Platonism of Julia, and the final rollicking bedroom farce, all display Byron at the height of his powers. It is evident here that he had found his métier and that his matured genius was in full bloom. In his deflation of sentiment and pretension he had a congenial subject to work on in the intellectual and moral superiority of Donna Inez. Juan's mother was a learned lady.

> She made the cleverest people quite ashamed,
>   And even the good with inward envy groan,
> Finding themselves so very much exceeded,
>   In their own way, by all the things that she did.
>   (I, 10)

There was sufficient satire in the simple truth, pointed up with occasional homely trivialities, à la Pope, or spiced with double- or triple-syllabled farcical rhyme:

> Her favourite science was the mathematical. . . .
>
> *   *   *   *   *   *   *   *   *   *   *
>
> Her thoughts were theorems, her words a problem,
> As if she deemed that mystery would ennoble 'em. . . .
>
> Some women use their tongues — she *looked* a lecture,
>   Each eye a sermon, and her brow a homily. . . .
>   (I, 12, 13, 15)

And then to cap the climax Byron borrowed a phrase from Pope's *Rape of the Lock* and turned it into something more stinging:

> To others' share let "female errors fall,"
> For she had not even one — the worst of all.   (I, 16)

Byron had already learned how to use outrageous rhyme for satiric purposes:

> In virtues nothing earthly could surpass her,
> Save thine "incomparable oil," Macassar!   (I, 17)

> What men call gallantry, and gods adultery,
> Is much more common where the climate's sultry.
>   (I, 63)

But the audacious rhyme that has become a classic of its kind is

> But — Oh! ye lords of ladies intellectual,
> Inform us truly, have they not hen-pecked you all?
>   (I, 22)

Byron had projected a narrator not himself, a friend of Juan's family, to tell the story, but he soon tired of him as he did of the archaisms and the pretense of a fictional character in *Childe Harold.* Before half the canto was written he had abandoned the fiction and had become himself the narrator; the author and commentator stepped on the stage as often as he pleased. The account of Juan's education is filled with obvious autobiography, though Byron departed from it whenever the temptation to clever satire intrigued him. There is little question that he is thinking of his own childhood when he describes Juan as

> A little curly-headed, good-for-nothing,
>   And mischief-making monkey from his birth;
> His parents ne'er agreed except in doting
>   Upon the most unquiet imp on earth. . . .   (I, 25)

But when he speaks of Juan being educated in the accomplishments of chivalry, it is obviously for the purpose of leading up to the clever climax:

> He learned the arts of riding, fencing, gunnery,
>   And how to scale a fortress — or a nunnery.   (I, 38)

Yet for the most part the account of Juan's education parallels his own and is a commentary on English education in general. No branch of knowledge was made a mystery, "excepting natural history." He was taught

> The languages, especially the dead,
>   The sciences, and most of all the abstruse,
> The arts, at least all such as could be said
>   To be the most remote from common use. . . .

> His classic studies made a little puzzle,
>   Because of filthy loves of gods and goddesses. . . .
>   (I, 40, 41)

The general hypocrisy in dealing with the classics he summed up by reference to a textbook he himself had known:

> Juan was taught from out the best edition,
>   Expurgated by learned men, who place,
> Judiciously, from out the schoolboy's vision,
>   The grosser parts; but, fearful to deface
> Too much their modest bard by this omission,
>   And pitying sore his mutilated case,
> They only add them all in an appendix,
> Which saves, in fact, the trouble of an index. . . .
>   (I, 44)

Byron gave his side of the separation story too with a disarming humor that belied the bitterness which still lurked at the bottom of his mind. Inez

> tried to prove her loving lord was *mad*,
> But as he had some lucid intermissions,
>   She next decided he was only *bad*. . . .

*   *   *   *   *   *   *   *   *   *

> Calmly she heard each calumny that rose,
> And saw *his* agonies with such sublimity,
> That all the world exclaimed, "What magnanimity!"
>   (I, 27, 29)

Although Byron said that the story of Juan and Julia was founded on the experience of an acquaintance, the details of the glowing adolescent love pangs of Juan are drawn with detachment and tenderness from his own memory. There is perhaps no finer example in *Don Juan*, or anywhere in Byron's poetry, of his consummate skill in balancing and blending critical analysis and feeling, in looking at the same experience from both the inside and the outside with sympathy, understanding, and amused tolerance. Here is an exemplification of Professor Lovell's statement that Byron's modernity consists of his setting up "a state of tension between the complexities of several points of view. This deliberate use of ambiguity saves him, as it does many a modern poet, from sentimentalism. . . ."[3]

Juan mooning in the lonely wood with feelings unknown to himself and inexpressible brings forth from the author amused comments on the nature poets and a sly reference to Wordsworth when he becomes "unintelligible."

> he did the best he could
> With things not very subject to control,
> And turned, without perceiving his condition,
> Like Coleridge, into a metaphysician.
>
> He thought about himself, and the whole earth,
> Of man the wonderful, and of the stars . . .
> How many miles the moon might have in girth,
> Of air-balloons, and of the many bars
> To perfect knowledge of the boundless skies; —
> And then he thought of Donna Julia's eyes. . . .
> *   *   *   *   *   *   *   *   *   *   *
> If *you* think 't was philosophy that this did,
> I can't help thinking puberty assisted.   (I, 91–93)

But in another mood he knew that Wordsworth was right. Nature does have power to solace the spirit, as he himself had given acknowledgment in *Childe Harold*. And he knew above all else that adolescent first love could be both ridiculous and

---

[3] Ernest J. Lovell, Jr., *Byron: The Record of a Quest*, 1949, p. 235.

beautiful. For Byron particularly it became the symbol and the core of the romantic ideal dream. However lightly he may speak, there is an undertone of nostalgic sympathy in the picture of Juan.

> Thus would he while his lonely hours away
>   Dissatisfied, not knowing what he wanted;
> Nor glowing reverie, nor poet's lay,
>   Could yield his spirit that for which it panted,
> A bosom whereon he his head might lay,
>   And hear the heart beat with the love it granted,
> With — several other things, which I forget,
> Or which, at least, I need not mention yet.   (I, 96)

Though he ridicules more mercilessly the self-deceiving Platonism of Donna Julia, he is inclined to give understanding and sympathy to the "natural feelings" of the young wife of an old husband. After all it is Platonism rather than Julia which gets the trouncing.

> Oh Plato! Plato! you have paved the way,
>   With your confounded fantasies, to more
> Immoral conduct by the fancied sway
>   Your system feigns o'er the controlless core
> Of human hearts, than all the long array
>   Of poets and romancers: — You're a bore,
> A charlatan, a coxcomb — and have been,
> At best, no better than a go-between.   (I, 116)

As for Julia's situation, it is at once humorous and pathetic. Byron has infused the objective picture of her hypocrisy with a tolerant sympathy for her frailty. It is the sympathy of one who has learned to accept human imperfections with a wry smile rather than in the agony of despair.

> A little still she strove, and much repented,
> And whispering "I will ne'er consent" — consented.
>   (I, 117)

In the bedroom farce that follows, Byron has made Julia somewhat less innocent and more calculating, and hypocritical without shame in putting her husband in the wrong while hiding Juan in her bed. But he has somewhat prepared the way in his digressive comments on human nature.

> Sweet is revenge — especially to women —
> Pillage to soldiers, prize-money to seamen.

> Sweet is a legacy, and passing sweet
>   The unexpected death of some old lady,
> Or gentleman of seventy years complete,
>   Who've made "us youth" wait too — too long already....
>
> But sweeter still than this, than these, than all,
>   Is first and passionate Love — it stands alone,
> Like Adam's recollection of his fall;
>   The Tree of Knowledge has been plucked — all's known —
> And Life yields nothing further to recall
>   Worthy of this ambrosial sin, so shown,
> No doubt in fable, as the unforgiven
> Fire which Prometheus filched for us from Heaven.
>   (I, 124–125, 127)

Discovered and disgraced, Julia again becomes a sympathetic character. Her farewell letter, sentimental and ridiculous — "written upon gilt-edged paper. . . . The wax was superfine, its hue vermillion" — is yet sincere and true.

Then the author steps in with some exuberant mockery about his epic, following this with new gibes at Wordsworth, Coleridge, Southey, "Because the first is crazed beyond all hope, / The second drunk, the third so quaint and mouthy," and his farcical boast that poor Roberts, the editor, took seriously: "I've bribed my Grandmother's Review, the British."

The moods change, like quicksilver, from comic to serious, and end in irony:

> But now at thirty years my hair is grey....
> I thought of a peruke the other day ...
>   I
> Have spent my life, both interest and principal,
> And deem not, what I deemed — my soul invincible.
>   (I, 213)

And then for two stanzas he is back unapologetically in the full mood of *Childe Harold*:

> No more — no more — Oh! never more, my heart,
>   Canst thou be my sole world, my universe! ...
> The illusion's gone for ever, and thou art
>   Insensible, I trust, but none the worse,
> And in thy stead I've got a deal of judgment,
> Though heaven knows how it ever found a lodgment.
>   (I, 215)

However high he may soar in sentiment, the temptation is always great to return to earth in the final couplet. But the moods melted one into another as naturally in his poetry as they did in his life. After some rueful reflections on ambition he sums up in another Childe Haroldish stanza:

> What is the end of Fame? . . .
> Some liken it to climbing up a hill,
>   Whose summit, like all hills, is lost in vapour;
> For this men write, speak, preach, and heroes kill,
>   And bards burn what they call their "midnight taper,"
> To have, when the original is dust,
> A name, a wretched picture and worse bust.   (I, 218)

But then he carries the *sic transit* theme back into comic irony with the reference to "Old Egypt's King Cheops."

The "seasick" scene that comes at the beginning of the second canto is a typical example of Byron's ironic method of deflating fine sentiment with a Swiftian realism of physical detail without either Swift's morbid revulsion at the necessary anatomical functions or his contempt for or renunciation of the feeling that gave rise to the sentiment. The scene begins with Juan's farewell to Spain as he sets out from Cadiz, which may be compared with Childe Harold's farewell to England. The latter shares the general mawkishness of other passages in the first canto of *Childe Harold;* whereas in *Don Juan* the hero is seen objectively though sympathetically as the victim of the indignities of nature which relentlessly intrude on ideal sentiments and visions.

The author, instead of suffering with the victim, indulges in amused detachment and commentary. Juan had just taken out Julia's letter and read it over again swearing that he could never forget her.

> "Sooner shall this blue ocean melt to air
>   Sooner shall Earth resolve itself to sea,
> Than I resign thine image, oh, my fair!
>   Or think of anything, excepting thee;
> A mind diseased no remedy can physic —"
> (Here the ship gave a lurch, and he grew sea-sick).
>   (II, 19)

Once seeing the possibilities of this farce, Byron carried it farther, for he easily succumbed to the temptation to shock delicate sensibilities:

"Sooner shall heaven kiss earth — (here he fell sicker)
  Oh, Julia! what is every other woe? —
(For God's sake let me have a glass of liquor;
  Pedro, Battista, help me down below.)
Julia, my love! — (you rascal, Pedro, quicker) —
  Oh, Julia! — (this curst vessel pitches so) —
Beloved Julia, hear me still beseeching!"
(Here he grew inarticulate with retching.)   (II, 20)

Then the author points up the experience in his own way:

Love's a capricious power. . . .
Against all noble maladies he's bold,
  But vulgar illnesses don't like to meet,
Nor that a sneeze should interrupt his sigh,
Nor inflammations redden his blind eye.

But worst of all is nausea, or a pain
  About the lower region of the bowels; . . .
And purgatives are dangerous to his reign,
  Sea-sickness death. . . .   (II, 22, 23)

In general the formula for tearing the mask from the face of pretension and sentiment — things are not what they seem: look! — is Swiftian, but the tone and final effect are different. Man is not to be bitterly condemned for allowing his fancy to get "astride of his reason" and kicking common sense out of doors. Rather he is the victim of the "clay-cold bond" that limits his spirit in its aspirations for an ideal world, and in his struggle to free himself from the clay, or in his pretense that it doesn't exist, he is often at the same time ridiculous and pathetic and he does not lose our sympathy. Byron could be as shocking as Swift in revealing the basic savagery of men under stress, as in the shipwreck scene that follows, but he never quite pictured them as Yahoos.

What shocked his contemporaries was not so much the horrific details of the suffering and the frailties of the men, including the cannibalism (almost all of which came, sometimes verbatim, out of travel books such as his "grand-dad's 'Narrative' ") as it was the light detachment and humor of the account.

There's nought, no doubt, so much the spirit calms
  As rum and true religion: thus it was,
Some plundered, some drank spirits, some sung psalms,
  The high wind made the treble, and as bass

> The hoarse harsh waves kept time; fright cured the qualms
>   Of all the luckless landsmen's sea-sick maws:
> Strange sounds of wailing, blasphemy, devotion,
> Clamoured in chorus to the roaring ocean.   (II, 34)

What was particularly revolting to fastidious readers was Byron's mingling of realistic details (told with matter-of-fact calmness) and humorous rather than moralizing comment. The ironies are piled one on another. Julia's letter, symbol of love and unselfish feeling which Juan had preserved through the shipwreck, was taken from him, torn up, and used for drawing lots to determine whose flesh should feed the others. And the lot fell to Pedrillo, Juan's pious tutor who had been kept from the rum kegs only by Juan's pistol. Pedrillo accepted his fate and requested that he be bled to death.

> And first a little crucifix he kissed,
> And then held out his jugular and wrist.
>
> The surgeon, as there was no other fee,
>   Had his first choice of morsels for his pains;
> But being thirstiest at the moment, he
>   Preferred a draught from the fast-flowing veins:
> Part was divided, part thrown in the sea,
>   And such things as the entrails and the brains
> Regaled two sharks, who followed o'er the billow —
> The sailors ate the rest of poor Pedrillo.   (II, 76–77)

But still we have Juan as the norm of human behavior against which to view these enormities. It was he who, when the ship was foundering, used a pistol to keep the men away from the rum while he admonished them: "let us die like men, not sink below / Like brutes."

Juan, though famished like the rest, refused to join the cannibals (and thereby saved his life, for many of those who gorged themselves on Pedrillo died in spasms). And amid all the horror and bestiality there is the picture of the father and his dying son in the longboat, told with sympathy but without sentimentality. Byron was aware, however, that he had gone out of his way to shock his readers. His defense was the one he usually employed in replying to attacks on *Don Juan*, the example of great writers of the past:

And if Pedrillo's fate should shocking be,
   Remember Ugolino condescends
To eat the head of his arch-enemy
   The moment after he politely ends
His tale: if foes be food in Hell, at sea
   'T is surely fair to dine upon our friends,
When Shipwreck's short allowance grows too scanty,
Without being much more horrible than Dante.

                                       (II, 83)

Thus far Byron had kept the narrative flowing with few interruptions, though he reserved the right to inject his own reminiscences, personality, and opinions at will. We are always conscious that it is Byron talking, and as this is a conversational poem he takes the liberties of conversation. His egotistic recollections and commentary require as little apology as they would in spirited talk among friends. In commenting on Don Juan's swimming prowess in reaching the shore when all the others perished, he adds:

   He could, perhaps, have passed the Hellespont,
     As once (a feat on which ourselves we prided)
   Leander, Mr. Ekenhead, and I did.   (II, 105)

And when he was describing the beauty of Haidée he said she was one

   Fit for the model of a statuary
     (A race of mere imposters, when all's done —
   I've seen much finer women, ripe and real,
   Than all the nonsense of their stone ideal).   (II, 118)

The fact that he here seemed to contradict directly what he had said in *Childe Harold* ("Where are the forms the sculptor's soul hath seized? / In him alone. Can Nature show so fair?" IV, 122) did not seem to bother him. Perhaps it was a measure of his acceptance of the real world that he was now willing to mold his ideal out of the clay rather than the cold marble.

   The idyllic love episode of Juan and Haidée on their Greek island points up both Byron's adherence to the ideal of innocence and the still unresolved conflict in his mind between the demands of the real and the ideal. He pictures Haidée with more warmth of approval than he lavished on any other heroine in his poetry. She was unsophisticated, innocent, a Noble Savage. She was "Nature's bride," devoid of the affectations and pretensions of women in civilized society. In the midst of this idyllic world there are intrusions of reality, but they are the author's intrusions of comment and reflection. Byron does not allow the ideal love itself to be corrupted; that is why Haidée must die young and Juan must be propelled by fate and Lambro into new adventures. Byron's half cynical comments on the side do not serve to denigrate, and are not intended to annul, the ideal love of Juan and Haidée but are consonant with the author's penchant for seeing several facets of every situation and emotional state at the same time. He is straightforward in his narrative ("I hate all mystery, and that air / Of clap-trap, which your recent poets prize") and when he introduces the piratical Lambro, Haidée's father, he does not take the trouble to build up dramatic premonition but lets the reader construct his own concept of trouble to come. And he makes sport of the classical comparison which was a part of the "clap-trap" of recent poets.

Haidée's teaching Juan her language awakens fond memories in the author.

> 'T is pleasing to be schooled in a strange tongue
>> By female lips and eyes . . .
>> As was the case, at least, where I have been;
> They smile so when one's right, and when one's wrong
>> They smile still more, and then there intervene
> Pressure of hands, perhaps even a chaste kiss; —
> I learned the little that I know by this:
>
> That is, some words of Spanish, Turk, and Greek,
>> Italian not at all, having no teachers. . . .
>>>>>> (II, 164, 165)

And then we are suddenly aware that Byron has slyly put on the mask of a fictional narrator, for it was precisely from female teachers that he learned Italian, with a Venetian accent! But on second glance we see it is still Byron with tongue in cheek, for he continues:

> Much English I cannot pretend to speak,
>> Learning that language chiefly from its preachers . . .
> I hate your poets, so read none of those.   (II, 165)

Without the intrusion of any facetiae but also without any mawkish sentimentality, Byron builds up the picture of a natural romantic love to its consummation and afterglow (Haidée watching her sleeping lover in her arms) with a skill that must command admiration. It is only after he has left the happy pair in their cave that the author returns to the less idyllic world and indulges in some reflections on women forced on him by his own experience.

> Some take a lover, some take drams or prayers . . .
> Some play the devil, and then write a novel.
>
> (II, 201)

But these observations belong to the civilized world and could not apply to the island paradise where love was uncorrupted.

> Haidée was Nature's bride, and knew not this;
>   Haidée was Passion's child, born where the Sun
> Showers triple light, and scorches even the kiss
>   Of his gazelle-eyed daughters; she was one
> Made but to love, to feel that she was his
>   Who was her chosen. . . .
>
> And now 't was done — on the lone shore were plighted
>   Their hearts; the stars, their nuptial torches, shed
> Beauty upon the beautiful they lighted:
>   Ocean their witness, and the cave their bed,
> By their own feelings hallowed and united,
>   Their priest was Solitude, and they were wed:
> And they were happy — for to their young eyes
> Each was an angel, and earth Paradise.   (II, 202, 204)

And yet Byron knew that this ideal natural love was a dream and he must perforce return to the actual world, however reluctantly, for it was a dream drawn with loving care from the deepest romantic longings of his youth and that was why in itself it must be left inviolate. It is perfectly clear that his cynical and worldly-wise observations do not belong to that locked-in dream. But Byron's commentary belongs to the whole of life, and he cannot suppress what he has known and what he has seen.

> Oh, Love! of whom great Caesar was the suitor,
>   Titus the master, Antony the slave. . . .
>
> Thou mak'st the chaste connubial state precarious,
>   And jestest with the brows of mightiest men. . . .
>
> (II, 205–206)

Love makes philosophers too. And while he is philosophizing he might as well open up a question that may have been puzzling his readers:

> But Juan! had he quite forgotten Julia?
> And should he have forgotten her so soon?

It is a "perplexing question," and he facetiously blames the moon,

> Else how the devil is it that fresh features
> Have such a charm for us poor human creatures?
>
> (II, 208)

It is the first questioning of that primal uncorrupted self which Juan in part is, a recognition that even the uncorrupted part shares with the sophisticated the taint of the flesh and the weight of the clay. Byron is as serious as he is facetious in his wail:

> I hate inconstancy — I loathe, detest,
>   Abhor, condemn, abjure the mortal made
> Of such quicksilver clay that in his breast
>   No permanent foundation can be laid;
> Love, constant love, has been my constant guest,
>   And yet last night, being at a masquerade,
> I saw the prettiest creature, fresh from Milan,
> Which gave me some sensations like a villain.
>
> But soon Philosophy came to my aid,
>   And whispered, "Think of every sacred tie!"
> "I will, my dear Philosophy!" I said,
>   "But then her teeth, and then, oh, Heaven! her eye!
> I'll just inquire if she be wife or maid,
>   Or neither — out of curiosity."
> "Stop!" cried Philosophy, with an air so Grecian
> (Though she was masqued then as a fair Venetian;)
>
> "Stop!" so I stopped — But to return: that which
>   Men call inconstancy is nothing more
> Than admiration due where Nature's rich
>   Profusion with young beauty covers o'er
> Some favoured object. . . .
>
> * * * * * * * * *
>
> In short, it is the use of our own eyes,
> With one or two small senses added, just
> To hint that flesh is formed of fiery dust.

> Yet 't is a painful feeling, and unwilling,
>   For surely if we always could perceive
> In the same object graces quite as killing
>   As when she rose upon us like an Eve,
> 'T would save us many a heartache, many a shilling,
>   (For we must get them anyhow or grieve),
> Whereas if one sole lady pleased for ever,
> How pleasant for the heart, as well as liver!
>
> (II, 209–213)

The true Romantic did hate inconstancy; it was the negation of his dream of ideal love and evidence of a human frailty that was intolerable to the romantic idealist. That the romantic ego was still dominant in Byron is indicated by the serious conclusion:

> The Heart is like the sky, a part of Heaven . . .
>   Its storms expire in water-drops; the eye
> Pours forth at last the Heart's blood turned to tears,
> Which make the English climate of our years.
>
> (II, 214)

The metaphor in the last line is as felicitous as it is unexpected. It is the kind of richly connotative phrase that makes *Don Juan* more quotable than anything else Byron wrote.

His contempt for even the mock-forms of the epic he had begun is expressed in the first line of the third canto: "Hail, Muse! *et cetera.*" Having established the pattern of his show, he could improvise as he wished. He had a like contempt for verisimilitude in the story. When he said "This story's actually true," he meant the truth of character and motivations rather than the "clap-trap" of situation and probability. It did not bother him that he had to stretch credulity considerably to have the longboat drift from the Gulf of Lyons, where the ship sank, to an island in the Cyclades without the sailors seeing any land between. On the other hand, he prided himself on the accuracy of setting and background. When he borrowed details he acknowledged his sources and generally added distinguishing touches of his own, as in the account of the shipwreck and in the description of the furniture of Lambro's palace. He told Murray that much of the latter was "taken from *Tully's Tripoli* (pray *note this*), and the rest from my own observation. Remember, I never meant to conceal this at all, and have only not stated it, because *Don Juan* had no preface nor name to it." As to charges of plagiary, he added, "*I* laugh at such charges, convinced that no writer ever borrowed less, or made his materials more his own."[4]

The observations on love and marriage which open the third canto were intended in part to point up by contrast the idyllic natural marriage of Juan and Haidée, but more particularly the picture of "Nature's bride" has opened the way for the expression of some homely truths that were deeply imprinted in Byron's mind. And in truth he could not but suggest that even this ideal and innocent love had the seeds of its own destruction inherent in it. At best love was "a foe to rest." The cynicism which follows runs the gamut of all the moods from serious to comic and leaves an after-taste not so much of bitterness as of sympathy for the human condition.

> In her first passion Woman loves her lover,
>   In all the others all she loves is Love . . .
>   One man alone at first her heart can move;
> She then prefers him in the plural number,
> Not finding that the additions much encumber. . . .
>
> 'T is melancholy, and a fearful sign
>   Of human frailty, folly, also crime,
> That Love and Marriage rarely can combine,
>   Although they both are born in the same clime;
> Marriage from Love, like vinegar from wine —
>   A sad, sour, sober beverage — by Time
> Is sharpened from its high celestial flavour
> Down to a very homely household savour.
>
> *   *   *   *   *   *   *   *   *
>
> Think you, if Laura had been Petrarch's wife,
> He would have written sonnets all his life?
>
> *   *   *   *   *   *   *   *   *
>
> But Dante's Beatrice and Milton's Eve
> Were not drawn from their spouses, you conceive.
>   (III, 3, 5, 8, 10)

It is true that Haidée after her "natural marriage" has become just a little more cunning, like Eve after eating the forbidden fruit. Though still innocent, she has managed to take advantage of her papa's absence to spend his substance rather lavishly in celebration of her nuptials close upon the false report of her father's

---

[4] *Letters and Journals*, V, 346–347. Letter of Aug. 23, 1821.

death. The halo of first love still hovers over the pair while they seek oblivion in each other's embraces, but they now recline on red velvet cushions instead of the hard floor of the cave, and the devil (in the person of the author) laughs a little quietly in the distance.

The return of Lambro the pirate-father, that "sea-solicitor," who was modeled in part on Ali Pacha ("He was the mildest mannered man / That ever scuttled ship or cut a throat"), has rightly been admired as one of the finest episodes in the poem. The very epithet applied to Lambro suggests that his profession was no more vicious or avaricious than that of many who enjoy social approval.

> Let not his mode of raising cash seem strange,
>   Although he fleeced the flags of every nation,
> For into a Prime Minister but change
>   His title, and 't is nothing but taxation. . . .
>   (III, 14)

Byron further excused him by making him a patriot Greek:

> He was a man of a strange temperament,
>   Of mild demeanour though of savage mood . . .
> His Country's wrongs and his despair to save her
> Had stung him from a slave to an enslaver.   (III, 53)

His fatherly feelings make him still more of a sympathetic character. But underneath we see his unforgiving qualities hardening as he perceives the wasting of his substance by his followers and his daughter.

In the meantime we return to Juan and Haidée, resting their feet on crimson satin and Persian carpets, dining at an ivory inlaid table spread with a hundred dishes. Now they were diverted by "Dwarfs, dancing girls, black eunuchs, and a poet." It is indicative again of the slight value Byron placed on the "machinery" of his narrative or the contradictions in it that he should have made this poet, a turncoat like Southey, the inditer and singer of "The Isles of Greece" which he wanted to insert at this point. The probability is that, having suppressed the cutting "Dedication" to Southey, he could not resist the opportunity offered by a "court poet" for a few gibes at his arch-enemy. Being paid "to satirize or flatter,"

> now he sung the Sultan and the Pacha —
> With truth like Southey, and with verse like Crashaw.
>
> (III, 79)

But Byron qualifies this by saying that he had genius, and though "a sad trimmer" he was "In company a very pleasant fellow." Moreover, he is given a kind of excuse for reciting this "National Air" because,

> having picked up several odds and ends
> Of free thoughts in his travels for variety,
>   He deemed, being in a lone isle, among friends,
> That, without any danger of a riot, he
>   Might for long lying make himself amends. . . .
>
> (III, 83)

Another reason for this deprecating ambiguity in introducing his fine lyric may well have been his tendency to qualify with a self-defensive gesture of ridicule whatever he felt most deeply. This has been remarked as a characteristic gesture which occurs again and again in *Don Juan*. Andrew Rutherford has seen its origins in Byron's childhood (the uneven temper of his mother and his sensitivity to his lameness) and in his associations with a cynical society, reinforced by his own "eighteenth-century distrust of uncontrolled emotion or enthusiasm." Rutherford concludes: ". . . at times one can see Byron's social-personal defence mechanism working in *Don Juan* as he draws back mockingly from the emotion which he has evoked, not because of any falsity or baseness in the emotion, but because he feels he has revealed too much of his deepest feelings — he has exposed himself to the danger of ridicule, which he forestalls by sneering or laughing himself, and momentarily discrediting the values which he has himself established."[5]

But certainly the opposite, or complementary, habit is just as prevalent in *Don Juan*. No sooner has Byron ridiculed something than he turns to its serious side. He laughs that he may not weep, and once he has had his fun he is likely to be doubly serious the day after. Commenting on the song of the equivocal poet ("The Isles of Greece") he says:

> His strain displayed some feeling — right or wrong;
>   And feeling, in a poet, is the source
> Of others' feeling. . . .

[5] *Byron, A Critical Study*, 1961, pp. 163, 165.

And with his eye still on the "trimmer-poet" he adds:

> but they are such liars,
> And take all colours — like the hands of dyers.
>
> (III, 87)

But then he turns deadly serious and speaks his own convictions:

> But words are things, and a small drop of ink,
>   Falling like dew, upon a thought, produces
> That which makes thousands, perhaps millions, think; ...
>   to what straits old Time reduces
> Frail man, when paper — even a rag like this,
> Survives himself, his tomb, and all that's his!
>
> (III, 88)

Another digression on digressions (he leaves his people to proceed alone, "While I soliloquize beyond expression: / But these are my addresses from the throne, / Which put off business to the ensuing session") leads to a discussion of what the French call "*longueurs*" ("We've not so good a *word*, but have the *thing*") and culminates in the example of Wordsworth's "Peter Bell":

> We learn from Horace, "Homer sometimes sleeps";
>   We feel without him, — Wordsworth sometimes wakes. ...
>
> (III, 98)

He pretends he is returning to the story again, but he has no intention of continuing the narrative in this canto. Juan and Haidée left alone after the feasting admire the twilight sky and that sets him off on another tack, a mood inspired by his evening rides with the Countess Guiccioli in the Pineta near Ravenna. The "Ave Maria" stanzas, associating the hour of prayer with the hour of love, are followed by a proclamation of his sentimental deism. The "Sweet Hour of Twilight!", "The shrill cicalas, people of the pine," and "Hesperus!" maintain the mood almost to the end of the canto, when he recoils from "this tediousness" as "being *too* epic."

When Byron opened the fourth canto with the statement that there is "Nothing so difficult as a beginning," he was speaking literal truth. He hated conventional openings and wriggled a good deal to avoid them. He sometimes took refuge in persiflage that had an undertone of seriousness and always expressed a feeling that was honest, even if only momentarily so. Looking back now on the rhetorical flights of the last canto that had lifted natural

love to a romantic pinnacle, he feels that he may have been
guilty of hubris,

> For oftentimes when Pegasus seems winning
> The race, he sprains a wing, and down we tend,
> Like Lucifer when hurled from Heaven for sinning;
> Our sin the same, and hard as his to mend. . . .
>
> (IV, 1)

Then follows some outright autobiography:

> Now my sere Fancy "falls into the yellow
> Leaf," and Imagination droops her pinion,
> And the sad truth which hovers o'er my desk
> Turns what was once romantic to burlesque.
>
> And if I laugh at any mortal thing,
> 'T is that I may not weep; and if I weep,
> 'T is that our nature cannot always bring
> Itself to apathy. . . .   (IV, 3, 4)

He is more sensitive about the accusation of being "*very*" fine"
than of having "a strange design / Against the creed and morals
of the land,"

> But the fact is that I have nothing planned,
> Unless it were to be a moment merry —
> A novel word in my vocabulary.   (IV, 5)

Returning to Juan and Haidée, he took up the theme he had
touched on before and elaborated it: "they could not be / Meant
to grow old, but die in happy Spring, / Before one charm or hope
had taken wing." It is the theme of the Thyrza poems.

> "Whom the gods love die young," was said of yore,
> And many deaths do they escape by this. . . .
>   perhaps the early grave
> Which men weep over may be meant to save.
>
> (IV, 12)

Yet the dream of ideal young love has a beauty of its own un-
tarnished by the knowledge that in real life it cannot last. The
author is not taking a superior attitude when he says that Juan
and Haidée are children still,

> But like two beings born from out a rill,
>   A nymph and her belovèd, all unseen
> To pass their lives in fountains and on flowers,
> And never know the weight of human hours.
>
> (IV, 15)

But in telling the story of this ideal pair Byron escapes both melodramatic sentiment and the hectic revolt against the conditions of life that made Childe Harold and Manfred beat their heads against the hard rock of human limitations. He could content himself with the comment that their story was "what we mortals call romantic, / And always envy, though we deem it frantic." (IV, 18)

Cold reality inevitably obtrudes when Haidée wakens from her uneasy dream to face her steely-eyed father. The warm-blooded Juan snatches his sabre, but finds himself looking into the barrel of Lambro's cocked pistol. And that brings to mind Byron's several near experiences of fighting a duel (he was always saved by his cooler-headed friends):

> It has a strange quick jar upon the ear,
>   That cocking of a pistol, when you know
> A moment more will bring the sight to bear
>   Upon your person, twelve yards off, or so. . . .
>
> (IV, 41)

Juan is left wounded after a valiant struggle and is carried away to a slave ship before the author becomes pathetic, "Moved by the Chinese nymph of tears, green tea!" He then turns back unapologetically to the sad end of Haidée, who died lingeringly of a broken heart, holding within her "A second principle of Life, which might / Have dawned a fair and sinless child of sin." The pathos of Haidée's death is unalloyed by any flippancy, for she was above all his other heroines the embodiment of his youthful ideals of innocence, beauty, and tenderness. She was, more than Theresa Macri (with whom he was disillusioned) the Maid of Athens, whom he had found not in the living flesh but rather in the song of "The Fair Haidée," which he translated before he left Greece and which he mentions in stanza 73.

This episode closed, Byron returned to the light vein and followed Juan's adventures with scarcely a look behind. It is significant that he does not allow himself to sentimentalize over Juan's loss and desolation as he had over Haidée's. It is true we

are told casually that when Juan came to himself off the shores
of Ilion he did not take much pleasure in the sight, "Another
time he might have liked to see 'em, / But now was not much
pleased with Cape Sigeum." But no mention is made of Haidée
and there is no dwelling on Juan's grief, while the author proceeds
to tell with some zest what he had seen at the site of Troy. We
next find Juan conversing with some fellow prisoners, a troop
of Italian singers.

Without doubt Byron had intended in due time to bring Juan
to Italy, for he had much prime material to furnish out his
adventures there. In the meantime he could not resist the opportunity to bring in some spicy details concerning the theatrical
characters he had known in Venice. In fact, it was fresh material
very much in his mind, for he had been in the midst of intrigues
with some of these singers and figurantes not long before he
wrote the canto. When the prisoners were paired off for the
slave market, Byron took delight in having Juan linked with "a
Bacchante blooming visage," a Romagnole whom he described
as having some of the qualities of the Countess Guiccioli, "With
eyes that looked into the very soul," and a "Great wish to
please." But all her power was wasted on Juan, for nothing
"Could stir his pulse, or make his faith feel brittle; / Perhaps his
recent wounds might help a little."

Byron had an excellent opportunity here to add some titillating
details to shock the English, but he had learned the value of
innuendo and preferred instead to twit his readers on their moral
squeamishness. Before he sent in the third and fourth cantos he
wrote Murray that he doubted that they "ought to be published,
for they have not the Spirit of the first: the outcry has not
frightened but it has *hurt* me, and I have not written *con amore*
this time."[6] And he bared his feelings precisely in the poem:

> Here I might enter on a chaste description,
>   Having withstood temptation in my youth,
> But hear that several people take exception
>   At the first two books having too much truth;
> Therefore I'll make Don Juan leave the ship soon,
>   Because the publisher declares, in sooth,
> Through needles' eyes it easier for the camel is
> To pass, than those two cantos into families.

(IV, 97)

[6] *Letters and Journals*, IV, 402. Letter of Feb. 7, 1820.

One penalty for depicting the passions in their true colors was that he had lost the "imprimatur" of the women. He had written to Hoppner after the first two cantos were published: "There has been an eleventh commandment to the women not to read it — and what is still more extraordinary they seem not to have broken it. But that can be of little import to them, poor things, for the reading or non-reading a book will never keep down a single petticoat. . . ."[7] And he spoke as slightingly of that patronage in the poem:

> What! can I prove "a lion" then no more?
>   A ball-room bard, a foolscap, hot-press darling?
> To bear the compliments of many a bore,
>   And sigh, "I can't get out," like Yorick's starling;
> Why then I'll swear, as poet Wordy swore
>   (Because the world won't read him, always snarling),
> That Taste is gone, that Fame is but a lottery,
> Drawn by the blue-coat misses of a coterie.
>
> (IV, 109)

And so the canto leaves Juan in the slave market at Constantinople awaiting his fate while watching the honest Turks bartering for the virgins.

[7] *Byron: A Self-Portrait,* ed. Peter Quennell, II, 493. Letter of Oct. 29, 1819.

15

Don Juan, Cantos V-X

BYRON BEGAN the fifth canto with some flippant stanzas on amorous writing intended to prepare the way for the scenes in the seraglio.

> When amatory poets sing their loves
>   In liquid lines mellifluously bland,
> And pair their rhymes as Venus yokes her doves,
>   They little think what mischief is in hand;
> The greater their success the worse it proves,
>   As Ovid's verse may give to understand;
> Even Petrarch's self, if judged with due severity,
> Is the Platonic pimp of all posterity.
>
> I therefore do denounce all amorous writing,
>   Except in such a way as not to attract;
> Plain — simple — short, and by no means inviting,
>   But with a moral to each error tacked. . . .
>
> (V, 1–2)

In the slave market Byron introduces a rather unusual character, an English soldier of fortune, with something of Hobhouse's good sense and *sang froid* but with more stoicism. This John Johnson, with all the sturdy qualities and some of the limitations of the true John Bull, serves as a foil or complement to the more sensitive, warm-blooded, and yet somewhat passive character of Don Juan. Since Byron had refrained from making Juan his complete alter ego, he could put some of his own words more appropriately in Johnson's mouth while at the same time keeping him a character in his own right. It is Johnson who refers to the Greeks as "Those servile dogs," who tells Juan: "Fortune at your time of life, / Although a female moderately fickle, / Will hardly leave you (as she's not your wife)." Johnson again philosophizes that "Time strips our illusions of their hue," that "Most men are slaves, none more so than the great," and "all are to be sold, if you consider / Their passions, and are dext'rous."

But after the pair are bought by a eunuch, the author steps in with his own comment, wondering if the merchant who sold his fellow beings ate a hearty dinner afterward. And he voices his own peculiar revulsion against being a slave to any physical appetite:

> I think with Alexander, that the act
>   Of eating, with another act or two,
> Makes us feel our mortality in fact
>   Redoubled; when a roast and a ragout . . .
> Can give us either pain or pleasure, who
> Would pique himself on intellects, whose use
> Depends so much upon the gastric juice?   (V, 32)

And speaking of mortality led easily to some reflections on the death of a commandant who was shot in front of Byron's house in Ravenna and brought upstairs to die. It was an experience that had made a deep impression on Byron. This is a prime example of how he molded the poem to record every nuance of his thought and feeling. The episode found its way into *Don Juan* in much the same way, and in some of the same phrases, as in his letters to Moore and Murray. The suddenness of the change from life to death raised the question: "then what is life or death?"

> But it was all a mystery. Here we are,
>   And there we go: — but *where?* five bits of lead,
> Or three, or two, or one, send very far!   (V, 39)

Byron had several times drawn back when tempted to describe the Oriental plants "et cetera" in the manner of Eastern travelers. Now before devoting several stanzas to the details of the life and decor of the seraglio, he opened up more fully on the describers of the picturesque.

> I won't describe; description is my "forte,"
>   But every fool describes in these bright days
> His wondrous journey to some foreign court,
>   And spawns his quarto, and demands your praise. . . .
>   (V, 52)

Byron's descriptions are alleviated by frequent digressions, as if his mind has wandered from the scene. The long galleries through which Juan and Johnson pass remind him of the huge rooms that dwarf man and bring on melancholy, and by premeditated casual association we are led to the Tower of Babel, Nimrod, and finally "the calumniated queen Semiramis," and the stanza to which he had been leading all the time. At the insistence of his friends in England he finally suppressed it because of its reference to a sex deviation and its sly innuendo concerning Queen Caroline — the calumniator of Semiramis had probably written " 'Courser' by mistake for 'Courier' " (Queen Caroline had been accused of having committed adultery with her courier).

The fact is that though Byron liked to tell a story, particularly one that was ironic or spicy, he was impatient with the details necessary to give it a realistic setting and verisimilitude. When he has to carry a narrative along for some space as he does in this canto to get Juan to Gulbeyaz, he does it in a careless and pedestrian way. That is why the digressions seem the much more lively parts of the poem. They are written *con amore*, while the rest is merely a chore. He makes the most of such things as Baba's hinting at the vast advantages if they would "condescend to circumcision." Juan says heroically, "they as soon shall circumcise my head!" but Johnson calmly promises to consider the proposition, after he has supped.

Juan glumly acquiesces when commanded by Baba, the eunuch, to dress as a girl.

> But tugging on his petticoat, he tripped,
>   Which — as we say — or as the Scotch say, *whilk*,
> (The rhyme obliges me to this; sometimes
> Monarchs are less imperative than rhymes).   (V, 77)

When Juan parts from Johnson and is led forth by Baba to some unknown adventure, he is still sullen but he manages a witticism (more Byronic than Juanian). Johnson says, "Keep your good name; though Eve herself once fell," and Juan replies, "the Sultan's self shan't carry me, / Unless his Highness promises to marry me." With such *divertissements* Byron carries the narrative along.

But his interest in the story increases and his metaphors become sharper when he comes to the encounter with Gulbeyaz, the Sultana who had ordered Juan purchased for her pleasure.

Byron thoroughly enjoys this confrontation of the haughty
Spaniard, who "could not stoop / To any shoe, unless it shod the
Pope," and the Sultan's favorite wife — " 'To hear and to obey'
had been from birth / The law of all around her." The behavior
of the woman spurned Byron had observed at first hand and he
described the scene with verve.

> Her first thought was to cut off Juan's head;
>   Her second, to cut only his — acquaintance;
> Her third, to ask him where he had been bred;
>   Her fourth, to rally him into repentance;
> Her fifth, to call her maids and go to bed;
>   Her sixth, to stab herself; her seventh, to sentence
> The lash to Baba: — but her grand resource
> Was to sit down again, and cry — of course.
>
> (V, 139)

But the grand irony, based on Byron's knowledge of the world
and of himself, was to have sympathy conquer both Juan's heroics
and his virtue.

> Juan was moved; he had made up his mind
>   To be impaled, or quartered as a dish
> For dogs, or to be slain with pangs refined,
>   Or thrown to lions, or made baits for fish,
> And thus heroically stood resigned,
>   Rather than sin — except to his own wish:
> But all his great preparatives for dying
> Dissolved like snow before a woman crying.
>
> (V, 141)

It was also a master stroke to have Baba arrive to announce that
the Sultan was coming just as Juan's heroic resolution was ebbing.
So far as Byron was concerned that episode was over. He turned
then to a mock appraisal of the virtues of the Sultan, who said his
prayers with "more than 'Oriental scrupulosity' " and "left to his
vizier all state affairs." The sack and sea settled all little dis-
turbances. "No scandals made the daily press a curse — / Morals
were better, and the fish no worse." His Highness did not fail to
notice the beauty of the new girl (Juan) among the damsels.

When the Sultana cast her sparkling eyes on her spouse, "As
suits a matron who has played a prank," the author reflects that
the Turks do well to shut their women up, for

Their chastity in these unhappy climes
   Is not a thing of that astringent quality
Which in the North prevents precocious crimes,
And makes our snow less pure than our morality. . . .

Thus in the East they are extremely strict,
   And wedlock and a padlock mean the same:
Excepting only when the former's picked
   It ne'er can be replaced in proper frame;
Spoilt, as a pipe of claret is when pricked:
   But then their own Polygamy's to blame;
Why don't they knead two virtuous souls for life
Into that moral centaur, man and wife?

                        (V, 157–158)

Having tacked a moral to "each error" as he had promised, Byron left the canto, and for the time being the poem too, for he had promised the Countess Guiccioli not to continue when she grew alarmed for his reputation. In the meantime Byron became absorbed in his historical dramas, in *Cain* (which raised more of a storm), and in the revolutionary activities of the Carbonari in Ravenna. After telling Murray of the promise that had been wrested from him, he continued, "The reason . . . arises from the wish of all women to exalt the *sentiment* of the passions, and to keep up the illusion which is their empire. Now *Don Juan* strips off this illusion, and laughs at that and most other things."[1] When Byron got the permission of his *amica* to resume the poem a year later (one may suspect he had already begun the sixth canto before that permission came), he took up the story in much the same spirit in which he had left it.[2] He wrote Murray: ". . . I obtained a permission from my Dictatress to continue it, — *provided always* it was to be more guarded and decorous and sentimental in the continuation than in the commencement. How far these Conditions have been fulfilled may be seen, perhaps, by and bye. . . ."[3]

[1] *Letters and Journals*, V, 321. Letter of July 6, 1821.

[2] It is entirely possible that he had written the sixth canto soon after he sent off the fifth on December 28, 1820, considering the similarity of tone in the seraglio scenes, and that he had held it back and finally suppressed it when Teresa Guiccioli asked him not to write any more. His first mention of his promise is in a letter of July 6, 1821. This seems the more likely in that the real break comes with the serious diatribe against war in the seventh and eighth cantos.

[3] *Letters and Journals*, VI, 95. Letter of July 8, 1822.

It is obvious in any event that the sixth canto was only a continuation of the fifth, necessary to complete the episode in the
seraglio and get Juan out of slavery and into the battle of Ismail.
The story itself again is pedestrian, redeemed only by the bright
remarks of the author along the way. Byron capped the episode
with his own moral:

> Polygamy may well be held in dread,
>   Not only as a sin, but as a *bore:*
> Most wise men, with *one* moderate woman wed,
>   Will scarcely find philosophy for more....
>   (VI, 12)

The accommodation of Gulbeyaz to the wishes of her lord and
master is recounted with a fine detached irony, for Byron is not
much involved with them as characters except as they furnish an
opportunity for comment on the ways of monarchs and women.
Monarchs are sublime "till they are consigned / To those sad
hungry jacobins the worms."

As narrator Byron assumes for the most part the role of omni-
scient observer, though sometimes he eschews knowledge of what
Juan could not know, and frequently he pretends ignorance when
it serves to pique the reader's curiosity or to add the spice of
innuendo, and always he is cavalier with details that might add
verisimilitude. He is as nonchalant as Hollywood in having Juan
speak, without language difficulty, to the Italians on the slave
ship, to the Englishman Johnson, and to the Turkish Baba and
Gulbeyaz. He had let Haidée teach Juan Greek because it served
his purpose to comment on the pleasure of learning a language
from a loving woman. But from that point on, language is no
longer a problem to Juan, or to Byron, until he comes to the
unpronounceable names of the Russians at the battle of Ismail.

New possibilities are opened up when Juan, in his feminine
disguise, returns to the seraglio, where there are "a thousand
bosoms . . . / Beating for Love, as the caged bird's for air." The
newcomer was much admired by all the odalisques, and especially
by Lolah, Katinka, and Dudù, who had a penchant for sentimental
friendship. It fell to the supple Dudù's lot to share her bed with
"Juanna." Byron describes Dudù's ample but quiet charms with
loving care. "I've seen your stormy seas and stormy women, /
And pity lovers rather more than seamen." The story of Dudù
and Juanna is told with amused tolerance for the little self-decep-

tions of women and the instinctive guile that Byron recognizes
as a part of innocence, but Dudù's innocence is more earthy than
that ascribed to an Ianthe or even a Haidée.

Though there is much that is farcical in the situation, Byron
handles it with tenderness for the most part. The narrative is as
usual interrupted with jocosities followed by more serious reflections, such as his confession: "I love wisdom more than she loves
me." The climax of the episode comes with Dudù waking the
whole Oda by screaming out in her dream of a pippin and a bee,
while Juan is apparently sleeping "As fast as ever husband by his
mate / In holy matrimony snores away." Byron ended the
matter with his usual withdrawal from omniscience and with pretended innocent candor.

The final episode of the canto is built on Gulbeyaz's reaction
to the news brought by the reluctant Baba that Juan had shared
the bed of Dudù. Always embarrassed by the necessity of
description, Byron usually fell back on a list of conventional
similes with tongue in cheek, and then broke off with a simulated
regret for the inadequacy of words ("Would that I were a
painter!"). His best descriptions are frequently in single lines or
couplets that turn a common metaphor into one that sparkles with
pertinence and freshness of suggestion. While Baba was watching
to see whether Gulbeyaz would change her mood or abate her
passion, she began to pace the room:

> And her brow cleared, but not her troubled eye;
> The wind was down, but still the sea ran high.
>
> (VI, 110)

And when she had ordered the "sack and sea" for Juan and Dudù,
Baba went his way grumbling about women and the trouble they
gave, "Which made him daily bless his own neutrality."

When Byron returned to *Don Juan* after the interregnum, he
carried with him a greater seriousness of purpose than merely "to
giggle and make giggle." Whether the sixth canto was written
earlier or not, it was in the spirit of the fifth and in any event was
necessary to complete the episode in the seraglio. But the Preface
published with Cantos VI, VII, and VIII is concerned alone with
the last two, which are mainly an attack on war and the politics
of tyranny. And in his correspondence of the time there is increasing emphasis on the value of *Don Juan* both as poetry and
as a satire on "abuses," i. e., mainly on the hypocrisies of society.

Whereas before he had belittled the criticism by depreciating his purpose — it was only meant to be "a little quietly facetious," "with as little poetry as possible" — now he spoke of his plan to display "the ridicules" of the various European societies, to have Juan "finish as *Anacharsis Cloots* in the French Revolution," or end in Hell. And he wrote to Murray: "I tell you, *it is poetry*. Your little envious knot of parson-poets may say what they please: time will show that I am not in this instance mistaken."[4] Moreover, he began to see *Don Juan* as a more important contribution to literature than any of the poems he had written in the romantic genre. "You see what it is to throw pearls to swine," he wrote to Shelley. "As long as I write the exaggerated nonsense which has corrupted the public taste, they applauded to the very echo, and, now that I have really composed, within these three or four years, some things which sh$^{d.}$ 'not willingly be let die,' the whole herd snort and grumble and return to wallow in their mire."[5]

The preface itself is written "in red-hot earnest" and is filled with indignation. Having suppressed his attack on "the intellectual eunuch Castlereagh" in the "Dedication," he made up for it now that John Hunt was his publisher and he no longer had to make concessions to John Murray's Tory friends.[6] "That he [Castlereagh] was an amiable man in *private* life, may or may not be true: but with this the public have nothing to do; and as to lamenting his death, it will be time enough when Ireland has ceased to mourn for his birth. As a minister, I, for one of millions, looked upon him as the most despotic in intention, and the weakest in intellect, that ever tyrannized over a country. It is the first time indeed since the Normans that England has been insulted by a

---

[4] *Letters and Journals*, V, 352. Letter of Aug. 31, 1821.

[5] *Letters and Journals*, VI, 67. Letter of May 20, 1822. Though Byron was here more immediately concerned about the reception of his poetic dramas, he also included among the things which should "not willingly be let die" *Don Juan*, which Shelley greatly admired.

[6] Cantos VI–XVI were published by John Hunt. After he had quarreled with Murray and turned over all his manuscripts to Hunt, Byron felt freer to express himself on political and other matters without the restraint which knowledge of Murray's squeamishness and caution had placed upon him. It is true that he sometimes wrote stanzas that he knew would shock Murray, but he was amenable to excision however much he may have protested against the "damned cutting and slashing" of his manuscripts. After Hunt became his publisher Byron also listened less to Hobhouse's prudent advice.

minister (at least) who could not speak English, and that Parliament permitted itself to be dictated to in the language of Mrs. Malaprop."

As for the moral objections to his earlier cantos he replied in the words of Voltaire: "La pudeur s'est enfuite des coeurs, et s'est refugiée sur les lèvres. . . . Plus les mœurs sont dépravés, plus les expressions deviennent mesurées; on croit regagner en langage ce qu'on a perdu en vertu."[7] The flood gates of his wrath were opened then on "the degraded and hypocritical mass which leavens the present English generation. . . . The hackneyed and lavished title of Blasphemer — which, with Radical, Liberal, Jacobin, Reformer, etc., are the changes which the hirelings are daily ringing in the ears of those who will listen — should be welcome to all who recollect on *whom* it was originally bestowed. Socrates and Jesus Christ were put to death publicly as *blasphemers,* and so have been and may be many who dare to oppose the most notorious abuses of the name of God and the mind of man. But persecution is not refutation, nor even triumph: the 'wretched infidel,' as he is called, is probably happier in his prison than the proudest of his assailants. With his opinions I have nothing to do — they may be right or wrong — but he has suffered for them, and that very suffering for conscience' sake will make more proselytes to deism than the example of heterodox Prelates to Christianity, suicide statesmen to oppression, or overpensioned homicides [Wellington] to the impious alliance which insults the world with the name of 'Holy!' "

With some lightening by the jocose absurdity of the comparisons, Byron has carried the same fierce earnestness into the opening stanzas of Canto VII (Tillotson, Wesley, and Rousseau "knew this life was not worth a potato"). He begins with an apostrophe to Love and Glory, and then replies to those who accuse him of "A tendency to under-rate and scoff / At human power and virtue, and all that," with his usual appeal to the example of Dante, Solomon, Cervantes, and others.

> Ecclesiastes said, "that all is vanity" —
>   Most modern preachers say the same, or show it
> By their examples of true Christianity. . . .
> Must I restrain me, through the fear of strife,
> From holding up the nothingness of Life?   (VII, 6)

[7] "Modesty has fled from hearts and has taken refuge on the lips. . . . The more depraved manners become, the more circumspect expression becomes; it is believed that one can gain in language what one has lost in virtue."

The account which follows of the siege of Ismail, the Turkish fortress at the mouth of the Danube, was no doubt intended to be a serious denunciation and savage satire on the supposed glories of war, the senseless slaughter commanded by ambitious monarchs and generals like Suwarrow, "Who loved blood as an alderman loves marrow," and the bootless heroism of thousands who perished in the fight. But "cheerfulness," or at least buffoonery, was always breaking in. He was soon making sport of the long Russian names:

> Achilles' self was not more grim and gory
> Than thousands of this new and polished nation,
> Whose names want nothing but — pronunciation.
>
> (VII, 14)

Scherematoff and Chrematoff and Mouskin Pouskin were all "proper men of weapons, as e'er . . . ran a sabre through skin." This levity has seemed to some critics to be out of tone with and to detract from the serious satire. It is probably true, as Steffan has suggested in his excellent analysis in the first volume of the "Variorum" *Don Juan,* that Byron was merely carrying over to the deadly earnest anti-war stanzas the habits of facetiousness he had practiced in the early cantos.[8] But it might also be argued that by taking the whole hooligan business lightly at times he has not only made his diatribe less like an unrelieved sermon (which his preface is for the most part), but has also thrown the irrationality of war into deeper perspective. It must be admitted, of course, that Byron could no more resist a play on words than Shakespeare could (and that probably accounts in part for his liking for and frequent quotation or adaptation of Shakespearean phrases). A sympathetic reader who has accepted the formless form of *Don Juan* will see this tendency only as another evidence of the conversational exuberance of the author and part of the revelation of a total personality which constitutes its charm. More downright readers will continue to complain, as Dr. Johnson did of Shakespeare's "quibbles," that he "is not long soft

[8] Truman Guy Steffan, *Byron's Don Juan,* Vol. I, *The Making of a Masterpiece,* Austin, Texas, 1957, p. 227. Steffan says, "His emotional comprehension and his technical sense of adjusting manner to matter had not kept pace with the development of his significant interests and broad intentions." But this may be narrowing Byron's intentions in the later cantos more than is justified. "To giggle and make giggle" was not wholly absent from his purpose to the end of the poem, nor did he conceive that inconsistent with his intent "To laugh at *all* things — for I wish to know / *What,* after *all,* are *all* things — but a *show?*" (VII, 2)

or pathetic without some idle conceit or contemptible equivoca-
tion." It might be said, however, that Byron's conceits were not
"idle" for the most part, but actually pointed up humorously
the matter he was seriously concerned with, as when he says that
he wonders "if a man's name in a *bulletin* / May make up for a
bullet in his body?" And he makes it clear before he leaves the
quibble on names that it has not arisen from mere nationalist
John Bull prejudice, for he includes some facetiousness on the lack
of originality in the names of the English soldiers of fortune in the
Russian army: "Sixteen called Thomson, and nineteen named
Smith."

The story of the battle is a story of ineptitude, greed, and
stumbling victory.

> The Russian batteries were incomplete,
>   Because they were constructed in a hurry....
>
> Whether it was their engineer's stupidity,
>   Their haste or waste, I neither know nor care,
> Or some contractor's personal cupidity,
>   Saving his soul by cheating in the ware
> Of homicide, but there was no solidity
>   In the new batteries erected there;
> They either missed, or they were never missed,
> And added greatly to the missing list.   (VII, 26–27)

He next makes sport of the great generals who distinguished
themselves in battle. The two who were most famous may have
been heroic, but were hardly heroes by Byronic standards. There
was "Potemkin — a great thing in days / When homicide and
harlotry made great." And the "dilettanti in War's art" were
given new heart by the "appointment of that lover of / Battles to
the command, Field-Marshal Souvaroff," whose dispatches were
"couched in pithy phrase." His orders were to "take Ismail at
whatever price." At this point Byron turns serious once more:

> "Let there be Light! said God, and there was Light!"
> "Let there be Blood!" says man, and there's a sea!
>   (VII, 41)

The day before the assault Juan and Johnson appear, having
escaped with the aid of Baba, with two girls from the harem.
After due explanations and proper disposal of the women, for
whose safety Juan was gallantly solicitous, they were assigned to
a regiment by Souvaroff, who knew Johnson as a former brave

warrior in the Russian armies. And then they "began to arm, / To burn a town which never did them harm."

The author pauses to consider the grandness of his epic story. He can't vie with Homer, "But still we moderns equal you in blood: / If not in poetry, at least in fact; / And fact is Truth, the grand desideratum!" In his reflections before the battle he considers the "shadows of glory," the dreams of "martial immortality," the romantically cloaked business of butchery, "Afflicting young folks with a sort of dizziness."

Byron's picture of the battle in Canto VIII is kaleidoscopic rather than panoramic or in any way consecutive, and the narrative is readily interrupted for, and frequently is only the illustrative preliminary to, the commentary. And yet the total of the "flame pictures" do add up to a portrait of the realistic horrors of war seldom equaled in poetic literature. His sermon boils down to a few platitudinous conclusions, whose reiteration is justified by the fact that though they are universally recognized they are everywhere disregarded in practice. First there is the commonplace that

> The drying up a single tear has more
> Of honest fame, than shedding seas of gore.
>
> (VIII, 3)

Another is that wars with all their glare

> except in Freedom's battles,
> Are nothing but a child of Murder's rattles.
>
> (VIII, 4)

Byron throughout made a distinction between battles for freedom, where the people were fighting against tyranny and for their own rights, and the wars of conquest wherein the soldiers and innocent civilians alike, as in the besieged city of Ismail, were pawns sacrificed for the whims and ambitions of their rulers and the "glory" of privileged military leaders. This dichotomy in his attitude toward war is everywhere made clear. Byron himself had from his earliest years dreamed of military glory, and his dream almost had fulfillment in the uprising of the *Carbonari* in Italy and at the very end when he was planning to lead his Suliotes against a Turkish fortress in Greece. But he always imagined himself leading a people in "Freedom's battles." His examples are Leonidas and Washington,

Whose every battle-field is holy ground,
Which breathes of nations saved, not worlds undone.
(VIII, 5)

A corollary of this attitude was his admiration for individual
heroism in battle, or self-sacrifice, or mercy, even in wars that in
themselves were "unholy." He could even admire the "Allah!
Allah! Hu!" of the Moslem warriors as they rushed recklessly into
battle sustained by their faith in the Mohammedan paradise
(though he would not be so sympathetic to the Christian who
did likewise). Although he understates Juan's bravery and attri-
butes his survival and his emergence as a hero to youthful *sang
froid* and chance, it is Juan's humanitarianism that he stresses, as
when he rescues the Turkish girl whom the hardened Russian
soldiers are about to kill.

But here as elsewhere the merit of the canto is in the digressions
and random comment, sometimes suggested by the events and
sometimes dragged in. " 'Carnage' (so Wordsworth tells you [in
his "Thanksgiving Ode"]) 'is God's daughter,' " and Byron adds
in a note: ". . . this is perhaps as pretty a pedigree for murder as
ever was found out by Garter King at Arms." Even his description of the battle is filled with figures intended to derogate it as an
occupation for mankind: "Three hundred cannon threw up their
emetic."

Juan and Johnson were advancing in the bloody mire, when
Juan "found himself alone, and friends retiring." Byron says in
effect that Juan's innocence made him a hero. He did not run
away, and though a creature of impulse, he was "always without
malice" in war or love. Instead of turning back he stumbled on
and fell in with a second column, was soon joined by Johnson,
and was among the first over the wall.

Byron recognized that the love of glory is a human motive
which operates in the best human beings, even when they are
not fighting wars for freedom. As Juan surmounted the wall,

he whose very body was all mind,
Flung here by Fate or Circumstance, which tame
The loftiest, hurried by the time and place,
Dashed on like a spurred blood-horse in a race.
(VIII, 54)

A single word is sufficient to set Byron off on a digression, but
as we have seen it is not always as far removed from the matter
in hand as at first it may appear. Juan's entering the town leads

to a quotation of Cowper's "God made the country and man made the town," and that recalls the fall of cities — Rome, Babylon, Tyre, Carthage, Nineveh — "and I begin to be / Of his opinion . . . / And pondering on the present and the past, / To deem the woods shall be our home at last." This launches several stanzas on Daniel Boone, the Noble Savage, "happiest amongst mortals anywhere."

Byron did not usually succumb to the illusions of the Noble Savage tradition, but like other romantics he was in some moods a victim of its allurements.

> Now back to thy great joys, Civilisation!
> And the sweet consequence of large society,
>   War — pestilence — the despot's desolation,
> The kingly scourge, the lust of notoriety,
>   The millions slain by soldiers for their ration. . . .
>   (VIII, 68)

And to clinch the point he follows with some gory details of the battle, Juan and Johnson wading through "a marsh of human blood." The city was taken, "And death is drunk with gore." Byron did not have to invent the horrors. They were all in the historical record, as he liked to point out. The episode of the Moslem fastening a death grip with his teeth on a Russian officer's heel was based on fact.

> But then the fact's a fact — and 't is the part
>   Of a true poet to escape from fiction
> Whene'er he can. . . .   (VIII, 86)

So to mingle the good with the bad in the account of the battle is necessary not only for the sake of variety but also and chiefly for the sake of truth. To leaven the pageant of cruelty and death, which makes "epic poesy so rare and rich," he tells of Juan's rescue of the little Turkish girl who is about to be murdered by "two villainous Cossacques." And even at this point he stops to ponder whether they should be blamed for their brutish natures, "or their sovereigns, who employ / All arts to teach their subjects to destroy." Though urged by Johnson to win fame by joining him in the last sally, Juan will not leave his protégée until her safety is provided for.

The soldiers, heated now by the hope of gain, perpetrate new atrocities. Yet the bravery of the Tartar khan briefly roused a tenth part of their human nature into pity and compassion. Juan

and Johnson tried to save him, but after his sons had all died fighting, he rushed on the enemy spears. Touched by such heroism,
even the Russians "Were melted for a moment." So too admiration is raised for the stubborn valor of the chief pacha who
refused to surrender, but in this sea of slaughter there was only
transient pity. So let it be seen "what a pious pastime war is."

In the end Byron made it perfectly clear that he was concerned
not principally with the barbarities of the heathen Turks and the
uncivilized Russians but with the senseless slaughter and suffering
brought about by the English alliances in the Napoleonic wars
and by English support of legitimacy and the unholy "Holy
Alliance."

> Howe'er the mighty locust, Desolation,
>   Strip your green fields, and to your harvests cling,
> Gaunt famine never shall approach the throne —
> Though Ireland starve, great George weighs twenty stone.
>   (VIII, 126)

Byron's raillery about the ladies who were disappointed that
"the ravishing did not begin" may strike some readers as a taste-
less anticlimax, but it fills out the picture of war as well as serving
as comic relief to the horror. The ravishing (sometimes with the
conscious or unconscious assistance of the victims) was a commonplace of war, and if it was slight on this occasion it was because
only a few hundred remained of the forty thousand who had
manned the wall, and the Russian soldiers were made chaste by
the chilly season and the "want of rest and victual."

Souvaroff's rhyming on the burning city turned Byron again
to the serious, "For I will teach, if possible, the stones / To rise
against Earth's tyrants," and he will teach "our children's children . . . *what things were* before the World was free!" There
will come a time, he says, when thrones will be looked upon with
as much wonder as the mammoth's bones.

And finally the author boasts that he has kept his word with
his readers. They have

> Had sketches of Love — Tempest — Travel — War —
>   All very accurate, you must allow,
> An *Epic*, if plain truth should prove no bar;
>   For I have drawn much less with a long bow
> Than my forerunners. Carelessly I sing,
> But Phoebus lends me now and then a string. . . .
>   (VIII, 138)

And he was honest in both statements. If he stretched credulity in having Juan, a youth and a foreigner, decorated with the order of St. Vladimir and sent with despatches announcing the victory to the Empress, that was merely a part of the machinery of the story to get his hero to St. Petersburgh and in the good graces of Catherine. In important matters of the human character and condition he did not stretch the long bow as much as most of his epic forerunners. And he sang carelessly because he had deliberately eschewed the "grand style" of epic writers for something more flexible and human.

The stanzas on Wellington which begin the ninth canto had first been written for the third but had been suppressed in deference to Murray and his advisers. Byron's attack on Wellington was based on the belief that he had been overpraised and overpaid for his victory at Waterloo and that he had "repaired Legitimacy's crutch."

> And I shall be delighted to learn who,
> Save you and yours, have gained by Waterloo?
> * * * * * * * * * *
> He whose whole life has been assault and battery,
>   At last may get a little tired of thunder;
> And swallowing eulogy much more than satire, he
>   May like being praised for every lucky blunder,
> Called "Saviour of the Nations" — not yet saved, —
> And "Europe's Liberator" — still enslaved. (IX, 4–5)

He suggests that Wellington send the sentinel before his gate "A slice or two from your luxurious meals: / He fought, but has not fed so well of late." Compared with Cincinnatus, Epaminondas, and George Washington, Wellington seems a rather mercenary savior of his country: "Great men have always scorned great recompenses." And finally,

> Never had mortal man such opportunity,
>   Except Napoleon, or abused it more:
> You might have freed fallen Europe from the unity
>   Of Tyrants, and been blest from shore to shore:
> And *now* — what *is* your fame? Shall the Muse tune it ye?
>   *Now* — that the rabble's first vain shouts are o'er?
> Go! hear it in your famished country's cries!
> Behold the World! and curse your victories!
>
> * * * * * * * * * *

> You *did great* things, but not being *great* in mind,
> Have left *undone* the *greatest* — and mankind.
>
> (IX, 9–10)

Fearing that his readers may have grown tired of his seriousness, Byron ends his speculations by quizzing both the machinery of formal poetry and his own lack of respect for form or pattern.

> But I am apt to grow too metaphysical . . .
> I quite forget this poem's merely quizzical,
>   And deviate into matters rather dry.
> I ne'er decide what I shall say, and this I call
>   Much too poetical: men should know why
> They write, and for what end; but, note or text,
> I never know the word which will come next.
>
> So on I ramble, now and then narrating,
>   Now pondering. . . .   (IX, 41–42)

But narrating is more of a bore for him than pondering, and he therefore lets the reader "suppose" Juan at St. Petersburgh, in a handsome uniform, "Made up by Youth, Fame, and an army tailor." Suppose him "Love turned a Lieutenant of Artillery," and attracting the attention of the Empress. The author especially "supplicates" the reader's supposition of Juan's position as favorite of Catherine.

It has frequently been suggested that the Russian cantos of *Don Juan* are the weakest because Byron was writing about what he had not seen and experienced, and by his own confession that always put a damper on his genius. Speaking of a spurious publication, "A Pilgrimage to Jerusalem," that had been ascribed to him, he wrote: "How the devil should I write about *Jerusalem*, never having yet been there?"[9] That is no doubt why he minimizes or generalizes the description of the physical setting, but even in the scene of the banquet of Juan and Haidée, where he was familiar with the Greek background, though he had not actually lived on an Aegean island, he drew on *Tully's Tripoli* for details of the furnishings of the rooms of Lambro's house. And again in the seraglio scenes he was irked by the need to describe, even though he had visited the Sultan's palace when he was in Constantinople (he had not been in the harem, of course).

---

[9] *Letters and Journals*, IV, 22. Letter of Dec. 9, 1816, to Murray.

The point is that description was neither his forte nor his purpose. A greater shortcoming in the Russian cantos might be said to be his lack of knowledge of the historical Catherine, though he had read something of her character and habits, particularly of her fondness for the grenadiers and lieutenants of artillery. But Byron makes no pretense to historical accuracy and is concerned with things he does know, the nature of women and the weaknesses of men. It is apparent that he is running the show and in any significant part his allusions are to what he does know, to Castlereagh in England, or to the *cavalier servente* in Italy. He knew what it was too for a boy to fall in love with an older woman, or into "self-love" as when some being "above / Ourselves . . . 'deigns to prove' / ('T is Pope's phrase) a great longing, though a rash one, / For one especial person out of many." This is a comment which may cast some light on Byron's later reflections on his infatuation for the "autumnal charms" of Lady Oxford.

Catherine "in juicy vigour" in spite of her years made Juan vain by her attentions. And this congenial subject sets up a digressive train that equals anything of a like nature in earlier cantos, both in felicitous phrasing of the commonplace and in the eye-twinkling revelation of unacknowledged feelings.

> The noblest kind of love is love Platonical,
>   To end or to begin with; the next grand
> Is that which may be christened love canonical,
>   Because the clergy take the thing in hand;
> The third sort to be noted in our chronicle
>   And flourishing in every Christian land,
> Is when chaste matrons to their other ties
> Add what may be called *marriage in disguise*.
>
>   (IX, 76)

Juan was much flattered by Catherine's "love, or lust; — / I cannot stop to alter words once written, / And the *two* are so mixed with human dust, / That he who *names one*, both perchance may hit on." And so he leaves the lovers on their "heaven-kissing hill," but not without a comparison between the frankly sensuous Catherine and "our own half-chaste Elizabeth," whose "vile, ambiguous method of flirtation, / And stinginess, disgrace her sex and station."

Byron was just as cavalier about the division of his "epic" into cantos as he was about the continuity of the subject matter. And the reason is of course that his real subject is the comic tragedy of man's confinement in the fiery flesh and his wriggling to get out of it. The episodes of the story are only useful for illustrative purposes, and the "machinery" is necessary only to move Juan into new situations. The tenth canto extricates Juan from "Royalty's vast arms" and transports him to England. The author is not hampered by the unfamiliar Russian scene because for the most part he by-passes it by digressing into fields in which he is the master, or by treating the affair of Juan and Catherine in realistic general terms that have more meaning for him than the historical or the fictional.

He begins with a half-skeptical tribute to science in the story of Newton and his apple, as a prelude to his praise of poetry which may be as far searching. The return to Juan "in the *bloom* / Of favouritism, but not yet the *blush*," only leads to another comment on youth and age. The digression on Jeffrey which follows is dragged in not because it has any relevance to the story or to the preceding discussion (except that an indelicate innuendo at the end of stanza 10 reminds him of a criticism of his temper and taste in the *Edinburgh Review*), but simply because it was on his mind at the moment, and in his view that was ample justification for its inclusion in a poem whose ultimate design was to explore the seas of thought and feelings of mobile mortal man. Having made up with Jeffrey, he would not quarrel with him or return to hatred.

When Byron finally returns to Juan and his situation as Catherine's favorite, we are told that he had become a very polished Russian and a little dissipated. Juan in his new spoiled state wrote pridefully to Spain, and all his near relations, finding him in such a happy station, prepared for emigration. His mother, Donna Inez, was glad to see that he had "brought his spending to a handsome anchor," commended him to God and warned him against "Greek worship" (though he could smother "*Outward* dislike"), informed him that she had married again and that he had a little brother, and "praised the Empress's *maternal* love." Here Byron exclaims:

> Oh for a *forty-parson power* to chant
> Thy praise, Hypocrisy!   (X, 34)

Though *gâté* Juan could not thrive long in this unnatural situation, for after all he was a sensitive plant and "In Royalty's vast arms he sighed for Beauty." When he grew sick, Catherine was perturbed and on his recovery sent him on a secret diplomatic mission to England. "So much did Juan's setting off distress her, / She could not find at first a fit successor." Juan was somewhat encumbered on his travels (like Byron) by a menagerie: "A bulldog, and a bullfinch, and an ermine." Besides his weakness for animals, he had a sentimental attachment for the little Turkish girl, Leila, "a pure and living pearl," and he took her along to protect her. In analyzing Juan's feeling for Leila, Byron may have been trying to understand his own for such young girls as Lady Charlotte Harley (the Ianthe of *Childe Harold*). It was not merely paternal or brotherly, "And still less was it sensual." Leila loved Juan too as her protector, but she refused to be converted and he was "the only Christian she could bear."

Byron touched on only a few high spots of the journey that offered opportunities for satiric or sardonic comment. Juan passed through Königsberg, "whose vaunt, / Besides some veins of iron, lead, or copper, / Has lately been the great Professor Kant." And at Cologne he saw "Eleven thousand maiden heads of bone. / The greatest number flesh hath ever known."[10] He came to Holland,

> That water-land of Dutchmen and of ditches,
> Where juniper expresses its best juice,
> The poor man's sparkling substitute for riches.
>
> (X, 63)

There he embarked for "the Island of the free."

Byron projected into Juan's thoughts and feelings his own mixed regard for his native shores. Always in the back of his mind was the thought that he might return there, and now he had an opportunity to contemplate what his feelings would be. Juan's half sophisticated, half innocent reactions fit the author's purpose very well. Even a foreigner like Juan could feel at first sight of "Albion's chalky belt — / A kind of pride that he should be among / Those haughty shopkeepers." Then the author steps on the stage:

[10] Byron's note: "St. Ursula and her eleven thousand virgins were still extant in 1816. . . ."

> I've no great cause to love that spot of earth,
>   Which holds what *might have been* the noblest nation;
> But though I owe it little but my birth,
>   I feel a mixed regret and veneration
> For its decaying fame and former worth.
>   Seven years (the usual term of transportation)
> Of absence lay one's old resentments level,
> When a man's country's going to the devil.   (X, 66)

Juan is introduced to the vexations of a landing at Dover, the custom house, "with all its delicate duties," the waiters "running mucks," and the "long, long bills, whence nothing is deducted."

> But, doubtless, as the air — though seldom sunny —
> Is free, the respiration's worth the money.   (X, 70)

He is off for Canterbury, and Byron exults in the speed compared with that in Germany, where they muddle along the road. Leila wonders, when told that the cathedral is "God's House," why he "suffered Infidels in his homestead," and she grieves that "Mahomet should resign / A mosque so noble, flung like pearls to swine."

The author steps in again to sentimentalize over a pot of beer and to exclaim "What a delightful thing's a turnpike road!" until brought up by the toll.

> Alas! how deeply painful is all payment!
> Take lives — take wives — take aught except men's purses.
>   (X, 79)

Juan saw London first from Shooter's Hill. It was a noble sight.

> The Sun went down, the smoke rose up, as from
> A half-unquenched volcano. . . .

Though he was not of their race Juan

> Revered the soil, of those true sons the mother,
> Who butchered half the earth, and bullied t'other.
>   (X, 81)

Byron was perhaps not quite sure how he would handle the satire in the English cantos, and he paused before going on. But he was sure of one thing:

> By and by,
> My gentle countrymen, we will renew
>   Our old acquaintance; and at least I'll try
> To tell you truths *you* will not take as true,
>   Because they are so.   (X, 84)

He will be a "male Mrs. Fry" (a reformer who tried to "improve" the inhabitants of Newgate jail). Why preach to "*poor* rogues"? Why not try your hand "at hardened and imperial Sin"? But he has prated too long; "by and by, I'll prattle / Like Roland's horn in Roncesvalles' battle." With that threat he ends the canto.

16

Don Juan, Cantos XI-XVII

IN THE FIRST TWO English cantos Byron was groping for a suitable way to display the "ridicules" of the society he had known. He had the materials in plenty but did not yet know how he would use them. Here on home ground it needed no effort to fill in the background or to find appropriate incidents or characters for comment or caricature. The description of London is more sure and more detailed and realistic than that of Constantinople or Petersburgh. Amid this *embarras de richesse* he hardly knows where to begin, and so he starts with a flippant but basically serious metaphysical speculation:

> When Bishop Berkeley said "there was no matter,"
> And proved it — 't was no matter what he said. . . .
> I would shatter
> Gladly all matters down to stone or lead,
> Or adamant, to find the World a spirit.   (XI, 1)

But now he can see with ironic yet poignant regret the dissipation of the romantic dream of Childe Harold-Manfred, the dream of escaping the flesh by some transcendent leap into the freedom of a world of spirit:

> What a sublime discovery 't was to make the
> Universe universal egotism,
> That all's ideal — *all ourselves!*   (XI, 2)

But "Indigestion" (a symbol of the "clay-cold bond") "perplexes our soarings." Then he adds facetiously that each shock of illness makes him more orthodox:

The first attack at once proved the Divinity
    (But *that* I never doubted, nor the Devil);
The next, the Virgin's mystical virginity;
    The third, the usual Origin of Evil;
The fourth at once established the whole Trinity
    On so uncontrovertible a level,
That I devoutly wished the three were four —
On purpose to believe so much the more.   (XI, 6)

From this he abruptly returned to Juan on Shooter's Hill
watching the sun set over murky London. He had almost ceased
to apologize, even with tongue-in-cheek mockery, for his digressions or to make artificial transitions to tie them to his story. Juan
is musing on the ideal life in Britain, "Freedom's chosen station,"
where "none lay / Traps for the traveller," when he is interrupted
by a knife and "Damn your eyes! your money or your life!"
Juan did not understand a word of English except "their shibboleth, 'God damn!'" He had of course understood John
Johnson well enough in Constantinople and was to talk without
any difficulty with all the English he met thereafter. Byron was
willing to sacrifice consistency in his story, however, whenever
it would serve his immediate purpose as it did here to comment
on the English "shibboleth." Juan understood the gesture, if not
the words, and shot the highwayman, and then wished he had
been less hasty:

"Perhaps," thought he, "it is the country's wont
    To welcome foreigners in this way: now
I recollect some innkeepers who don't
    Differ, except in robbing with a bow. . . ."
                                        (XI, 15)

And then as Juan proceeded toward his hotel in the West End
a flood of memories, both nostalgic and critical, surged up to fill
the picture. There were the pretentious names in the suburbs:
"Groves" devoid of trees, and "Mount Pleasant," "containing
nought to please." Juan encountered "coaches, drays, choked
turnpikes, and a whirl / Of wheels, and roar of voices, and confusion," but when he crossed the bridge and saw the lamps of
Westminster, the grand structure of the Abbey, the line of lights
up Charing Cross and Pall Mall, he (Byron and not Juan) felt
his heart swelling with pride, but he did not fail to notice, as
Juan stopped at the door of his fine hotel,

            as usual several score
Of those pedestrian Paphians who abound
In decent London when the daylight's o'er. . . .

                            (XI, 30)

   Rumors of his strange adventures had preceded Juan, "his wars
and loves," and he found himself "extremely in the fashion, /
Which serves our thinking people for a passion." His official
duties soon brought Juan in contact with politicians and "their
double front, / Who live by lies, yet dare not boldly lie."

         Now what I love in women is, they won't
         Or can't do otherwise than lie — but do it
         So well, the very Truth seems falsehood to it.

                            (XI, 36)

But Byron could not leave the subject without a recognition of
the complexity of truth:

         And, after all, what is a lie? 'T is but
         The truth in masquerade; and I defy
         Historians — heroes — lawyers — priests, to put
         A fact without some leaven of a lie.   (XI, 37)

   Both the ministers and their underlings were polite to Juan,
but Byron took his fling at them nevertheless.

         The very clerks . . .
         Were hardly rude enough to earn their pay:

         And insolence no doubt is what they are
         Employed for. . . .   (XI, 40–41)

   Juan was a bachelor, "which is a matter / Of import both to virgin and to bride." He had seen the world, "which is a curious
sight, / And very much unlike what people write." The "Blues"
talked to him in bad French or Spanish, and Miss Araminta Smith,
who at sixteen had translated "Hercules Furens" into "as furious
English," set down his sayings in a common-place book.
   Byron could not resist the temptation here to comment on
the literary coteries, the "ten thousand living authors" to be met
at assemblies or small parties, and the eighty "greatest living
poets," acclaimed by the magazines. Some think that Coleridge
has the sway, "And Wordsworth has supporters, two or three; /
And that deep-mouthed Boeotian 'Savage Landor' / Has taken

for a swan rogue Southey's gander." And finally he cannot leave the contemporary literary scene without some gibes at Keats, though latterly, under the influence of Shelley, he had somewhat tempered the harshness of his judgment.

> John Keats, who was killed off by one critique,
> > Just as he really promised something great,
> If not intelligible, without Greek
> > Contrived to talk about the gods of late,
> Much as they might have been supposed to speak.
> > Poor fellow! His was an untoward fate;
> 'T is strange the mind, that very fiery particle,
> Should let itself be snuffed out by an article.
>
> > > > > > > > > (XI, 60)

Then without apology for the digression he returns to Juan, who had been left in peril between "live poets and *blue* ladies." His mornings he spent in business, "a laborious nothing," his afternoons "in visits, luncheons, / Lounging and boxing; and the twilight hour / In riding round those vegetable puncheons / Called 'Parks,' where there is neither fruit nor flower." Then comes dinner and gaiety where the "door . . . opens to the thousand happy few / An earthly Paradise of *Or Molu.*"

This was the world as Byron had known it. But "I look for it — 't is gone, a globe of glass!" The "*Où sont?*" stanzas that follow constitute a nostalgic critique of the whole world of fashion he had known in his years of fame, and a summary of the changes that had taken place in the seven years of his exile. Where are Napoleon, Castlereagh, Grattan, Curran, Sheridan, "the unhappy Queen"? And "Where are those martyred saints the Five per Cents? / And where — oh, where the devil are the Rents?" Where is Brummell? Where is George the Third, and where is "Fum" the Fourth, our "royal bird"? Where are the "Honourable Mistresses and Misses?" Some are "laid aside like an old Opera hat." "Where are the Lady Carolines and Franceses / Divorced or doing thereanent." "Some maids have been made wives, some merely mothers."

Byron was having so much fun with his cleverly turned topical allusions and innuendoes that he almost forgot Juan, but it was not all meaningless horseplay, for in enumerating the changes he had seen in seven years he ended with a serious political commentary:

> I have seen crowns worn instead of a fool's cap —
> I have seen a Congress doing all that's mean —
> I have seen some nations, like o'erloaded asses,
> Kick off their burthens — meaning the high classes.
>   (XI, 84)

With Juan poised for some adventure in English society not quite yet determined, the author gives his alter ego some sage advice for dealing with his English environment:

> But "*carpe diem*," Juan. . . .
>   and above all keep a sharp eye
> Much less on what you do than what you say:
> Be hypocritical, be cautious, be
> Not what you *seem*, but always what you *see*.
>   (XI, 86)

Then he turns directly to his English readers and tells them: "You are not a moral people, and you know it." And he reminds them that this is only a work of fiction,

> Though every scribe, in some slight turn of diction,
> Will hint allusions never *meant*.   (XI, 88)

It is important to remember in reading *Don Juan* that Byron usually tells the truth even when he is jesting. When he says that the work is only fiction and that "I sing of neither mine nor me," he means it literally. He has determined that in this part of Juan's story he is going to present him with detached irony and sympathy in an English setting, acting on and reacting to people who are composites and types rather than actual people the author had known in his years of fame in England. Juan will be one part of his *ideal* self and therefore not real, and he can look on him with an objective eye. He will not caricature real people, as he had Annabella in the Donna Inez of the first canto. But they will not be the less real because they are fictional, for their ingredients will be distilled from a lifetime observation of human traits. This is not to say that the author will not draw on recollections of real places and events, such as in the description of Newstead Abbey as "Norman Abbey," the country estate where Juan meets the microcosm (which considers itself the macrocosm) of English society. And of course the author will step on the stage with his own reminiscences and comment. But Juan's adventures will be kept intact as his own with people as complex and vividly real as imagination working on the authentic stuff of life can make them, and as all great fictional characters are, even when caricatured.

A general discourse from the throne begins the twelfth canto; the rueful contemplation of middle age — "Love lingers still, although 't were late to wive: / And as for other love, the illusion's o'er" — and the defense of the miser, who has a "pleasure that can never pall," that outlasts love or lust or wine. Cash even rules love, for (with a thrust at Malthus) "sages write against all procreation, / Unless a man can calculate his means / Of feeding brats the moment his wife weans." When he reintroduces Juan it is for the purpose of illuminating the general setting in which he finds himself; the real story is yet to come. It is evident that Byron has not yet formulated a definite plan.

Juan was still in London, "Where every kind of mischief's daily brewing." When tired of other play he "flirted without sin / With some of those fair creatures who have prided / Themselves on innocent tantalisation." There is a competition among the women for the privilege of taking in charge Leila's education, and in passing Byron bares some of the cynicism of the marriage mart as he had witnessed it: "I've known them court an heiress for their lover." He assures his reader that it is "always with a moral end / That I dissert" and that is what puts his "Pegasus to these grave paces."

> But now I'm going to be immoral; now
> I mean to show things really as they are,
> Not as they ought to be: for I avow,
> That till we see what's what in fact, we're far
> From much improvement with that virtuous plough
> Which skims the surface, leaving scarce a scar
> Upon the black loam long manured by Vice....
>
> (XII, 40)

It seems clear from this and from what he said in succeeding stanzas (these first twelve cantos were only the beginning of the poem, and if his Pegasus didn't founder he would "canter gently through a hundred") that he had really begun to feel he had finally found a medium through which he could "moralize his song" as worthily as Pope without the limiting formalism and stultifying effects which inevitably dogged his efforts to use the couplet. It was one step further toward acceptance of the limita-

tions of his world and of himself which in turn unleashed his
genius for its full flight. It was with great zest that he prepared
to display "that Microcosm on stilts, / Yclept the Great World."

The care of Leila fell to Lady Pinchbeck, and Byron hints
that it was a good choice, for the lady had been a little gay in
youth and therefore was the wiser. He painted her with some of
the fondness he had felt for Lady Melbourne, whose merit was in
seeing his. Juan was a favorite with Lady Pinchbeck "Because she
thought him a good heart at bottom, / A little spoiled, but not so
altogether."

Juan had an awkward part to play in "The royal game of
Goose," which is good society, "The single ladies wishing to be
double, / The married ones to save the virgins trouble." Among
the perils to the bachelor of birth and fortune are the mothers
and the brothers who demand what his intentions are, "For talk
six times with the same single lady, / And you may get the
wedding-dresses ready." But worse is that "amphibious sort of
harlot . . . your cold coquette" whose "innocent flirtation" is
"Not quite adultery, but adulteration." And the worst

> Is when, without regard to Church or State,
>   A wife makes or takes love in upright earnest.
> Abroad, such things decide few women's fate . . .
> But in old England, when a young bride errs,
> Poor thing! Eve's was a trifling case to hers.
>
> (XII, 64)

The reason is that " 't is a low, newspaper, humdrum lawsuit /
Country." But "a genial sprinkling of hypocrisy, / Has saved the
fame of thousand splendid sinners" who are among the proudest
of the aristocracy and grace the highest society, "So gentle,
charming, charitable, chaste."

To Juan, "coming young from lands and scenes romantic,"
passion in England seemed "half commercial, half pedantic." At
first he did not think the women pretty, for it takes a while to
become adjusted to a new climate and a new complexion, and he
had to learn to appreciate "our pure pearls of price, / Those
polar summers, *all* Sun, and some ice."

> Like Russians rushing from hot baths to snows
>   Are they, at bottom virtuous even when vicious:
> They warm into a scrape, but keep of course,
> As a reserve, a plunge into remorse.   (XII, 73)

Byron drew on all his experience of the comparative religion of love abroad and at home in his discussion of the nuances of attitudes. The English woman, like the soil, "may give you time and trouble, / Well cultivated, it will render double." Nine times out of ten she may be urged only by caprice or coquetry, but if she takes to a *grande passion* it may turn out a tornado.

Juan, the author admits, had become a little blasé, and it was not to be wondered at that, considering his experience, "his heart had got a tougher rind." And being thrust into high society, even with the best intentions to avoid it, he was exposed to temptations. And so at the end of "the twelfth canto of our Introduction" the stage was set, and he tantalizes his readers with the possibilities in the story itself which is to follow.

> But what, and where, with whom, and when, and why,
> Is not to be put hastily together. . . .   (XII, 86)

The thirteenth canto begins with a mocking statement of his serious purpose, which is not to be taken lightly merely because he speaks of it in jest:

> I now mean to be serious; — it is time,
> Since Laughter now-a-days is deemed too serious. . . .
> (XIII, 1)

In the second stanza Byron introduces Lady Adeline Amundeville, the most complex and interesting heroine in all his narrative poetry. Haidée was charming as "Nature's bride" but she was scarcely realized as an individual, and even Julia, though subtle in her self-deception, was a fairly simple character. But Adeline has depths which the author in creating her delighted in exploring. It is possible to see in her some of the unspoiled as well as the spoiled qualities of Annabella Milbanke when she rose upon Byron's horizon a fresh garden flower in Lady Melbourne's hot-house drawing room. And at this detached distance he is equally inclined to analyze her virtues with her weaknesses, rather than make her a simple caricature as he did in Donna Inez. But she shares some of the features of Lady Frances Webster and perhaps half a dozen other women. Finally it is the quintessence of the feminine mind and heart that he is trying to penetrate, and Adeline escapes easy identification. He describes her as

> The fair most fatal Juan ever met,
> Although she was not evil nor meant ill;
> But Destiny and Passion spread the net. . . .
> (XIII, 12)

Her charms "made all men speak, and women dumb." She was chaste "to Detraction's desperation" and married to a man she loved well.

Lord Henry Amundeville has some of the features of Lord Holland in his political activities, something of William Lamb in his complacency in relation to his wife (he was "Cool, and quite English, imperturbable"), and probably shared traits with a dozen of Byron's acquaintances among the Whig aristocracy. He was a great debater, and "few Members kept the House up later." He liked the gentle Spaniard for his gravity and docility and honored him for looking up to his mentor in politics. It is the relationship Byron recalled with Lord Holland when he deferred to the older and experienced politician before he made his maiden speech in the House of Lords.

Juan stood well with both the "Ins and Outs" of politics, and was a welcome guest at "Blank-Blank Square," the town house of the Amundevilles. Byron thus piques his readers' curiosity at the same time that he deliberately avoids writing a *roman à clef*. He doesn't want to run the risk of "Reaping allusions private and inglorious, / Where none were dreamt of"; besides, since there is scarce a season when some splendid house is not rocked by the "heart-quake of domestic treason," he might stumble on them unawares.

Fascinated by Adeline, he returns to an analysis of her character. Her virtue was sufficient shield from the crowd of coxcombs who surrounded her. As for coquetry, "she disdained to wear it — / Secure of admiration." She was "polite without parade," giving attention of the kind that flatters, "A gentle, genial courtesy of mind, / To those who were, or passed for meritorious." She had a "calm patrician polish" in her speech that keeps down enthusiasm, just as the Mandarin by his manner will not let you guess that "anything he views can greatly please." But then "rash Enthusiasm in good society / Were nothing but a moral inebriety." Adeline, however, was not indifferent.

> (*Now* for a common-place!) beneath the snow,
> As a Volcano holds the lava more
>   Within — *et caetera*. Shall I go on? — No!
> I hate to hunt down a tired metaphor....
>
> I'll have another figure in a trice: —
>   What say you to a bottle of champagne?

Frozen into a very vinous ice,
  Which leaves few drops of that immortal rain,
Yet in the very centre, past all price,
  About a liquid glassful will remain;
And this is stronger than the strongest grape
Could e'er express in its expanded shape:

'T is the whole spirit brought to a quintessence;
  And thus the chilliest aspects may concentre
A hidden nectar under a cold presence. . . .
And your cold people are beyond all price,
When once you've broken their confounded ice.
                                    (XIII, 36–38)

For the most part Byron was content to take the "tired meta-phor" or the commonplace simile and give it new vigor with an unexpected turn of phrase or a striking juxtaposition or rhyme. But occasionally the champagne of his imagination emerges with a few drops of its immortal rain. These cold people, he says, are fascinating to the romantic voyager, "a North-West Passage / Unto the glowing India of the soul."

The English winter, "ending in July, / To recommence in August," was now ended, and the turnpikes "glow with dust" as carriages retreat to country houses. Byron had found his machinery at last for displaying that microcosm, the great world of English society, in all its true colors, brilliant and dun. Here as in other situations into which he had thrown his hero, he had divided allegiances. It is evident in the zest of his description of the exodus from London as in the later account of life in the country house of Lord and Lady Amundeville that he is haunted by a nostalgic sense of pleasure in the recollection of details of that gay life into which he had been swept as a youth. This sense overlays but does not cloud the satiric picture.

Lord Henry and Lady Adeline depart for their "Gothic Babel," a thousand years old. Their country house, Norman Abbey, was of course Newstead Abbey, Byron's fondness for which is re-flected in the loving description, from the "Druid oak" and the "lucid Lake" to the "glorious remnant" of the church with a virgin and child in a niche over the grand arch of the one stand-ing wall. Nothing quite matched Byron's nostalgia for Newstead. He had lived there only briefly, but somehow it symbolized his lost youth, and some of his happiest memories were associated with it: his courting of Mary Chaworth, his skull-cup parties with Hobhouse and other friends, his sojourn there with Augusta when they were snowbound, and again before his engagement. For the moment he has forgotten his satiric purpose in the sweet melancholy of the reminiscence. But it returns as he goes on to describe the portraits of the ancestors of the Amundevilles on the walls. There were stern judges whose brows did not suggest that they would lean much "from might to right," attorneys-general, "hinting more . . . / Of the 'Star Chamber' than of 'Habeas Corpus.'" But the description must end; though Homer had his "Catalogue of ships," the modern author must be more moderate: "I spare you then the furniture and plate."

The promised party was set for "mellow Autumn." There follows a comparison between the Italian autumn and the English, in which Byron's nostalgia for his native land shows through the mockery. England does not have festoons of red grapes as in the "sunny lands of song," but she has the "purchased choice of choicest wines" and "The very best of vineyards is the cellar." And although she has not the climate that makes the southern autumn day appear like a second spring, she has "sea-coal fires," and out doors "what is lost in green is gained in yellow." If she misses the "effeminate *villeggiatura* — / Rife with more horns than hounds," she has the chase and the Melton jacket.

> If she hath no wild boars, she hath a tame
> Preserve of bores, who ought to be made game.
>   (XIII, 78)

The list of the guests assembled at Norman Abbey is an hilarious bit of foolery that has meaning in its madness. Byron has used tag names that in themselves constitute a critique of the "bores" his exile had given him the freedom to dissect. One may suspect that the names sometimes have subtleties of reference or innuendo that might lead to clues if one could follow the sinuosities of Byron's roguish mind, but the pursuit is hardly worth the trouble. There was the Duchess of Fitz-Fulke (significantly mentioned first — her "frolic Grace" furnished the core of the intrigue as the story proceeded), the Countess Crabby, the Ladies Scilly, Busey, Miss Eclat, Miss Bombazeen, Miss Mackstay, Miss O'Tabby, "And Mrs. Rabbi, the rich banker's squaw; / Also the honourable Mrs. Sleep, / Who looked a white lamb, yet was a black sheep: / With other Countesses of Blank — but rank." Among the élite, money in the bank is the passport that shrouds "The *passée* and the past; for good society / Is no less famed for tolerance than piety."

The party consisted of thirty-three of the highest caste, but he mentions only a few. There were Parolles, "the legal bully," the "young bard Rackrhyme," Lord Pyrrho, "the great freethinker," and Sir John Pottledeep, "the mighty drinker," the Duke of Dash, and the "six Miss Rawbolds — pretty dears! / All song and sentiment; whose hearts were set / Less on a convent than a coronet." There was also the "*preux Chevalier de la Ruse,*" a soldier of fortune who had a "magic power to please — The dice seemed charmed, too, with his repartees." Others were Jack Jargon, "the gigantic guardsman," General Fireface, "Who ate, last war, more yankees than he killed," and the Welsh judge, Jefferies Hardsman, who was such a wag that the condemned man "had the Judge's joke for consolation." There was a Parliamentary orator, who "revelled in his Ciceronian glory" and who had a memory "excellent to get by rote" and wit enough to "hatch a pun or tell a story."

This "heterogeneous mass" Byron found too dull even for comedy.

> Society is now one polished horde,
> Formed of two mighty tribes, the *Bores* and *Bored*.
>
> (XIII, 95)

If he had believed this completely, instead of only in a yawning moment, he would not have continued. But he still found that society intriguing even if some of its members were bores, and he liked some of them, as he had liked that "damned bore" "Monk" Lewis.

The activities of the guests at the country house mainly consisted in passing the time until they gathered to dine, for "happiness for Man — the hungry sinner! — / Since Eve ate apples, much depends on dinner."

> For *ennui* is a growth of English root,
>   Though nameless in our language: — we retort
> The fact for words, and let the French translate
> That awful yawn which sleep cannot abate.
>
> (XIII, 101)

The elderly turned over books in the library or criticized the pictures, walked through the garden, or read their lectures on the morning papers, while keeping their eyes on their watches, "Longing at sixty for the hour of six." The ladies rode or walked, read or gossiped, discussed the fashion, or wrote letters. "The earth has nothing like a she epistle." It, "like a creed, ne'er says all it intends," but is as "full of cunning as Ulysses' whistle." Byron may well have had in mind some of Annabella's letters written before their marriage, or his sister's after he left England, full of "megrims and mysteries": ". . . I can't make out whether your disorder is a broken heart or the earache."[1]

After the banquet and the wine came the duet — "(My heart or head aches with the memory yet)." Sometimes there was a dance, but not on field days, for the men were too tired. Small talk or flirtation filled up the hours till ten, when they retired.

> But all was gentle and aristocratic
>   In this our party; polished, smooth, and cold,
> As Phidian forms cut out of marble Attic.
>   There now are no Squire Westerns, as of old;
> And our Sophias are not so emphatic,
>   But fair as then, or fairer to behold:
> We have no accomplished blackguards, like Tom Jones,
> But gentlemen in stays, as stiff as stones.   (XIII, 110)

Whatever resolution Byron may have made to be serious and to stick to his story, he found it easier to hold himself to the first than to the second resolve. The speculations that ran through his head were serious enough, though the expression from habit and from diffidence was still flippant. More and more he was obsessed by questions of reality and appearance, and of the mind of man, "that very fiery particle." These were the speculations that overflowed into his Ravenna Journal in 1821 and his later "Detached Thoughts." While his thinking on these subjects was not profound, it was honest and it cut through some of the rationalizations necessary for the maintenance of the consistency of more subtle philosophers' systems. If "we could but snatch a certainty, / Perhaps Mankind might find the path they miss — / But then 't would spoil much good philosophy."

Byron was free to admit that he had no purpose in his speculations, and he laid his whole plan in the poem before his readers:

> For which my sole excuse is — 't is my way;
>   Sometimes *with* and sometimes without occasion,

[1] *Astarte*, 1921, p. 285. Letter of June 3, 1817.

> I write what's uppermost, without delay;
>   This narrative is not meant for narration,
> But a mere airy and fantastic basis,
>   To build up common things with common places.
>   (XIV, 7)

As Bacon says, a straw will show the way the wind blows, and such a straw is poetry, "according as the Mind glows."

At least he has offered his readers variety — Love, War, a tempest — "Also, a seasoning slight of lucubration; / A bird's-eye view, too, of that wild, Society." If this world has not been described much of late, it is because there is "a sameness in its gems and ermine." There may be "much to excite," but there is "little to exalt." There is monotony in the characters and commonplace even in their crimes. "It palls — at least it did so upon me, / This paradise of Pleasure and *Ennui*."

What was "uppermost" in Byron's mind having been exploited and explored, he could get on with the story. Juan, a foreigner in a strange environment, was nevertheless "all things unto people of all sorts" and "most things to all women." He was successful in the hunt, for he was a good rider, but in his heart he scorned it. And unlike the English gentlemen he didn't fall asleep after dinner, a quality that made him more agreeable to women. He was a good listener, and was graceful in the dance. It was no wonder that he was a favorite, "A little spoilt, but by no means so quite." The Duchess of Fitz-Fulke, "who loved *tracasserie*, / Began to treat him with some small *agacerie*." This "full-blown blonde," uninhibited in the use of her womanly powers, is treated rather sympathetically by Byron; though she is not a type that could hold the sentimental romantic permanently, he rather delights in contrasting her unhypocritical brashness with the subtler self-deceptions of Adeline. She had previously made "a dead set" at Lord Augustus Fitz-Plantagenet, who began to look a little black at this new flirtation of hers. The women felt sorry for him but never even mentioned the Duke.

> Theirs was that best of unions, past all doubt,
> Which never meets, and therefore can't fall out.
>   (XIV, 45)

Lady Adeline disapproved of her Grace's free conduct without admitting to herself, or perhaps knowing, the real cause of her disquiet.

> And waxing chiller in her courtesy,
> Looked grave and pale to see her friend's fragility,
> For which most friends reserve their sensibility.
>
> (XIV, 46)

It is not the author's purpose at present to inquire too closely into Adeline's motives, even though "To trace all actions to their secret springs / Would make indeed some melancholy mirth." Besides, "the roots of things . . . are so much intertwisted with the earth." For whatever reason, Adeline resolved to impede the affair before the pair made some "sad mistake." Her innocence gave her the courage to be bold, for she did not need "those palisades by dames erected, / Whose virtue lies in never being detected."

Having nothing to hide, she called in her husband for advice, and asked him to counsel Juan, but he declined because he thought the boy "had more brain than beard" and could take care of himself; besides, "Opposition only more attaches." And as he was called to the Privy Council, he "calmly kissed her, / Less like a young wife than an aged sister." Lord Henry was "a cold, good, honourable man," but it was obvious that he lacked what "pretty women — the sweet souls! — call *soul*." This leads to speculation on the "undefinable '*Je ne sçais quoi*'" that women demand in love. Neither man nor woman can show quite *how* they would be loved.

> The Sensual for a short time but connects us —
> The Sentimental boasts to be unmoved;
> But both together form a kind of Centaur,
> Upon whose back 't is better not to venture.
>
> (XIV, 73)

Adeline's intentions were of the best, but "Intense intentions are a dangerous matter." She was not *then* in love with Juan, or she would have had strength to fly from that "wild sensation."

> She was, or thought she was, his friend — and this[2]
> Without the farce of Friendship, or romance
> Of Platonism, which leads so oft amiss
> Ladies who have studied Friendship but in France
> Or Germany, where people *purely* kiss.   (XIV, 92)

[2] Referring to Annabella Milbanke's starting a correspondence with him by saying she wanted to be his friend, Byron remarked to Thomas Medwin: "Friendship is a dangerous word for young ladies; it is Love full-fledged, and waiting for a fine day to fly." (*Conversations of Lord Byron*, I, 38.)

As usual, Byron made sport of Platonism as a kind of innocent hypocrisy, but there was one kind of friendship with women which he believed in, for he had experienced it (with Lady Melbourne and a few others):

> If free from Passion, which all Friendship checks,
>   And your true feelings fully understood,
> No friend like to a woman Earth discovers,
> So that you have not been nor will be lovers.[3]
>
>   (XIV, 93)

Having laid the foundation for a prime intrigue that would burst high society wide open, Byron ends the canto by warning his reader not to jump to any conclusions. Whether Juan and "chaste Adeline" became friends in this or any other sense will be discussed later. He is content "to leave them hovering, as the effect is fine. . . ." If the reader tries to anticipate he will only make mistakes. But great things spring from little. Who would think that as great a passion as ever brought a man and woman to the brink of ruin should have sprung from "a harmless game at billiards"?[4] Truth is always stranger than fiction; "if it could be told, / How much would novels gain by the exchange!"

Byron was rather delighted at having set the stage for a fictional exposé of English society, but he was a little uncertain how to proceed, for fiction was unnatural to him. He had cultivated the habit of self-revelation and of speaking his own thoughts to such a degree that reality was always breaking in, not only in the author's digressive comment but also in the characters and the situations. And so he was constantly dancing back and forth from fiction to reality and was always on the brink of revealing something personal. For others it might be difficult to tell the bare truth; for him it was difficult to avoid it. Byron's problem, as he confesses a little later, is in "rend'ring general that which is especial." He can only try.

---

[3] This is another curious example of Byron's transferring almost verbatim (except for the necessities of the rhyme) to the stanzas of *Don Juan* the ideas he had expressed in conversation and letters. He wrote to Lady Hardy: "I have always laid it down as a maxim, and found it justified by experience, that a man and a woman make far better friendships than can exist between two of the same sex; but *these* with this condition, that they never have made, or are to make, love with each other." (*Letters and Journals,* VI, 137. Letter of Nov. 10, 1822.)

[4] In 1813 Byron wrote Lady Melbourne how "Platonism" became imperiled over a game of billiards with Lady Frances Webster.

Adeline was honorable, but "ran a risk of growing less so." Few of the "soft sex" are very stable. "They differ as wine differs from its label, / When once decanted . . . / yet both upon occasion, / Till old, may undergo adulteration." Adeline had heard some rumors of Juan's past history, but women view such matters "with more good humour" than men do. Besides, in England his conduct had grown more strict, for he had "The art of living in all climes with ease."

In the portrait of Juan that follows Byron drew more details from his own features than he perhaps was aware of, or at least than his readers would be.

> His manner was perhaps the more seductive,
>   Because he ne'er seemed anxious to seduce. . . .
> * * * * * * * * * *
> Sincere he was — at least you could not doubt it,
>   In listening merely to his voice's tone.
> The Devil hath not in all his quiver's choice
> An arrow for the Heart like a sweet voice.
>
> By nature soft, his whole address held off
>   Suspicion: though not timid, his regard
> Was such as rather seemed to keep aloof. . . .
> * * * * * * * * * *
> He neither brooked nor claimed superiority —
>
> That is, with Men: with Women he was what
>   They pleased to make or take him for; and their
> Imagination's quite enough for that:
>   So that the outline's tolerably fair,
> They fill the canvas up. . . .   (XV, 12–16)

Adeline had an intense interest in Juan and, following the course of a prototype Byron must have had in mind, Miss Milbanke, began to ponder how to save his soul. When she advised him to get married, Juan replied that he had no objection except that those he had a preference for were wed already. But Adeline did not desist, for there is nothing women like better than matchmaking. They generally have a host of unpromising male candidates and "a blooming glut of brides." These "zealous matrons . . . favour, *malgré* Malthus, Generation," for they are "Professors of that genial art, and patrons / Of all the modest part of Propagation."

The prospective brides that Adeline turned up for Juan gave Byron an opportunity for some riotous fooling with tag-names — Miss Reading, Miss Raw, Miss Flaw, Miss Showman, and Miss Knowman, and "two fair co-heiresses Giltbedding" — and then reality broke in.

> There was Miss Millpond, smooth as summer's sea,
>   That usual paragon, an only daughter,
> Who seemed the cream of Equanimity,
>   Till skimmed — and then there was some milk and water,
> With a slight shade of blue too, it might be,
>   Beneath the surface; but what did it matter?
> Love's riotous, but Marriage should have quiet,
> And being consumptive, live on a milk diet.
>
> (XV, 41)

Byron turned serious again as he introduced "a certain fair and fairy one," Aurora Raby, "A lovely being, scarcely formed or moulded, / A rose with all its sweetest leaves yet folded." She grew quietly like a flower, her heart serene and apart from the world. It would be futile to speculate on the model for Aurora within Byron's experience in English society. It is possible that she was suggested by some such unopened flower he had met briefly — the briefer the meeting the more favorable for the idealization — during his years of fame, or it might even be that she was what he had imagined and hoped Annabella might be when he first saw her. At any rate more attention is given to her personality than that of any character other than Adeline, who, it "happened," omitted her from the list of eligibles for Juan: "She marvelled 'what he saw in such a baby / As that prim, silent, cold Aurora Raby?'" Aurora was not dazzled by Juan as the other women were because "she did not pin her faith on feature." Nor was she impressed by his fame, though that was such as "plays the deuce with Womankind," for he had the reputation of "Faults which attract because they are not tame." But the mystery of Aurora's character naturally attracted Juan.

Juan's conference with Adeline ended with the call to dinner, and Byron takes the opportunity to make sport of the various dishes with foreign names, chiefly French, that make up the gourmet menu of English gourmands.

> But oh! ye modern Heroes with your cartridges,
> When will your names lend lustre e'en to partridges?
>
> (XV, 67)

At the dinner table Juan was awkwardly placed between Adeline and Aurora. The latter maintained an indifference which piqued Juan's interest, while "Adeline's malicious eyes / Sparkled with her successful prophecies." When at last Aurora was drawn into a conversation with Juan, and even smiled once or twice, Adeline began to fear she would "thaw to a coquette." But Juan had a winning way, a proud humility, deference to women, tact, and the art of drawing people out. He also had good looks, and though Aurora admired Minerva more than the Graces, even Socrates, "that model of all duty, / Owned to a *penchant*, though discreet, for beauty."

Byron was aware that he had said a few stanzas back that Aurora did not "pin her faith on feature," and that the reader might convict him of a contradiction.

> But if a writer should be quite consistent,
> How could he possibly show things existent?
>
> If people contradict themselves, can I
>   Help contradicting them, and everybody. . . .
> *   *   *   *   *   *   *   *   *   *
> 'T is wonderful what Fable will not do!
> 'T is said it makes Reality more bearable:
>   But what's Reality? Who has its clue?
> Philosophy? No; she too much rejects.
> Religion? *Yes;* but which of all her sects?
>
> (XV, 87–89)

But why, he says, "will I thus entangle / Myself with Metaphysics?"

> I always knock my head against some angle
>   About the present, past, or future state:
> Yet I wish well to Trojan and to Tyrian,
>   For I was bred a moderate Presbyterian.   (XV, 91)

He is only a "temperate theologian" and "meek as a metaphysician," but in politics he feels it his duty "to show John / Bull something of the lower world's condition,"

> Because my business is to *dress* society,
>   And stuff with *sage* that very verdant goose.
>
> (XV, 93)

And now for further variety he is going to try the supernatural. And he asks the reader if he has ever seen a ghost. He has no intention to sneer at such things, for reasons that he hints are associated with his own experience, and especially not at night, and so he will wait till morning (and the next canto) to rhyme on them.

> Between two worlds Life hovers like a star,
> 'Twixt Night and Morn, upon the horizon's verge.
> How little do we know that which we are!
> How less what we may be!   (XV, 99)

Returning to what he had said of the balance between fable and truth, Byron began the sixteenth canto with some flippant boasting of his muse, which despite her follies or her flaws is the "most sincere that ever dealt in fiction." She treats all things and retreats from none. His epic will contain "A wilderness of the most rare conceits / . . . some bitters with the sweets, / Yet mixed so slightly, that you can't complain." The truest episode is the story of a ghost which he is about to tell.

On retiring for the night Juan felt restless — thinking of Aurora — and went for a walk in the Gothic gallery where the moon cast an eery light on the old pictures on the walls. As he "mused on Mutability, / Or on his Mistress — terms synonymous," he thought he heard "A supernatural agent — or a mouse." It was no mouse but a monk, in cowl and dusky garb, who passed and repassed noiselessly and then vanished. He returned to his room and finally got to sleep, but the next morning at breakfast he was abstracted, not knowing whether to tell what he had seen, "At risk of being quizzed for superstition." Pensive and pale over his tea, he was observed by Adeline, who turned pale herself, while the Duchess of Fitz-Fulke "played with her veil, / And looked at Juan hard, but nothing uttered." Aurora Raby "Surveyed him with a kind of calm surprise." It is clear that Byron had now established the tensions he had intended to set up in the mind and feelings of Juan in his relations with these three women.

Adeline "had a twilight tinge of '*Blue*'" but was far enough from the "sublimer azure hue" to "deem Pope a great poet." Aurora was more Shakespearean.

> The worlds beyond this World's perplexing waste
> Had more of her existence. . . .   (XVI, 48)

Quite different was "her gracious, graceful, graceless Grace," whose mind, "If she had any, was upon her face," where you

might trace "A little turn for mischief." Her taste in poetry ran
to the *Bath Guide*, sonnets to herself, or *bouts rimés*.

Juan began to rally and the company dispersed. And the author
details some of the activities at a country estate. First a picture
dealer comes with "a special Titian, warranted original" for Lord
Henry's opinion. Then "a modern Goth, I mean a Gothic /
Bricklayer of Babel, called an architect" came with a plan to restore the Abbey at a trifling cost of some thousands. Lord Henry
also had to give his judgment on a mortgage, a prize ox, a prize
pig, and "two poachers caught in a steel trap, / Ready for gaol,
their place of convalescence." And then there was a pregnant
country girl

> in a close cap
> And scarlet cloak (I hate the sight to see, since —
> Since — since — in youth, I had the sad mishap. . . .
> (XVI, 61)

It is the duty of the Justice of the Peace to "keep the game / And
morals of the country from caprices" —

> Preserving partridges and pretty wenches
> Are puzzles to the most precautious benches.
> (XVI, 63)

The poor girl was made to wait, for Lord Henry was occupied
with dogs and horses and preparations for the "Public day" at the
hall; he was "a great electioneer, / Burrowing for boroughs like
a rat or rabbit."

The portrait of Lord Henry as a fence-riding politician, "A
friend to Freedom" and yet "No less a friend to Government,"
strengthens the supposition that this side of his fictional character
was intended as a gentle ribbing of Byron's political patron Lord
Holland, to whom he had always showed great deference as a
friend and guide in Whig Society but from whose middle-of-the-
road views he had deviated in the radicalism of his first speech in
Parliament on the Frame Bill. Lord Henry's liberalism did not
stand in the way of his defense of privilege: "he exactly the just
medium hit / 'Twixt Place and Patriotism." He rationalized his
holding of "some sinecures he wished abolished," and he could
not "quit his King in times of strife." But the dinner-bell interrupts these speculations.

Juan was still so abstracted by the ghost he had seen that he was

> but slightly harmonized
> With the substantial company engrossed
> By matter, and so much materialised,
> That one scarce knew at what to marvel most
> Of two things — *how* (the question rather odd is)
> Such bodies could have souls, or souls such bodies!
>
> (XVI, 90)

Adeline was playing the gracious hostess, that is, the political wife, to perfection, but observing her "vivacious versatility" (or "what is called mobility"), Juan "began to feel / Some doubt how much of Adeline was *real*."

The Duchess of Fitz-Fulke seemed much at ease, her laughing blue eyes observing the "ridicules" of the "fashionable bees" and storing it up "for mischievous enjoyment." When the guests retired, Adeline sparked the ridicule of the squires and squiresses with her innocent "faint praise," which "served to set off every joke." Only Juan and Aurora did not join in these witticisms. Aurora looked as though she approved Juan's silence; perhaps she mistook it for charity. And her esteem kindled in him

> some feelings he had lately lost,
> Or hardened; feelings which, perhaps ideal,
> Are so divine, that I must deem them real: —
>
> The love of higher things and better days;
> The unbounded hope, and heavenly ignorance
> Of what is called the World, and the World's ways;
> The moments when we gather from a glance
> More joy than from all future pride or praise. . . .
>
> (XVI, 107–8)

And so the way is prepared for one of Byron's (and life's) little ironies. Juan retired "full of sentiments, sublime as billows / Heaving between this World and Worlds beyond." In his night-gown he sat apprehensive of the ghost's return. When he heard the footsteps of the Black Friar his blood curdled,

> For Immaterialism's a serious matter;
> So that even those whose faith is the most great
> In Souls immortal, shun them *tête-à-tête*.
>
> (XVI, 114)

His fright increased when the door opened with an infernal creak and the cowled monk stood in the light of his candles. Then "his own internal ghost began to awaken . . . to quell his corporal shaking," his fear turned to wrath, and he advanced while the ghost retreated. It paused in the darkness of the hall. His fright returned when he put forth his arm and touched only the wall. But his curiosity would not allow him to retreat, for he observed that the ghost's blue eyes sparkled in the moonlight, and that the grave had spared it a sweet breath, a straggling curl, a red lip, and pearly teeth. He put forth his other arm and it "pressed upon a hard but glowing bust."

> Back fell the sable frock and dreary cowl,
>   And they revealed — alas! that e'er they should!
> In full, voluptuous, but *not o'er*grown bulk,
> The phantom of her frolic Grace — Fitz-Fulke!
>
> (XVI, 123)

In the fragment of a seventeenth canto which Byron wrote before his energies and attention became absorbed in his Greek adventure he tantalized his readers by leaving it an open question whether Juan's ideal feelings, revived in him by Aurora Raby, were "materialized" by the Duchess of Fitz-Fulke. What happened in the "tender moonlight situation" he will not tell.

> I leave the thing a problem, like all things. . . .
>
> (XVII, 13)

Perhaps that was the best ending for a poem, which by its very nature, and by virtue of the life that it embodied, must forever remain unconcluded. It should be considered a slice of life and of the mind and personality of an unusually vibrant, witty, and honest human being. As a whole it can perhaps be better and more fairly judged as a novel-satire in verse than as a poem in the ordinary sense. That Byron had plans, perhaps rather definite ones, for its continuation seems evident from what he said both in the poem and in letters and conversation. Whether it would have been improved in a continuation is a speculation beyond criticism. That would have depended on the development of the personality of which it was so clear a reflection.

17

The Vision of Judgment

The Vision of Judgment stands apart from Byron's other satires, both those in the heroic couplet and those in the ottava rima, in being unified in structure and compact in expression. Byron has resisted the temptation to excessive digression and has obviously taken delight in the machinery of his fable, which has a kind of consistency often absent from his other satires where he considered the narrative only a peg on which to hang his commentary. In these areas as well as in the sparkling wit of individual lines and the farcical realization of the characters it is a satiric masterpiece. His subtle and "tolerant" picture of the personnel of the angelic world, both blessed and fallen, is a significant achievement. Their celestial "ichor" is very earthly, but still it raises them to a height sufficiently above mundane views and limitations to make them admirable judges of the earthly scene.

As the preface indicates, the poem was written in "red-hot earnest," but the ludicrousness of Southey's own "Vision," of which it was a parody, kept the author's indignation from weighing down the humor of the poem. Byron's quarrel with Southey was long standing and is too complicated to discuss in detail. Besides it is not really essential to an appreciation of the satire. It is sufficient to know that Southey's laureate apotheosis of George III on his death, written in solemn and dull hexameters, was quite enough, apart from the thinly veiled attack in the preface on Byron as the leader of the "Satanic School" of poetry, to spark the satire. In his "true dream" or vision Byron would train his telescope on the gates of heaven and show what really happened when George III arrived there for judgment.

Byron's satire in the poem is three-pronged: political, theological, and literary. First, there is the attack on George III and his ministers as agents and symbols of tyranny and oppression. This subject, as usual, tends to stir Byron's indignation to the point that the satire loses its lightness and slips into philippic, though an occasional ironic turn or hyperbole may save the stanzas from becoming solemn diatribe, as when he says that George died bereft of sense and sight, "but left his subjects still behind, / One half as mad, and t'other no less blind." Despite the defensive tone of the preface, intended to allay suspicions of impiety in his light treatment of "saints, angels, and spiritual persons," Byron deliberately flaunted a theological *lèse majesté* in reducing to their human equivalents the whole hierarchy of anthropomorphic "supernatural personages" accepted by conventional religionists, and particularly by believers and defenders (like Southey) of the established religion, "for by many stories, / And true, we learn the Angels are all Tories." But all this is contributory, and it all leads directly to the satire on Southey as renegade whose hired pen would scribble encomiums of saints or devils with equal fervor and whose cacophonous hexameters could set Michael's teeth on edge and drive the demons howling back to hell. If in the course of this satire the author could shock the pious English reader or expose his hypocrisies, so much the better.

The poem opens with St. Peter dozing at the celestial gate. "His keys were rusty, and the lock was dull," so few people had come through of late. Since the Napoleonic wars the devils had drawn most souls another way. The angels were bored and singing out of tune. "The Guardian Seraphs had retired on high, / Finding their charges past all care below." The only one busy was the Recording Angel,

> Who found, indeed, the facts to multiply
>   With such rapidity of vice and woe,
> That he had stripped off both his wings in quills,
> And yet was in arrear of human ills.   (St. 3)

Even the assistants assigned to the job could not keep up the record of the crime and slaughter,

> Till at the crowning carnage, Waterloo,
> They threw their pens down in divine disgust —
> The page was so besmeared with blood and dust.
>   (St. 5)

In evaluating George III's reign, Byron was careful to distinguish between his private virtues — he was a good farmer and constant "to a bad, ugly woman" — and his public acts: "A worse king never left a realm undone!" His funeral made some pomp, but no tears were shed save "by collusion." There was elegy enough, "Bought also" (like the Laureate's). "Of all / The fools who flocked to swell or see the show, / Who cared about the corpse?" Byron's tongue-in-cheek "God save the king!" is not without its logic, considering the ending, and may be considered a kind of humorous dramatic premonition. And he uses the conventional pious exclamation as the opening for an ironic impiety:

> It is a large economy
>> In God to save the like; but if he will
> Be saving, all the better; for not one am I
>> Of those who think damnation better still:
> I hardly know too if not quite alone am I
>> In this small hope of bettering future ill
> By circumscribing, with some slight restriction,
> The eternity of Hell's hot jurisdiction.
>
> I know this is unpopular; I know
>> 'Tis blasphemous; I know one may be damned
> For hoping no one else may e'er be so. . . .
>> (St. 13–14)

In the scene at the heavenly gate when George arrives, Byron has taken delight in picturing the angels with jovial familiarity as spirits possessed of amiable human weaknesses, and at the same time free enough of the common human vices of the creators of their fable to judge them with ironic detachment. The commotion of George's arrival makes St. Peter start and exclaim: "There's another star gone out, I think!" But before he could go back to sleep a cherub "flapped his right wing o'er his eyes" to waken him, and Peter said, a little annoyed: "Well, what's the matter? / Is Lucifer come back with all this clatter?"

> "No," quoth the Cherub: "George the Third is dead."
>> "And who *is* George the Third?" replied the apostle:
> "*What George? what Third?*" "The King of England," said
>> The angel. "Well! he won't find kings to jostle
> Him on his way; but does he wear his head?
>> Because the last we saw here had a tustle,
> And ne'er would have got into Heaven's good graces,
> Had he not flung his head in all our faces." (St. 18)

The angel then answered: "Peter! do not pout: / The King who comes has head and all entire, / And never knew much what it was about." He was only a puppet, pulled about on his wire, but he must be judged nevertheless.

Then in a rush of mighty wind Satan came to dispute for George's soul. St. Peter was frightened by his "glance of supernatural hate."

> He pottered with his keys at a great rate,
>   And sweated through his Apostolic skin:
> Of course his perspiration was but ichor,
> Or some such other spiritual liquor.   (St. 25)

The arrival of the archangel Michael, "Radiant with glory," sets the stage for the contest. The author apologizes for his poor earthly comparisons, "for here the night / Of clay obscures our best conceptions, saving / Johanna Southcote, or Bob Southey raving." For a full appreciation of the irony, one should keep in mind the fact that Byron's poem is a parody of Southey's "Vision," wherein he gives a detailed solemn description of the "Celestial City." Byron's triumph throughout is in lighting Southey's solemnities with a human and a humorous touch. Perhaps the peak of his success here is in the description of the meeting of Michael and Satan. They met in the neutral space before the gate of heaven,

> And therefore Michael and the other wore
>   A civil aspect: though they did not kiss,
> Yet still between his Darkness and his Brightness
> There passed a mutual glance of great politeness.
>   (St. 35)

Satan's argument for the possession of the soul of George III is simple and direct:

> "I claim my subject: and will make appear
>   That as he was my worshiper in dust,
> So shall he be in spirit, although dear
>   To thee and thine, because nor wine nor lust
> Were of his weaknesses; yet on the throne
> He reigned o'er millions to serve me alone." (St. 39)

At this point, in reviewing George's career, Satan assumes Byronic solemnity in his denunciation of tyranny. It is true, he says, that the king was only a tool ("I have the workmen safe"), but from all the rolls of history, "produce a reign / More drenched with gore, more cumbered with the slain. / He ever warred with freedom and the free." He grants his "neutral virtues," but that doesn't assuage the oppression which he caused millions to suffer. "The New World shook him off; the Old yet groans / Beneath what he and his prepared." And finally he was "The foe to Catholic participation / In all the license of a Christian nation."

> But here Saint Peter started from his place
>   And cried, "You may the prisoner withdraw:
> Ere Heaven shall ope her portals to this Guelph,
>   While I am guard, may I be damned myself!"
>   (St. 49)

But the suave and diplomatic Michael broke in:

> "Good Saint! and Devil!
>   Pray, not so fast; you both outrun discretion.
> Saint Peter! you were wont to be more civil:
>   Satan! excuse this warmth of his expression,
> And condescension to the vulgar's level:
>   Even Saints sometimes forget themselves in session."
>   (St. 51)

Michael asked Satan to call his witnesses against George, and at the wave of his swarthy hand a "cloud of witnesses," like "Hell broke loose," came from every nation to testify. Michael accused him of abusing his call for witnesses. "I did not mean / That you should half of Earth and Hell produce."

> Satan replied, "To me the matter is
>   Indifferent, in a personal point of view:
> I can have fifty better souls than this
>   With far less trouble than we have gone through
> Already; and I merely argued his
>   Late Majesty of Britain's case with you
> Upon a point of form; you may dispose
> Of him; I've kings enough below, God knows!"
>   (St. 64)

In bringing in Wilkes and Junius as spokesmen for the cloud of witnesses, Byron of course was prompted by the fact that Southey had damned them in his "Vision," but once having introduced them Byron enjoyed delineating the impish spirit of Wilkes and quipping about the great to-do over the identity of Junius, and he offers his own solution:

> 'Tis, that what Junius we are wont to call,
>> Was *really* — *truly* — nobody at all.

> I don't see wherefore letters should not be
>> Written without hands, since we daily view
> Them written without heads. . . .   (St. 80–81)

Satan was about to call as additional witnesses George Washington, Horne Tooke, and Franklin, when the devil Asmodeus elbowed through the crowd and dropped down a heavy burden, which is soon perceived to be Robert Southey.

> "Confound the renegado! I have sprained
>> My left wing, he's so heavy; one would think
> Some of his works about his neck were chained.
>> But to the point; while hovering o'er the brink
> Of Skiddaw (where as usual it still rained),
>> I saw a taper, far below me, wink,
> And stooping, caught this fellow at a libel —
> No less on History — than the Holy Bible."

> > > > > > > > > (St. 86)

Satan interposed that he had been expecting this man for some time.

> "A sillier fellow you can scarce behold,
>> Or more conceited in his petty sphere:
> But surely it was not worth while to fold
>> Such trash below your wing, Asmodeus dear:
> We had the poor wretch safe (without being bored
> With carriage) coming of his own accord."

> > > > > > > > > (St. 88)

But now that he was here they could see what he had done. " 'Done!' cried Asmodeus, 'he anticipates / The very business you are now upon, / And scribbles as if head clerk to the Fates.' " But Michael, the fair judge, said that they should hear what he had to say.

> Now the bard, glad to get an audience, which
>> By no means often was his case below,
> Began to cough, and hawk, and hem, and pitch
>> His voice into that awful note of woe
> To all unhappy hearers within reach
>> Of poets when the tide of rhyme's in flow;
> But stuck fast with his first hexameter,
> Not one of all whose gouty feet would stir.   (St. 90)

Before Southey could get his "spavined dactyls" under way there was a general bustle in the spiritual throng, for the Angels had "enough of song / When upon service." And even George, "mute till then, exclaimed, 'What! what! / *Pye* come again? No more — no more of that!'" In this line Byron embalmed the poet laureate in amber along with his notorious predecessor, who had brought the laureateship to the lowest ebb of fawning sycophancy. But Byron, who on meeting Southey had called him the "best-looking bard" he had seen, could not rest without giving him his due in the poem. The "varlet" was not ill-favored and possessed a sort of grace that made his whole aspect "by no means so ugly as his case."

Michael stilled the tumult and gave Southey a chance to defend himself. He said

> He meant no harm in scribbling; 'twas his way
> Upon all topics; 'twas, besides, his bread,
>   Of which he buttered both sides. . . .
>
> He had written praises of a Regicide;
>   He had written praises of all kings whatever;
> He had written for republics far and wide,
>   And then against them bitterer than ever;
> For pantisocracy he once had cried
>   Aloud, a scheme less moral than 'twas clever;
> Then grew a hearty anti-jacobin —
> Had turned his coat — and would have turned his skin. . . .
>
> He had written Wesley's life: — here turning round
>   To Satan, "Sir, I'm ready to write yours,
> In two octavo volumes, nicely bound,
>   With notes and preface, all that most allures
> The pious purchaser; and there's no ground
>   For fear, for I can choose my own reviewers. . . ."
>   (St. 96–97, 99)

When Satan declined, he offered to write Michael's life. "Mine is a pen of all work . . . / I would make you shine / Like your own trumpet. By the way, my own / Has more of brass in it, and is as well blown." Then he offered his "Vision": "yes — you shall / Judge with my judgment! and by my decision / Be guided who shall enter heaven or fall. / I settle all these things by intuition. . . . When I thus see double, / I save the Deity some worlds of trouble."

And nothing could stop him from reading his "Vision." At the fourth line

> the whole spiritual show
> Had vanished, with variety of scents,
> Ambrosial and sulphureous. . . .
>
> The Angels stopped their ears and plied their pinions;
> The Devils ran howling, deafened, down to Hell . . .
> Michael took refuge in his trump — but, lo!
> His teeth were set on edge, he could not blow!
> (St. 102–103)

At the fifth line St. Peter, "an impetuous saint," raised his keys and knocked the poet down. He fell into his lake but did not drown.

> He first sank to the bottom — like his works,
>   But soon rose to the surface — like himself;
> For all corrupted things are buoyed like corks,
>   By their own rottenness. . . .   (St. 105)

All that the author saw farther in "this true dream," before his telescope vanished, was that in the confusion

> King George slipped into Heaven for one;
> And when the tumult dwindled to a calm,
> I left him practising the hundredth psalm.   (St. 106)

To let King George slip into heaven was to emphasize that the satire was aimed at Southey and that the poor mad king was less of a sinner than those who praised him for virtues he did not possess. It is in keeping too with the "tolerance" and good humor that make *The Vision of Judgment* so devastating in its exposure of the political and religious hypocrisies of the poem which it parodies. In its concept as in its phrasing it rises to some sublime heights of both the ridiculous and the poetic, and enriches the memory with some unforgettable lines. Swinburne was justified in saying that in it Byron gave satire wings to fly with.

18

A Retrospective View

BYRON WAS of the world worldly — he had nothing of the transcendental Romanticist's sense of being a seer poet, the voice of some divine afflatus. More than Wordsworth he was "a man speaking to men," not in the language of inspired poetry, but in that of reason and honest feeling.

Byron's slight regard for poetry as an end in itself resulted in verbal carelessness (as well as a reluctance to revise or polish), a cavalier attitude toward formal beauty or symmetry, and a willingness to digress and ramble even in his Popean satires. But his very contempt for poetry contributed to a uniqueness in his literary product which must be considered a compensation for the resultant imperfections of style and structure. Literature as an aesthetic entity, a thing in itself to be admired like a painting or a statue for its artistic qualities, never won his sympathies. He valued the literature of the past for the life, ideas, or feelings it embodied, whether in the work of Fielding, Rousseau, or Shakespeare. And in his own literary productions he aimed first at truth and accuracy in the expression of attitudes and emotions and cared little for mere ingenuity, or the prettiness of a well turned phrase, much as he enjoyed a clever epigram or rhyme once he was embarked on the expression.

Yet it would be a mistake to accept unqualifiedly the assumption that Byron's poetry is all bad technically. Negligent and offhand as he seemed to be in matters of form and structure, his manuscripts show that he often sought with meticulous care for the words that would match accurately the nuances of his thought or mood. And frequently when he did not revise it was because he had miraculously lighted on the most felicitous phrase in the first spring of his imagination.

What bothers some readers of Byron, particularly those who have a preference for poetry that conforms to certain literary rules and proprieties, is that he does not "play the game." He never lets the poem govern what he has to say — he is always the master of the make-believe — he can never for long maintain a "persona" or fictional character. The puppeteer always shows himself to his audience and keeps them aware that he is there, that he will say directly what others might prefer to say in fiction.

Byron's poetic reputation suffers particularly in a period in which the current critical taste demands compactness of phrase and richness of overtone or symbolic suggestion. But Byron boasted: "When I speak, I *don't hint*, but *speak out*." He did, however, make his poetry a supple instrument for the revelation of truth as he saw it — truth of intellectual speculation and truth of mood (a relativistic truth in both areas of expression).

He can be subtle when one least expects it. When he says in *Don Juan* that he hates inconstancy he both means it and doesn't mean it. One has to be most on guard when he is mocking. Does he really mean to renounce all amorous writing as he announces at the beginning of the fifth canto, or is the irony forthright and meant to emphasize the opposite point of view? He means to eschew the kind of amorous writing that Petrarch indulged in — he is going to deal with love realistically and not sentimentally — and he is making sport of the pious critics who have thought his realism conducive to immorality. But even more in his metaphysical speculations, he balances the tensions of unresolved attitudes. His ironic comments on Bishop Berkeley's "sublime discovery" that makes the "Universe universal egotism . . . *all ourselves!*" gives him an inward glimpse of the true nature of his own romantic longings, never abandoned wholly even in his most mocking moments in *Don Juan*. And he can say with both irony and conviction:

> I would shatter
> Gladly all matters down to stone or lead,
> Or adamant, to find the World a spirit.

It may be that Byron's final appeal to a disillusioned world, whether in the nineteenth century or the twentieth, is that he is as honest as we wish we could be. It may be the honesty of an anarchic mind, but it has its wholesome qualities, the strength of its weaknesses in formal poetic expression and in consistency.

Professor Lovell finds striking parallels between Byron's attitudes and those of several twentieth century writers and sees a perfect statement of the Byronic credo in Robinson Jeffers' introduction to his own *Selected Poetry* (1937): ". . . I decided not to tell lies in verse. Not to feign any emotion that I did not feel . . . not to say anything because it was popular, or generally accepted, or fashionable in intellectual circles, unless I myself believed it; and not to believe easily." Lovell says: "The result, in the poetry, is often a view of nature or civilization which may be flatly contradicted elsewhere, but it is also one which is cruelly inclusive in its method, refusing to achieve unity by the mere exclusion of the 'unpoetic,' one which often expresses a lively awareness that the obvious attitude is not the only possible attitude, and thus one which can still speak directly, conversationally, and with force and good humor to the mind of the present century."[1]

Yet, while present-day readers lean strongly toward the realistic and satiric in Byron, and while it is the fashion to point out that he had one foot (presumably the sound one) firmly planted in the eighteenth century — in its rationalism, its common sense, and its distrust of what Byron called "entusymusy" — it is still important to remember that the other foot, even though halt, stood as firmly in the romantic nineteenth century. The core of his thinking and the basis of his poetry is romantic aspiration. The final picture is one of a man who, reluctantly, because he is still the romantic, has come to terms with an imperfect world — at least to the point of finding it an amusing place. His romantic zest for life and experience lends vigor to both the comic and the tragic aspects of the discrepancy between reality and appearance, between imperfections and pretensions.

[1] Ernest J. Lovell, Jr. *Byron: The Record of a Quest,* pp. 210, 237.

Selected Bibliography

I. BIBLIOGRAPHIES

Wise, Thomas J.: *A Bibliography of the Writings in Verse and Prose of George Gordon Noel, Baron Byron. . . .* 2 vols. Privately printed, London, 1932–1933. The most detailed bibliography of Byron's first editions. Includes much miscellaneous material: facsimiles of title pages, manuscript poems, and autograph letters.

Coleridge, E. H., ed.: *The Works of Lord Byron, Poetry.* London, 1898–1904. Vol. VII contains an extensive bibliography of Byron's works, including successive editions and translations.

Pollard, H. G.: "Byron," in *Cambridge Bibliography of English Literature.* 1941. Contains a selected but extensive bibliography of biographical and critical works on Byron.

Chew, Samuel C.: *Byron in England.* London, 1924. Has a useful bibliographical appendix of Byroniana.

————: "Byron," in *The English Romantic Poets, A Review of Research.* A publication of the MLA, revised ed., 1956. A selected critical bibliography.

Marchand, Leslie A.: "Recent Byron Scholarship" in *Essays in Literary History,* presented to J. Milton French, ed. Rudolf Kirk and C. F. Main. New Brunswick, N.J., 1960. A bibliographical essay that evaluates biographical and critical studies of Byron published in the past thirty years.

Annual bibliographies appear in *PMLA* and in the *Keats-Shelley Journal.*

II. EDITIONS

Poetry

The Works of Lord Byron, Poetry. Ed. E. H. Coleridge. 7 vols. London, 1898–1904. The most complete edition of Byron's poetry to date. Part of the standard thirteen-volume Murray edition of Byron, it contains a number of poems not theretofore published, from the Murray MSS. and other sources, and valuable prefaces and notes by the editor.

The Complete Poetical Works of Lord Byron. Ed. Paul Elmer More. Boston, 1905. Cambridge Edition. The best complete one-volume edition, including all new material from E. H. Coleridge's seven-volume edition.

Byron's Don Juan. A Variorum Edition. By Truman Guy Steffan and Willis W. Pratt. 4 vols. Austin, Texas, 1957. The first volume is a general introduction by Steffan. Volumes two and three give the variants from all extant manuscripts and editions. Volume four contains the notes, edited by Pratt.

Lord Byron: *Childe Harold's Pilgrimage and Other Romantic Poems.* Ed. Samuel C. Chew. New York, 1936. The Odyssey Series in Literature. A good selection with useful notes.

Lord Byron: *Don Juan and Other Satirical Poems.* Ed. Louis I. Bredvold. New York, 1935. The Odyssey Series in Literature. All the important satires, except that it does not have the fourteen stanzas of the seventeenth canto of *Don Juan.*

The Best of Byron. Ed. Richard Ashley Rice. New York, 1942. The selection is good although *Childe Harold* and *Don Juan* are necessarily given only in part. The introduction and notes are full and often illuminating.

George Gordon, Lord Byron: *Selected Poetry and Letters.* Ed. Edward E. Bostetter. New York, 1951. Rinehart Editions. A brief but good selection.

The Selected Poetry of Lord Byron. Ed. Leslie A. Marchand. New York, 1951. Modern Library College Editions (also in regular Modern Library edition). Contains all of *Childe Harold* and a large selection of Byron's other poems, except *Don Juan.*

Lord Byron: *Don Juan.* Ed. Leslie A. Marchand. Boston, 1958. Riverside Editions. The whole of *Don Juan* from the text of E. H. Coleridge's edition, with ample notes.

Letters

The Works of Lord Byron, Letters and Journals. Ed. Rowland E. Prothero. 6 vols. London, 1898–1901.

Lord Byron's Correspondence. Ed. John Murray. 2 vols. London, 1922. Revealing letters, mainly to Lady Melbourne, Hobhouse, and Kinnaird. Many of those in the second volume bowdlerized with silent omissions.

Byron: A Self-Portrait, Letters and Diaries, 1798 to 1824. Ed. Peter Quennell. 2 vols. London, 1950. A selection including about fifty theretofore unpublished letters and the complete text of others which had been published with omissions.

III. Memoirs by Contemporaries of Byron

Blessington, Countess of: *Conversations of Lord Byron*. London, 1834. A shrewd contemporary interpretation somewhat colored by the writer's personality, based on conversations at Genoa just before Byron left for Greece.

Broughton, Lord [John Cam Hobhouse]: *Recollections of a Long Life*. Ed. Lady Dorchester. 6 vols. London, 1909–1911. Extracts, often jumbled and condensed, with omissions and confusion in the chronology, from the diaries of Hobhouse. Vols. I and II cover the years of Hobhouse's close association with Byron.

Dallas, R. C.: *Recollections of the Life of Lord Byron, from the Year 1808 to the End of 1814. . . .* London, 1824. Dallas was Byron's literary agent and saw his early volumes through the press.

Gamba, Pietro: *A Narrative of Lord Byron's Last Journey to Greece*. London, 1825. A hero-worshiping account by the brother of Byron's last mistress, Teresa Guiccioli.

Hobhouse, J[ohn] C[am]: *A Journey through Albania and Other Provinces of Turkey . . . during the Years 1809 and 1810*. 2nd ed. 2 vols. London, 1813. Though Hobhouse does not mention Byron often, he does give interesting details of their common experiences and observations during the first year of Byron's Eastern journey.

Hunt, J. H. Leigh: *The Autobiography of Leigh Hunt*. Ed. J. E. Morpurgo. London, 1949.

————: *Lord Byron and Some of His Contemporaries. . . .* London, 1828. Hunt's somewhat prejudiced account, modified in his more tolerant *Autobiography*, shows some aspects of Byron's character and details of his life not elsewhere recorded.

Kennedy, James: *Conversations on Religion, with Lord Byron and Others, Held in Cephalonia. . . .* London, 1830. Although Byron often sported with Kennedy's Methodistic seriousness, this book reveals not only his fundamental skepticism of religious dogma but also his serious interest in religious speculation.

Lovell, Ernest J., Jr., ed.: *His Very Self and Voice: Collected Conversations of Lord Byron*. New York, 1954. An omnium gatherum (except for Blessington and Medwin) of contemporary conversations. Useful for reference, but fragmented by chronological arrangement.

Medwin, Thomas: *Conversations of Lord Byron: Noted during a Residence with His Lordship at Pisa, in the Years 1821 and 1822*. London, 1824; also Paris, 1824. Though inaccurate in details, Medwin captures something of the racy style of Byron in conversation and letter writing, and reveals some things which other memoirists discreetly withheld.

Millingen, Julius: *Memoirs of the Affairs of Greece.* . . . London, 1831. One of Byron's doctors at Missolonghi, Millingen gives some unique details of Byron's last days in Greece.

Moore, Thomas: *Memoirs, Journal and Correspondence of Thomas Moore.* Ed. Lord John Russell. 8 vols. London, 1853–1856. Many references to Byron, both during his life and while Moore was gathering material for his "biography" of Byron.

Parry, William: *The Last Days of Lord Byron.* . . . London, 1825. By one of the most sympathetic and clear-headed of Byron's companions at Missolonghi.

Polidori, J. W.: *The Diary of Dr. John William Polidori, 1816.* Ed. W. M. Rossetti. London, 1911. A day-by-day account of Byron's Rhine journey and sojourn in Switzerland by his Anglo-Italian private physician.

Rogers, Samuel: *Recollections of the Table-Talk of Samuel Rogers.* Ed. A. Dyce. London, 1887. Contains much personal gossip and many anecdotes about Byron during his years of fame.

Stanhope, Colonel Leicester: *Greece in 1823, 1824 & 1825.* . . . London, 1828. A Benthamite member of the London Greek Committee, often at odds with Byron, Stanhope fills in many details of Byron's life at Missolonghi.

Trelawny, E. J.: *Recollections of the Last Days of Shelley and Byron.* London, 1858. Trelawny is picturesque but very unreliable in details and often prejudiced in his analysis of Byron's character.

————: *Records of Shelley, Byron, and the Author.* London, 1878. A new edition of the above, with additions and changes, and some contradictions, as in his account of Byron's lame foot.

IV. BIOGRAPHIES

Galt, John: *The Life of Lord Byron.* London, 1830. Chiefly useful for Galt's account, from personal observation, of Byron during parts of his journey to Greece.

Moore, Thomas: *Letters and Journals of Lord Byron: with Notices of His Life.* 2 vols. London, 1830. The first "official" biography, authorized not by his family or executors but by his publisher, John Murray. Limited by some voluntary and involuntary suppressions, it is still valuable for its collection of contemporary anecdotes and for the first extensive publication of Byron's letters and journals.

Elze, Karl: *Lord Byron: A Biography.* English translation, London, 1872. Contains some new material and documents.

Jeaffreson, J. Cordy: *The Real Lord Byron*. 2 vols. London, 1883. Some new material, not documented; an often acute analysis of Byron's character.

Mayne, Ethel: *Byron*. 2 vols. London, 1912 (revised, 1 vol., 1924). The first biography to make use of *Astarte* and of a mass of new letters edited by Prothero and Murray. Sympathetic but sometimes gushing.

————: *The Life and Letters of Anna Isabella Lady Noel Byron*. London, 1929. Has much new material from the Lovelace Papers throwing light on Byron's marriage.

Maurois, André: *Byron*. English translation, London, 1930. A readable and sympathetic Gallic interpretation.

Marchand, Leslie A.: *Byron: A Biography*. 3 vols. New York, 1957. The most complete biography, embodying much new material from manuscripts and recently published letters.

V. Biographical Studies

Borst, William A: *Lord Byron's First Pilgrimage*. New Haven, 1948. A close study of the personal and political attitudes that colored Byron's reaction to the experience of his early travels as reflected in *Childe Harold*.

Cline, C. L.: *Byron, Shelley and Their Pisan Circle*. Austin, Texas, 1952. The political and personal drama of Byron's residence in Tuscany, centering on the repercussions of the episode of the affray with a dragoon, but reaching out to his whole association with the English colony in Pisa.

Elwin, Malcolm: *Lord Byron's Wife*. London, 1962. A publication drawn from documents and letters in the Lovelace Collection, now owned by Byron's descendent Lord Lytton. The total picture is not very favorable to the character of Lady Byron.

Erdman, David V.: "Byron and Revolt in England," *Science and Society*, XI (1947), 234–248.

————: "Lord Byron and the Genteel Reformers," *PMLA*, LVI (1941), 1065–1094.

————: "Lord Byron as Rinaldo," *PMLA*, LVII (1942), 189–231. The best account of Byron's political activities and attitudes is to be found in these three articles by Erdman.

Fox, Sir John C.: *The Byron Mystery*. London, 1924. A lawyer's examination of the evidence connected with the Byron separation and the relations of Byron and his half-sister.

Knight, G. Wilson: *Lord Byron: Christian Virtues*. London, 1952. Knight is convincing in part but, like the Countess Guiccioli, he is a little too eager to put a halo around his hero's head.

————: *Lord Byron's Marriage*. London, 1956. An attempt to unlock the mystery of the Byron separation. Rather cavalier in the use of biographical evidence, but some shrewd guesses help to illuminate Byron's character. The overstressing of Byron's homosexual tendencies has led to questionable conclusions concerning the poet's relations with women.

Lovelace, Earl of: *Astarte*. Privately printed, London, 1905 (new ed., with additional letters, ed. Mary Countess of Lovelace, 1921). Lopsided in its interpretations, but contains many valuable letters and other documents touching the Byron marriage and separation and Byron's attachment to his sister.

Marshall, William H: *Byron, Shelley, Hunt, and The Liberal*. Philadelphia, 1960. A close study of Byron's involvement with Hunt and Shelley in the ill-fated periodical.

Moore, Doris Langley: *The Late Lord Byron*. London, 1961. Byron's posthumous reputation as seen in the lives and quarrels of his surviving friends and relations. The author's account of the burning of the Memoirs is the most complete and accurate one that has been written.

Nicolson, Harold: *Byron, the Last Journey*. London, 1924. A detached analysis of the confusion and discord of Byron's last days, often regarded as cynical by tender-minded Byron admirers.

Origo, Iris: *The Last Attachment*. London, 1949. The story of Byron and the Countess Teresa Guiccioli, told with detachment and sympathy, from many original sources. Includes the complete Italian text and English translations of Byron's letters to Teresa.

Pratt, Willis W.: *Byron at Southwell*. Austin, Texas, 1948. Traces the biographical background of Byron's early volumes of poetry with some new material from documents in the University of Texas Library.

Quennell, Peter: *Byron, the Years of Fame*. London, 1935. Discerning and sometimes brilliant interpretations of Byron's life, friendships, and loves in Regency London. Some new material, but mostly from well-known sources, without much attention to specific references or chronology.

————: *Byron in Italy*. London, 1941. The interpretation of the Italian years gains in liveliness from the quotation of Byron's entertaining letters from Italy.

VI. CRITICAL ESSAYS AND STUDIES

Arnold, Matthew: Preface to *The Poetry of Byron*, 1881 (reprinted in *Essays in Criticism, Second Series*, 1888). Arnold was strongly attracted to Byron, but his Victorian earnestness would not permit him to give whole-hearted approval, though he granted him "sincerity and strength." For an interesting background of nineteenth century criticism of Byron see H. J. C. Grierson, "Lord Byron: Arnold and Swinburne," in *The Background of English Literature*, London, 1926.

Bostetter, Edward E.: "Byron," in *The Romantic Ventriloquists*. Seattle, 1963. Byron stands alone among the Romantics in not having deceived himself into a belief in the reality of the transcendental dream. *Don Juan* is a record of Byron's "release and growth as man and artist."

————: "Byron and the Politics of Paradise," *PMLA*, LXXV (1960), 571–576. A study of the political and religious radicalism of *Cain*.

Bottrall, Ronald: "Byron and the Colloquial Tradition in English Poetry," *The Criterion*, XVIII (1939), 204–224. Bottrall maintains that Byron renewed the English poetic tradition with his colloquial force.

Bowra, C. M.: "*Don Juan*," in *The Romantic Imagination*. Cambridge, Mass., 1961. Byron retained his Romantic longings, but "tested them by truth and reality."

Boyd, Elizabeth F.: *Don Juan, A Critical Study*. New Brunswick, N. J., 1945. A thorough study of the personal and literary ingredients of the poem.

Calvert, William J.: *Byron: Romantic Paradox*. Chapel Hill, N. C., 1935. The dichotomy of Byron's clinging to classicism as a critical principle but leaning to Romantic self-expression in his poetry.

Chew, Samuel C.: *The Dramas of Lord Byron: A Critical Study*. Göttingen, 1915. A penetrating critical analysis, but it somewhat overstresses the importance of the dramas in Byron's total work.

Eliot, T. S.: "Byron," in *From Anne to Victoria*, ed. Bonamy Dobree. London, 1937; also in *On Poetry and Poets*, London, 1957. Eliot is severe in his judgment of *Childe Harold* but praises *Don Juan*.

Elton, Oliver: *A Survey of English Literature, 1780–1830*. London, 1912. The chapter on Byron is sympathetic and judicious and often penetrating in its analysis.

Fairchild, Hoxie N.: *The Romantic Quest*. New York, 1931. One of the keenest analyses of the Byronic mind, "too idealistic to refrain from blowing bubbles and too realistic to refrain from pricking them."

————: "Byron," in *Religious Trends in English Poetry*, Vol. III. New York, 1949. Pictures the war in Byron between skepticism and belief ending in Sentimental Deism. The Romantic religion of self-deification is thwarted in Byron by the "realistic sense of human limitation."

Fuess, Claude M.: *Lord Byron as a Satirist in Verse*. New York, 1912; reprinted, 1964. Good as a summary of historical and literary background of the satires, but inadequate as a critical analysis. He sees Byron as "shallow and cynical" and with "no positive attitude towards any of the great problems of existence."

Johnson, E. D. H.: "Don Juan in England," *ELH*, II (1944), 135–153. Emphasizes how completely Byron misjudged the moral temper of his English middle class readers in his accusations of cant and hypocrisy.

————: "A Political Interpretation of Byron's *Marino Faliero*," *MLQ*, III (1942), 417–425. Byron's interest in a political revolution in England led by aristocrats and gentlemen is reflected in many passages in the drama.

Leavis, F. R.: "Byron's Satire," in *Revaluation*. London, 1936. Byron's balance of the "Romantic-aristocrat high decorum" and the "irreverently familiar" marks a falling off from the urbanity of Augustan satire. Variety, flexibility, and individuality are among Byron's merits.

Lovell, Ernest J., Jr.: *Byron: The Record of a Quest*. Austin, Texas, 1949. An analysis of Byron's concept and treatment of Nature. A postscript on "The Contemporaneousness of Byron" gives an excellent statement of the attitudes which make him peculiarly congenial to the twentieth century.

————: "Irony and Image in Byron's *Don Juan*," in *The Major English Romantic Poets: A Symposium in Reappraisal*, ed. Clarence D. Thorpe *et al.* Carbondale, Ill., 1957. Lovell stresses Byron's "basically ironic theme of appearance versus reality," but tries to show, less convincingly, that he belongs to the age of the "New Critics."

Marchand, Leslie A.: "Byron and the Modern Spirit," in *The Major English Romantic Poets: A Symposium in Reappraisal*, ed. Clarence D. Thorpe *et al.* Carbondale, Ill., 1957. Stresses Byron's hardheadedness, his refusal to believe that the romantic dream was other than the mind's creation, and yet his clinging to the dream as a part of man's life.

Marshall, William H.: *The Structure of Byron's Major Poems.* Philadelphia, 1962. Displays some acumen, but distorted by a critical system which gives more attention to the Oriental tales than to *Don Juan.*

Pratt, Willis W.: "Byron and Some Current Patterns of Thought," in *The Major English Romantic Poets: A Symposium in Reappraisal,* ed. Clarence D. Thorpe *et al.* Carbondale, Ill., 1957. Tries to link Byron's confusions and disenchantments with those of twentieth century poets.

Praz, Mario: *The Romantic Agony.* Translated from the Italian by Angus Davidson. London, 1933 (2nd ed., 1951). Considers the Byronic hero as a kind of "devil's disciple," and the embodiment of the ideal of "*l'homme fatal*" and the "*caractère maudit.*"

Ridenour, George M.: *The Style of Don Juan.* New Haven, 1960. One of the most penetrating and judicious of the modern critical studies of the poem and of Byronic attitudes. The author points up Byron's use of "the Christian myth of the Fall" and the "classical theory of the styles" without forcing the poet into any Procrustean system.

————: "The Mode of Byron's *Don Juan,*" *PMLA,* LXXIX (1964), 442–446. A refutation of Marshall's contention that Byron's irony in *Don Juan* is "terminal," the voice of many speakers inconsistent among themselves. Ridenour maintains that Byron speaks in his own voice and has a fundamental consistency in his comic vision.

Russell, Bertrand: "Byron and the Modern World," *Journal of the History of Ideas,* I (1940), 24–37; included, slightly abridged, as a chapter in his *History of Western Philosophy,* London, 1945. Byron is pictured as the aristocratic rebel whose "revolt of solitary instincts against social bonds" has promoted freedom but has hindered social cooperation.

Rutherford, Andrew: *Byron: A Critical Study.* Palo Alto, Cal., 1961. A useful introduction to the major poems with stress on the superior merits of the ottava rima satires. The criticism is perceptive and sometimes penetrating.

Slater, Joseph L.: "Byron's Hebrew Melodies," *Studies in Philology,* XLIX (1952), 75–94. The closest study of the background and themes of Byron's lyrics.

Steffan, Truman Guy: "The Devil a Bit of Our Beppo," *Philological Quarterly,* XXXII (1953), 154–171. A study of the verbal changes and improvements in the original manuscript.

————: "The Token-Web, the Sea Sodom, and Canto I of *Don Juan,*" *Studies in English,* University of Texas (1947), pp. 108–168.

Traces the personal history and the Venetian environment of Byron which contributed realism to the first canto.

Strout, Alan Lang: *John Bull's Letter to Lord Byron*. Norman, Oklahoma, 1947. A new edition, with critical and historical introduction, of one of the most acute and sympathetic of the contemporary critiques of Byron.

Swinburne, Algernon Charles: Preface to *A Selection from the Works of Lord Byron*. London, 1865; reprinted in *Essays and Studies*, 1875. A glowing tribute.

————: "Wordsworth and Byron," *Nineteenth Century*, XV (1884), 583–609, 764–790; reprinted in *Miscellanies*, 1884. Hostile to Byron.

Trueblood, Paul G.: *The Flowering of Byron's Genius*. Palo Alto, Cal., 1945. A systematic analysis of *Don Juan* aimed at showing a progressive seriousness of purpose. Misses overtones of humor and caprice in the effort to establish a thesis.

West, Paul: *Byron and the Spoiler's Art*. New York, 1960. An attempt to relate the drives and motivations of Byron's personality to his poetry. West sees Byron's main skill in comic verse. He analyzes his poetic techniques, his imagery and ironic turns, and makes some perhaps too facile parallels with other writers from Baudelaire to Hemingway.

————, ed.: *Byron: A Collection of Critical Essays*. Englewood Cliffs, N. J., 1963. A Spectrum Book. A good selection of essays and chapters from recent books on Byron's poetry.

INDEX

To Works of Byron Discussed in This Book

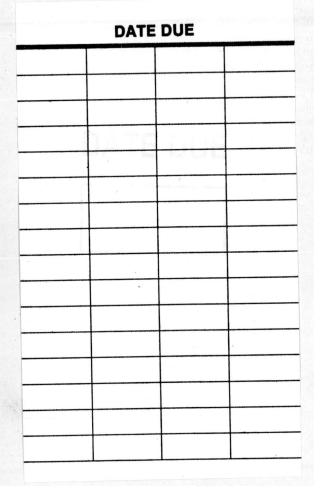

DATE DUE